A Life-Long Springtime

The Life and Teaching of George Congreve SSJE

— LUKE MILLER —

Sacristy
Press

Sacristy Press
PO Box 612, Durham, DH1 9HT

www.sacristy.co.uk

First published in 2022 by Sacristy Press, Durham

Sacristy Limited, registered in England & Wales, number 7565667

British Library Cataloguing-in-Publication Data
A catalogue record for the book is available from the British Library

ISBN 978-1-78959-198-9

For Jacqui

Contents

"We Christians," said S. Clement in his loveliest passage, "having learnt the new blessings, have the exuberance of life's morning's prime in this youth which knows no old age, in which we are always growing to maturity in intelligence, are always young, always mild, always new. For they must necessarily be new, who have become partakers of the new World. And that which participates in Eternity is wont to be associated to the incorruptible: so that to us appertains the designation of the age of childhood, a life-long springtime. Because of the truth that is in us, our hearts saturated with the truth cannot be touched by old age: but wisdom is ever blooming, ever remains constant, the same."[1]

George Congreve

The value of a book is not measured by the large editions which are all sold off, but by the eternity wherewith its teachings may live in some few readers, learners, and practitioners.[2]

Richard Meux Benson

---

[1] George Congreve SSJE, Sermon on "Holy Fear", SSJE/6/5/3/1.

[2] Richard Meux Benson SSJE, Correspondence from Cowley, letter to Mrs Comper, Easter Monday 1904, SSJE/6/1/2/9/6.

Preface and Acknowledgements

Sometime in 1989, looking for something to do in a quiet moment between things at St Stephen's House, I came across one of Fr Congreve's books on a shelf of old texts not important enough to be in the library. Realizing that here was an author who had lived in those same buildings on Marston Street, Oxford, I took up and read. I don't know now which passage it was that arrested the attention, but there began an interest which has sustained me over thirty years.

After ordination I thought, in my innocence, that there would be time between parochial responsibilities to complete the Oxford extramural BD, as it then was. I was encouraged at that point by Peter Hinchliff who supervised initial work. At St Edward's House, then the Mother House, I received—after careful initial inquisition as to my intentions from the Superior, Father Naters—the opportunity to read Congreve's papers in the SSJE archive. I had many happy days off in the library delving into the boxes. Sean Murphy's hospitality gave me an unexpected study in which to work for one day at this time. The Fathers could not have been more welcoming, though they warned me not to eat with them as the food was so poor! It was there that I first came across the extraordinary correspondence between Congreve and Benson, at the beginning of 1890, which precipitated Benson's resignation, and I knew I was on to something historical even if no one was interested in the beautiful spiritual elements of Congreve's legacy; but busyness in life meant that nothing ever came to fruition.

Congreve has, however, often been my inspiration for a point in a homily or some other piece of writing. Geoffrey Rowell told me to keep up the studies. In 2013, I gave a series of talks for the Catholic League at Walsingham, linking Congreve and St Thérèse of Lisieux. (One of the founders of the Catholic League was Father Fynes-Clinton of whom Congreve wrote, "he seems a fine young man".) With the huge and continuing encouragement of Mark Woodruff, these talks were published by the Catholic League along with Congreve's splendid meditation written on Robben Island, "The Sorrow of Nature", as *The Sorrow of Nature: The Way of the Cross with George Congreve SSJE and St Thérèse of Lisieux.*

Ironically it was the conclusion of the life of the English congregation of SSJE which spurred further work. Charles Card-Reynolds and the other trustees of the Fellowship of St John have been unfailingly kind and supportive, and I am very grateful to them for permission to make extensive use of the archive which passed into their care and which they placed in the Lambeth Palace Library in 2012. The series of slightly chaotically arranged boxes which I knew has been thoroughly and carefully archived and indexed by Simon Sheppard. Congreve wrote, "Nothing tires my head as much as copying manuscripts. I am sure it is bad for you." Thanks to Simon, you can now find those words at SSJE/6/5/2/4/13, f. 13. His help, and that of his colleagues at the Church of England Record Centre in Bermondsey, meant copying manuscripts was not so bad at all for me during study leave, granted by the Diocese of London in 2015, during which I read the Congreve archive systematically and drew together the years of notes into some sort of continuous text. My thanks to the diocese, and more recently to the Bishop of London, for time in the last stages of writing to get everything in order.

Serenhedd James has now completed for the Fellowship of St John his work, *The Cowley Fathers* (Canterbury Press, 2019) which will stand as the definitive general history of the English Congregation of SSJE. His interest, care, encouragement, correction and quotation of my work has been a constant support in the process of writing. Douglas Dales was a veritable Barnabas and gave immensely valuable advice in structuring the book. He also read it in its entirety, as did Nigel Aston, Robert Beaken, Barry Orford, Stephen Platten and Mark Woodruff. Their trenchant comments have helped to make it much better than it would have been. All the mistakes and omissions are, of course, mine. It is an especial pleasure to know the prayers and support of Brother James Koester SSJE, the Superior of the American Congregation, and others of the Brethren who have also read the draft.

I have seized on opportunities to draw on the material and forge it into something better through discussion. These have especially included presenting a paper at the conference organized by the Fellowship of St John on the Cowley Fathers, at St Stephen's House; a lecture at Pusey House at the invitation of the Principal, George Westhaver; the annual Sheffield Lecture on Catholic Mission at St Matthew's, Carver Street, at the invitation of Grant Naylor and the Bishop of Sheffield; and the "Gift of Catholic Mission" conference in London arranged by Michael Bowie and Susan Lucas. A more devotional presentation was made for a Lent Day at St Mary's, Wellingborough; I am more grateful than I can say to Robert Farmer for his gift to me on that occasion of a copy of *Christian Progress* inscribed by Congreve.

All this has been supported in the last three years through the appointment, by the Principal and House Council, to an Honorary Research Fellowship at St Stephen's House, and I take this opportunity to give a public thank you to the institution where for me (and in a way for Father Congreve) this began.

Writing is one thing, finding a publisher is another. Many of those already named have given assistance and advice, and I am grateful to Stephen Platten for his introduction to the enormously helpful team at Sacristy Press. Declan Kelly and his team at Lambeth Palace Library have been unfailingly generous with time in helping to find pictures and check things in the period when the library move and COVID restrictions have meant that the archives are closed. I gratefully acknowledge their permission to reproduce the illustrations. The Rector of Bilton, Tim Cockell, kindly arranged for the picture of Richard Assheton and he and the Assheton family kindly gave permission for its use.

Jacqui has always encouraged me when I have thought I was wasting time, effort and indeed money on all of this. To her unselfish love and kindness I am extraordinarily indebted, till death us do part—and in God's grace beyond—and maybe she will accept this in lieu of all those flowers I should buy but never do.

Congreve wrote beautifully, but his books are out of print and he is not well known. I have therefore quoted extensively, both from his published and his unpublished writings, in order to allow him, as far as possible, to speak for himself. Discussion of issues is largely left to the footnotes, rather than intruding an authorial voice into the text. Congreve was a man of his time and uses ideas and language which reflect his own culture and Victorian assumptions. I have quoted what he wrote and tried to explain his views. Specifically, I have made use—always in quotations and in context—of his way of describing the people of Africa, India and elsewhere. Words such as "native", "Kafir" and "coloured" were for him neutral, and I hope that his love of those he variously described is properly expressed and the nuance of his views explained in the discussion in the text.

The book is structured loosely around the course of Congreve's life, although in order to maintain themes I have taken material from his entire oeuvre in each chapter. An introduction sets his life, in very general terms, in the context of the political, ecclesiastical, international and intellectual developments of the age in which he lived. There follows a narrative of his background and early life before he came to Cowley, and the reasons for his move to join the Society. This is, in fact, nearly half his life, but both the archive material and the importance of his contribution, it seems to me, fall almost entirely in the second half of his sojourn on earth. The second chapter explores Congreve's beginning of the religious life and his later teaching on its nature.

One of Congreve's major themes was the way that God is revealed by "glimpses" through beauty and through the natural world. Because of his association with Ninian Comper, in the early part of his religious life, this theme is taken next. Historically speaking, the heart of the book is Chapter 4 which explores the events around the resignation of Benson, but also explores the debate within SSJE about the best way to structure relationships within a religious community, so central to the failures of Benson's leadership. I argue that Congreve's intervention saved the Society from collapse at that point. Chapter 5 looks in more detail at the balance between activity and contemplation in the religious life, but also has a bearing on our modern concerns for wellbeing amongst the clergy and church workers. It is in this chapter that Congreve's missiology is explored. Congreve's first trip beyond Europe and his first encounter with South Africa is also narrated here.

There follow two chapters on his second period in South Africa: an extraordinarily fertile five years spent in Cape Town at the very beginning of the twentieth century. The work he did for the Society in Cape Town and the nature and activity of the mission during the Boer War are described. There is further understanding of nature, with its place in the economy of salvation and the nature of Christian hope is explored. The contributions of Africans to the Mission are discussed, along with issues of race relations. There are extensive quotations from what was some of Congreve's loveliest writing.

Chapter 8 moves the focus to Congreve's teaching about war, drawing both on his own background as the scion of a military family and on his writing and speaking during the Boer War and the First World War. He is challenging, interesting and relevant in restating what may be thought outdated positions but which have much to say to us today. Finally, Chapter 9 sets out Congreve's creative understanding of the Christian in old age, as he looks with clear sight at decay and death rather than avoiding the issues by simply attempting to extend middle age. The concluding chapter is an attempt at an assessment of Congreve's contribution and legacy, asking why—if he is so helpful—he has been so singularly forgotten.

This is not a history of the Society of Saint John the Evangelist, nor of Anglo-Catholicism, nor of the British Empire. It is not a book about aesthetics, or the care of nature, or the religious life. It is neither family nor military history. It is not a book of spirituality nor a source of prayers and meditations. It does touch on all these things and more, but what gives coherence is the underlying object which was Congreve's great focus and theme. Always he was seeing how things point to God and, if I have been successful, that will be the thread which draws it all together. In his book, *The Interior Life* (p. 190.), Congreve wrote of a portrait, "The artist's aim was not to reproduce an image of a certain person's features, but to express the infinite mystery of a human soul created in the image of God." If this work comes somewhere near achieving that, then it will have served its purpose.

Introduction

Just before George Congreve was born in 1835, there was a revolution in England. It is not usually described as such, but an enormous upheaval of the British polity resulted from three momentous legislative acts: the repeal of the Test and Corporation Acts in 1828, Catholic Emancipation in 1829, and the Reform Act of 1832 effected a definitive shift away from a confessional state in which membership of the Church of England was the prerequisite for participation in education, government and (most of) society. The theology and teaching of the Church of England was no longer explicitly the underpinning of the way that society was ordered. Prior to this revolution of 1828–32, Parliament was "a kind of lay assembly" of the church and the Church was—in theory—"guarantor of order and morality, and . . . of political Liberty". Now the Church was to be simply an institution (albeit a powerful and influential one) within the state.[1] As is often the case with revolutions, to the casual observer in many ways nothing seemed to change, but the consequences took decades to work out, decades during which Congreve grew to maturity, was ordained as a Church of England priest and became a member of the Society of Saint John the Evangelist, the community of priests supported by lay brothers living a life dedicated to God in which he was to serve until his death in 1918.

When he was a boy, Congreve's family were living in County Wicklow; it was there he grew up, and member of an ancient English family though he was, he always thought of himself as Irish.[2] At this time the whole island of Ireland was governed from Westminster. The changes to the

1   Kenneth Hylson-Smith, *The Churches in England from Elizabeth I to Elizabeth II: Vol. 2, 1689–1833* (London: SCM Press, 1997), p. 309.
2   William Hawks Longridge SSJE (ed.), *Spiritual Letters of Father Congreve* (London: Mowbray, 1928), letter of 16 May 1888, p. 20.

position of the Church of England had repercussions in the complex politics of Ireland, bringing violence to the fore.[3]

In later life Congreve recognized the "hopeless ignorance and narrowness" of the Church of England in Ireland. "I see now that our way of religion must have been to the Roman Catholics a perpetual scandal, for though there were hidden Saints and lives of prayer among us, yet there was a pagan ignorance and contempt of every Catholic tradition." He went on to note, however, that there was wrong on all sides. A neighbouring member of the English aristocracy survived being shot in the head. Congreve remembered, "A relation of mine was at the railway station and heard a countryman bringing the news to a Roman Catholic priest, who had just taken a place in the railway carriage. 'Did they give him warning?' asked his Reverence. 'They did.' 'Then why didn't he take it?'"[4] He recalled his own "shock of religious horror" when he saw a procession of students walking cassocked and barefoot near the seminary at Maynooth. He was shocked at the idea that young boys like him were being "trained and disciplined to go into the world to spread the awful doctrines of the Church of Rome and nobody could stop them".[5] Congreve's often repeated concern to seek "cordiality" between people of different religious outlooks was forged in youthful experience of deep sectarianism and conflict. Although his father was a member of the Royal Irish Constabulary, nothing in Congreve's surviving writings refers to the famine of 1848 when he was thirteen. The politics of Ireland were, however, one of the few issues related to the world which feature in his correspondence, especially when Gladstone in 1884 and Asquith in 1914 attempted to resolve the "Irish Question".[6]

Within the Church of England, there were broadly two responses to the changes in the constitutional position of the Church. There were those who welcomed—or at least acquiesced in—the right of the state to direct

---

[3]   Hylson-Smith, *Churches in England*, p. 314.

[4]   Mildred Violet Woodgate, *Father Congreve of Cowley* (London: Geoffrey Bles, 1956), p. 3.

[5]   Ibid.

[6]   Congreve, Correspondence with Fr Benson, letter dated "Caldy, Weds" [1886], SSJE/6/5/2/1.

the church: forgoing independence in order to retain influence. Their opponents characterized them as "Erastians" following the view named (possibly unfairly) after the sixteenth-century Swiss reformer Erastus, that the State is supreme over the Church.[7] The other view found voice when the Professor of Poetry at Oxford, John Keble, preached the Assize Sermon at the University Church in 1833. A sermon before the Assizes began was an example of the old constitutional ideals, the church recalling the judiciary to the principles on which they should judge before the courts sat. Keble used the opportunity to decry "National Apostasy" and asserted the Church's independence. This sermon is usually understood to be the beginning of what has come to be called the Oxford Movement.[8] With Keble the two great leaders of the movement were John Henry Newman, the vicar of the University Church in Oxford, and Edward Pusey, Regius Professor of Hebrew.

Others swiftly began to identify with Pusey, Keble and Newman, including Richard Meux Benson, like Pusey a member of Christ Church, who was attracted by the commitment and zeal of the new movement. They campaigned by producing pamphlets or tracts, and thus became known as "Tractarians". Their argument was that the Church is independent of the state because it is "catholic". The Church of England in Ireland in which Congreve was brought up was self-consciously Protestant, defining itself against the Roman Catholic Irish church, and in the rest of the British Isles most members of the Church of England took a similar view. There had, however, been a stream of "High Churchmen" who emphasized, as the Tractarians now insisted, that there had been no fundamental hiatus when the Church of England split from Rome in the sixteenth century.[9] Keble, Pusey and Newman argued that because the contemporary Church had a direct continuity with the undivided

---

7 Owen Chadwick, *The Pelican History of the Church: Vol. 3, The Reformation* (London: Penguin Books, 1964), p. 150.

8 But see Peter Nockles, "The Oxford Movement: Historical Background, 1780–1833", in Geoffrey Rowell (ed.), *Tradition Renewed: The Oxford Movement Conference Papers* (Allison Park, PA: Pickwick Publications, 1986), p. 24.

9 Richard Sharp, "New Perspectives on the High Church Tradition: Historical Background 1730 to 1780", in Rowell (ed.), *Tradition Renewed*, pp. 4–23.

western Church, it was independent of the state. The Church of England was not, they argued, Protestant, but Catholic. While, as time went on, some—prime among them Newman—came to the conclusion that to be catholic required them to become Roman Catholics, Keble and Pusey remained in the Church of England.

In the face of these divisions of opinion in the Church, just as in contemporary politics, "parties" (though without formal membership) began to develop. Alongside the Tractarians, who also became known as "Anglo-Catholics", the inheritors of the great Evangelical revival of the previous century became more self-conscious. There was also a third group, the "Broad Church", who accepted the new settlement of Church and state and took the anti-dogmatic position that there can be an acceptance of a wide range of views on theological issues.[10]

Whatever the proximate political and legal beginnings of the Anglo-Catholic movement, it was above all spiritual and theological. Much Anglo-Catholic theological thinking started by drawing out the implications of the belief in the incarnation, that in Jesus Christ God became fully a human being so that human beings can participate in God.[11] In a retreat given in the 1880s, Congreve wrote:

> Not only is the incarnation a fact of history, a fact which still exists and is as powerful as ever, but . . . it is the very basis of all reality, of every substance of all existence. By Christ all things were made . . . all history is but the glory of the working out of His purpose, who, being God was made man.[12]

The understanding that the incarnation was for all people led the Anglo-Catholics to serve the poorest, and as the nineteenth century progressed,

---

[10]   Hylson-Smith, *Churches in England*, p. 314. Perry Butler, "From the Early Eighteenth Century to the Present Day", in Stephen Sykes and John Booty (eds), *The Study of Anglicanism* (London: SPCK, 1988), pp. 32–7.

[11]   Geoffrey Rowell, *The Vision Glorious: Themes and Personalities of the Catholic Revival in Anglicanism* (Oxford: Oxford University Press, 1983), p. 15.

[12]   George Congreve SSJE, *Cowley Retreats No. 1: The Incarnation and the Religious Life* (Oxford: Society of Saint John the Evangelist, 1930), p. 5.

there developed the phenomenon of the "slum priest". In his eighties, in the years just before the First World War, Benson would travel to London to go to St Peter's, London Docks and work with the people there, and the clergy at St James's, Liverpool had a significant impact on Congreve when he came to serve in his first parish on the Wirral in the 1860s.[13]

Many of these younger clergy brought not only learning and holiness, but art and theatre. Congreve was to be a significant patron of church art himself but he was not a "ritualist", one of those who made use of elaborate ceremonial vestments and rich decoration in their churches, partly in conformity with contemporary Roman Catholic practice, and partly because it gave their churches a sense of the numinous and a touch of heaven in ordinary.[14] In common with the early leaders, Benson had a nuanced position on vestments and other externals: prepared to use them, but not seeing them as crucial.[15] Congreve similarly wrote to a correspondent, about some chasubles, that they were in his view legal and "quite worth restoring" but that he was happy in private and small services with the "linen vestment".[16] Others placed much more emphasis on the right to use ritual actions and aids, devoting much time to study and research to prove their use to be in accordance with both Scripture and the teaching of the Church of England.

The SSJE were more interested in the pastoral and spiritual application of ritual practices, supporting the reintroduction of confession and, for example, research into the anointing of the sick: Father Puller, one of Congreve's younger contemporaries in the Society, wrote a book on

---

13 Nigel Scotland, *Squires in the Slums: Settlements and Missions in Late Victorian Britain* (London: I. B. Tauris, 2007). For a vivid description of Benson at St Peter's, London Docks, see Mildred Violet Woodgate, *Father Benson of Cowley* (London: Geoffrey Bles, 1953), pp. 173–5.

14 John Shelton Reed, *Glorious Battle: The Cultural Politics of Victorian Anglo-Catholicism* (Nashville, TN: Vanderbilt University Press, 1996), p. 25.

15 Serenhedd James, *The Cowley Fathers: The History of the English Congregation of the Society of Saint John the Evangelist* (Norwich: Canterbury Press, 2019), pp. 49, 131.

16 Congreve, Copies of letters to friends and associates: letter to Mrs Torr, 1 October 1898, SSJE/6/5/2/7.

this subject, based on lectures he had given with the encouragement of Father Waggett, another friend and contemporary of Congreve's.[17] Others however were more militant in support of "externals". In the 1870s, when opposition to Anglo-Catholicism was strongly expressed and attempts were made to use the law to enforce simpler worship, they were prepared to lose their livings and even go to prison over the issue, following through on their view that the State and its laws cannot regulate the Church.[18]

All the Tractarian leaders, but perhaps especially Pusey, had called for a renewal of personal holiness as the means by which the nation could be called back from apostasy to faithfulness, and the infelicities of constitutional arrangements corrected. Personal holiness took different forms. Where Pusey disengaged from the pleasures of this world—an asceticism for which Benson too was singularly noted—Keble, by contrast, "was generally more willing to see God in nature and in life's simple pleasures"—in which he was strikingly like Congreve.[19]

The quest for personal holiness led to attempts to form communities of "religious" living under vows of poverty, chastity and obedience—in effect, the re-establishment of monasticism in the Church of England.[20] In this, Pusey was a pioneer. The first communities were for women, but soon attempts were made to establish communities for men. Benson became the vicar of Cowley St John to the east of Oxford in 1850. A man of deep personal prayer and austerity, he joined a guild called the Brotherhood of the Holy Trinity in 1852; the guild called its members to live under a rule (on which Pusey had advised) in an ordered and dedicated fashion. This led in time to Benson and two other priests establishing the Society of Saint John the Evangelist, living together in

---

[17] Frederick William Puller SSJE, *The Anointing of the Sick in Scripture and Tradition, with some Considerations on the Numbering of the Sacraments* (London: SPCK, for the Church Historical Society, 1904).

[18] Reed, *Glorious Battle*, p. 164.

[19] Frederick H. Borsch, "Ye Shall Be Holy: Reflections on the Spirituality of the Oxford Movement", in Rowell (ed.), *Tradition Renewed*, p. 69.

[20] Peter F. Anson, *The Call of the Cloister* (London: SPCK, 1955).

a mission house in his parish.[21] From the beginning they had plans for overseas missions, especially in India and North America. During the first years after his own ordination, Congreve had shared this concern, and it was that which brought him into contact with Benson and the SSJE in the mid-1860s.

The mid-nineteenth-century world was shrinking and had been for some time. In December 1825, the steam paddle ship *Enterprize* [*sic*] docked in Calcutta, 113 days after leaving the pool of London. It was the first time that a steam vessel had made such a long journey, albeit large parts had been under sail.[22] Faster and better links were important following the establishment in 1818 of wider and firmer dominance of the British in India. During the first three decades of the nineteenth century, the continuing growth of British hegemony in India had led to a significant debate about Christian mission—in India specifically, but also across the expanding British Empire. This debate took place in the context of the changes to the religious constitution that had spawned the Oxford Movement. The outcome defined the shape of missionary endeavour in the Empire and is the background to the foreign missionary work of the Society of Saint John the Evangelist, and Congreve's part within it.

As she became clearly the dominant power in India, there were those who argued that Britain should act as the Mughals had done before, allowing local Indian life to continue without interference under a framework of security and taxation. This was largely the view taken at the turn of the eighteenth and nineteenth centuries by those such as Warren Hastings who were directly instrumental in establishing the position of the British in India. They felt that any attempt to bring Christianity to India would lead to resistance and revolt. This view was long-lived. In the mid-nineteenth century Lord Ellenborough, the last President of the Board of Control of the East India Company, stated that "Christian

---

[21] James, *Cowley Fathers*, pp. 1–10.

[22] David K. Brown, *Before the Ironclad: Warship Design and Development 1815–1860* (Barnsley: Seaforth Publishing, 2015), p. 50. *Enterprize* had spent sixty-four days steaming and the rest under sail.

education" was responsible for the "almost unanimous mutiny in the Bengal army" in the uprising of 1857.[23]

At the beginning of the century, however, Christian evangelicals in Britain who were campaigning against the transatlantic slave trade were horrified with a position, however politically astute, which meant leaving unchallenged slavery and social practices in India, such as infanticide and suttee (the burning alive of a widow on the funeral pyre of her husband).[24] Samuel Wilberforce and others demanded the gospel should be preached in India not only to save souls, but to reform society. They found allies among political Radicals and philosophical Utilitarians who believed the irrationality of superstition would hinder the development of India (and, as free traders, they were concerned that the monopoly of the East India Company inhibited trade). When the East India Company's charter was renewed in 1793, the effort of Wilberforce to allow Christian missionary activity in areas controlled by the Company was defeated in the Commons; opportunities to abolish suttee were turned down around 1800. The debate continued, however, and when in 1813 the East India Company's trading monopoly was abolished, the country was opened to missionary activity, though without any government funding.

The refusal of government to sponsor missionary activity was crucial for the future. It meant that the endeavour to evangelize India was not an activity of the state, but was placed in the hands of churches and of missionary bodies established for the purpose.[25] Coming a decade and a half before the repeal of the Test and Corporation Acts, this government neutrality about whether and by whom missions were conducted could be said to be the first part of the "national apostasy" Keble denounced. The policy articulated separation of Church and State, with a clear view that the new dominions, whatever polity they were to have, would not be

---

[23] Max Warren, "The Church Militant Abroad: Victorian Missionaries", in Anthony Symondson (ed.), *The Victorian Crisis of Faith* (London: SPCK, 1970), pp. 57–70, here at p. 64.

[24] Tom Holland, *Dominion: The Making of the Western Mind* (London: Little, Brown, 2019), p. 401.

[25] Percival Spear, *A History of India: Vol. 2* (Harmondsworth: Penguin, 1965), p. 123.

confessional states. Any idea evaporated that India might be converted to Christianity by conquest, as large parts of it had been converted to Islam from the eleventh to the fifteenth centuries, or by mass baptisms following the conversions of rulers, such as brought the Russians to Christianity in the ninth.

The debates continued, and by 1828 it was recognized by British administrators that "we have a great moral duty to perform in India". Suttee was abolished in British India that year, though the concern that the ban might be overturned in Parliament led to Raja Rammohun Roy travelling to Britain to defend the abolition on the grounds that suttee had no real part in true Hinduism—simultaneously defending his own religion from British interference and winning the praise and thanks of evangelical Christians.[26] Meanwhile, in India steps were taken with the support of local communities to suppress Thuggee, ritual murder and robbery in the name of the goddess Kali. In keeping with the principle that westernization was counterproductive to empire, other Indian customs—prime among them the caste system—were left untouched.[27]

Congreve wrote vividly, after his own visit to India, of the huge task the missionaries perceived themselves to be facing:

> Imagine yourself passing, as once was my lot, through a Hindu Méla or sacred pilgrimage. A million Hindus filled the plain where the Ganges and Jumna meet. We who are looking on there, with our English conventionality and self-possession are but an atom in that tempest of spiritual forces. Two thousand ascetics march past us, through the crowd that worships, down to bathe in and adore the sacred river: the air trembles with the spiritual fervour of the multitude. The Englishman standing by to see the sight knows himself to be an alien to these million worshippers of the Ganges that surround him, these two thousand enthusiastic

---

[26] Holland, *Dominion*, p. 403.

[27] Spear, *History of India*, pp. 120–5.

ascetics, as if he had just alighted there from another planet . . .
Could there be any place for Christ in such a gathering?[28]

He described the little Church Missionary Society tent, and the missionary there handing out one small book.

The Church Missionary Society, founded in 1799 by William Wilberforce, the former (and repentant) slave trader John Newton and others, with its headquarters in William Goode's study in the Rectory of St Andrew-by-the-Wardrobe in the City, was an attempt to organize missionaries into groups and to focus work.[29] Prior to the founding of the Mission Societies many individuals had attempted to go to foreign mission fields with no training, and some of them barely literate.[30] The rise of Anglo-Catholicism led to further organizations for prayer and fundraising at home, linked with a different style of mission abroad.

Anglo-Catholics brought two distinctive policies to the attempt to evangelize in non-Christian environments. The first was inculturalization. Previous missions had brought British ways along with British belief. In 1849, when an evangelical Society for the Suppressing of Human Sacrifices in West Africa was established, its aims were not only "prohibitions of human sacrifice, twin murder and trial by ordeal, but also provision for such things as the right of the mission house to be an asylum, the Presbyterian conception of Sunday observance, and Victorian dress fashions".[31] By contrast, Anglo-Catholics sought to work with local customs and ways, training local catechists and teachers and trying to enable local cultures to become Christian rather than attempting

---

[28]   George Congreve SSJE, *The Interior Life, and Other Addresses* (London: Mowbray, 1913), p. 318.

[29]   The study is the present writer's kitchen.

[30]   Peter Hinchliff, "The Selection and Training of Missionaries in the Early Nineteenth Century", in G. J. Cuming (ed.), *Studies in Church History, Vol. 6: The Mission of the Church and the Propagation of the Faith* (Cambridge: Cambridge University Press, 1970), pp. 131–5.

[31]   J. F. A. Ajayi, *Christian Missions in Nigeria, 1841–1891: The Making of a New Elite* (London: Longman, 1965), p. 65, quoted in Warren, "Church Militant", p. 64.

wholesale westernization. When the Cowley Fathers sent their catechist Bernard Mizeki to his own people, and to martyrdom, they were working in just this tradition. Congreve himself only went to South Africa late in life and was "too late in foreign lands to learn a new language", but others were expected to preach and minister in Xhosa.[32]

The second distinction of Anglo-Catholic mission endeavour—as might be expected for those who were "High Church", that is, had a high view of the institution of the church as ordained by God and not merely a human construct—was what Pusey called "Church Mission". The Roman Catholic Church had an international hierarchy, while the individual missionaries and the Mission Societies were often from the non-conformist and non-episcopalian churches. Pusey argued that the way forward was for Church of England missionary bishops, since:

> [f]or the wants of mankind an institution is needed, unvarying in
> its main character, independent of man . . . supported by God . . .
> and having His permanency imparted to it. Such an institution
> He has given us in His Church against which "the gates of hell
> shall not prevail". The Church is, in prophecy as in history and
> fact, *the* preacher of the Gospel and the converter of the heathen
> . . . Her succession of Bishops mount up, by a golden chain, link
> by link, to the apostles.[33]

The difficulty was that consecrating overseas bishops was complex and cumbersome. An act of Parliament was needed in 1786 to enable the consecrations of those who would work in territories not under the Crown (for this reason Samuel Seabury, the first Bishop for North America, had to be consecrated in the non-established Scottish Episcopal Church). Each new see also required legislation. By 1841 when the Colonial Bishoprics Fund was set up, there were only seven overseas bishops

---

[32] Henry Power Bull SSJE, "George Congreve", in *The Cowley Evangelist*, May 1918, p. 101.

[33] E. B. Pusey, *Parochial Sermons* (Oxford and London, 1865), No. 11, quoted in Ruth Teale, "Dr Pusey and the Church Overseas", in Perry Butler (ed.), *Pusey Rediscovered* (London: SPCK, 1983), p. 187.

serving in America, Canada, the West Indies, Calcutta and Australia. Pusey campaigned for their increase, working with key supporters such as his school friend Edward Coleridge (Coleridge was a Master at Eton from

1824 to 1857, and thus overlapped with the boy Congreve who was at the school 1850–4). Also important was the support of Bishop Blomfield of London.[34] Over time more sees were established and endowed. The first Lambeth Conference of world-wide Bishops of what was by now called the Anglican Communion was held in 1867, by which time there were fifty bishops in the colonies and thirty-five dioceses in America.[35]

By the time Congreve made his visits to South Africa in the 1890s and 1900s, relations between the Bishop and the mission of the Society of Saint John the Evangelist were both cordial and important. Some other issues had been thrashed out over the fifty years or so since the campaigners had worked for the establishment of a bishopric in Cape Town. Pusey had attempted to elide the Crown from the appointment process for bishops in the missions, but in this he was defeated. During the 1860s, the overseas churches began to develop forms of synodical government and to work out, through a number of complex legal cases, where authority lay for local churches. The colonial sees began to grow in independence and to assert local governance.[36] These complexities played into the situation following the breakdown of relations between Benson and the American Father Grafton, one of Benson's original collaborators in founding the Society, and in the division which ensued between the American and English congregations of the SSJE.[37]

---

[34]   On Pusey's crucial role, see Teale, "Dr Pusey", p. 186. On Coleridge, Teale, *op. cit.*, p. 192 and G. F. Maclear, *St Augustine's Canterbury: Its Rise, Ruin, and Restoration* (London: Wells Gardner, Darton and Co., 1888).

[35]   Butler, "From the Early Eighteenth Century to the Present Day", in Sykes and Booty (eds), *Study of Anglicanism*, pp. 37–9.

[36]   Peter Hinchliff, "Church-State Relations", in Sykes and Booty (eds), *Study of Anglicanism*, pp. 360–2.

[37]   On the breakdown of relationships, see Eldridge H. Pendleton SSJE, *Press On, the Kingdom: The Life of Charles Chapman Grafton* (Cambridge, MA: Society of Saint John the Evangelist, 2014), pp. 68–81.

One of the legal cases, which led ultimately to the rejection by the Anglican (as it was by now accurate to call it) Church in South Africa of the ultimate authority of the Privy Council, involved the deposition for heresy of the Bishop of Natal, John Colenso, by the Bishop of Cape Town, Robert Gray. The heresy involved included embracing the new biblical criticism which challenged the historicity of parts of the biblical narrative. The intellectual ferment of the nineteenth century forms a background to Congreve's life and thought. It was a time during which many Anglo-Catholics moved from positions which were largely conservative in terms of the so-called "higher criticism" to more nuanced views. Pusey was strongly opposed to modern biblical interpretation, as was Benson. Congreve appears to have been more open to the new thinking, but his own interests were more pastoral and aesthetic, delighting in poetry and beauty rather than agonizing over points of biblical history or interpretation. In this, he is strikingly modern. To a correspondent who wrote for advice for a parishioner whose faith had been shaken by the discovery of the Archeopteryx, he wrote that just because "the development of material things is in one line", that does not mean that "we can ignore the moral and spiritual dimensions of man".[38] It was Benson who was fascinated by the continual discoveries of science, as Congreve noted in 1909: "anything about this half discovered planet [Pluto] fascinates" the Father Founder.[39]

It was transparently clear to Congreve that the work of mission was a supernatural one: "A work like ours is an organised attack on the kingdom of Satan."[40] The conviction of the beginning of the century that conversion is civilizing was taken right through the work. This was held true at home as it was abroad. There is some evidence to suggest that support for the work in the industrialized slums in Britain came from many people in the English establishment because they felt that having a gentleman in

---

[38] Congreve, Copies of letters to friends and associates: letter to Richard Assheton, undated, SSJE/6/5/2/6, f. 100.

[39] Congreve, letter to Br John, 8 January 1909, SSJE/6/5/2/2/10, f. 1.

[40] John M. Schofield, "St Cuthbert's Mission: an Historical Sketch" (1971), SSJE/9/2/4/4, p. 29.

Figure 1: George Congreve aged 52, his greatest
and most productive years yet to come.

every community was a way of preventing revolution.[41] The same mixed motives applied on the foreign mission field. For example, in 1895 Lord Rosebery said:

> [L]iberal imperialism implies, first, the maintenance of the empire; secondly, the opening of new areas for a surplus population; thirdly, the suppression of the slave trade; fourthly, the development of missionary enterprise, and fifthly, the development of our commerce.[42]

Congreve certainly believed that Christianity leads to the growth of civilization; but for him, and for missionaries in the slums of Britain and in countries abroad, their first desire was for the salvation of souls. They believed that without Christ people could not be saved, and there was a real urgency about the work of mission as a result. Congreve did, however, believe that when people act in ways which are open to Christ, then Christ works in them. Speaking of the self-sacrifice of those fighting the First World War, he reflected on:

> the splendid self sacrifice of other loyal and dear fellow subjects of the King who have never heard of Christ to whom nevertheless He has whispered the glorious secret of sacrifice for justice and truth and whose deeds and sufferings His love has ennobled.[43]

Congreve loved South Africa, the country and its peoples. It was another world from his earlier experience. At the beginning of his life there were hardly any European settlements in Africa, and the so-called "scramble for Africa" took place when he was already in late middle age. Lord Rosebery's comments, made just before Congreve first travelled to Africa, are a reminder that slavery remained an acute concern for

---

[41] Brian Green, "Launching the Lifeboats: A History of the Public School Mission Movement", unpublished BA dissertation (Birkbeck College London, 2000), p. 6.

[42] Quoted in Warren, "Church Militant", p. 66.

[43] Congreve, "Sacrifice", in *The Cowley Evangelist*, October 1916, p. 219.

many contemporaries, both in terms of halting what remained of the transatlantic and trans-Saharan trade, and the fear of a re-imposition of slavery under other names and other forms in the exploitation of African peoples through the development of the colonial system. Congreve was particularly alert to this in what he observed during and in the aftermath of the Boer War. There was also the concern of slavery within Africa itself. Britain and the other colonial powers asserted political dominance in Africa some decades after the abolition of slavery, and ostensibly specifically to bring slavery to an end. Congreve shared the contemporary view that the spread of the British Empire would help to stamp out an evil which some estimates suggest that, even at the height of the transatlantic trade, had meant there were more enslaved Black African people within the African continent than outside it.[44]

Towards the end of Congreve's long life, steam ships plied the Atlantic carrying thousands of people, and he himself had travelled from London to South Africa twice and visited India. There were aeroplanes in the skies and motor cars on the road, while the telephone bothered the peace and quiet of the Mission House. Technological change was incessant, as it is today. His was a world at once very similar to and very different from what we know now; but because he strove to speak about what is eternal and "real", he has much to teach later times. In his lifetime Congreve was well regarded as a great spiritual writer. He did not write systematically, but his talks and sermons were collected in a number of volumes, and he contributed prefaces for others' books. His influence continued for a while after his death but has waned, so he is now largely unknown. Congreve would have expected that. He wrote in a panegyric for a dear friend:

> A poet or master in music leaves his life's work behind him to sing on perhaps for many generations; a good Christian makes his life music to God, gives it all out to God without fear from

---

[44]   Roland Oliver and Anthony Atmore, *The African Middle Ages, 1400–1800* (Cambridge: Cambridge University Press, 1981), pp. 195–7; Hugh Thomas, *The Slave Trade: The History of the Atlantic Slave Trade, 1440–1870* (London: Papermac, 1988), pp. 798–9.

day-to-day, and when he comes to die, has nothing to leave behind him to be his monument in this world; he gave his life to God, and its secret dies out of the ages, but is with God, and with those whom it helped to find God.[45]

A hundred years after his death, what is left behind of Congreve still has much to teach of the things of God which break through and transfigure the sorrows of this world, and even those who may disagree with his thought cannot but be struck by the beauty of his writing:

> One Christmas morning, as I was standing before the Sacristy window, ready to go into the Hospital Chapel at Cowley St John, for the early Celebration, I could not help observing a sky impressive in its extraordinary stillness and sadness. A solid grey continent of cloud lay poised in the empty vault of heaven before sunrise. Without change or motion, it stretched from north to south for miles, and suggested irresistibly the long-suffering endurance of man's toilsome life uninspired, unkindled by love from a higher world . . .
>
> With the pathos of that impression in my mind, I went into the chapel to celebrate the Holy Mysteries. We heard the Christmas Gospel: "And the Word was made flesh, and dwelt among us . . ." He who is "the outshining of the Father's glory" came to us in our darkness; we received Him, worshipped, and gave thanks.
>
> When the service was finished, as I returned from the Altar to the Sacristy, and faced the window once more, there appeared again my image of the endurance of fallen man without grace; there, as before, was the almost immeasurable length of cloud-continent stretching across the empty heavens. It lay without motion, the very same in form as I had seen it an hour ago; but now all the weight of its sorrow was lifted, changed, transmuted by the fire of a hidden sunrise.

---

[45] George Congreve SSJE, *Christian Progress, with other Papers and Addresses* (London: Longmans, Green & Co., 1910), p. 14.

The world of mere dulness [*sic*], those leagues (as it were) of lifelong endurance, lay as still as ever, unchanged in any way, except that now every vapour-film in so many miles of cloud-bank was suffused, alive with the fervour of light, the rapture of the manifestation of a new day. Here was the image for me of the difference between a life of patient human toil without the desire of God, and the same life quickened and transformed by the revelation of the love of God in Christ.[46]

In many ways, George Congreve helps those who read his works to see the world in a new light, quickened and transformed by the revelation of the love of God in Christ.

---

[46] George Congreve SSJE, *Christian Life, a Response, with other Retreat Addresses and Sermons* (London: Longmans, Green & Co., 1899), pp. 125–6.

CHAPTER 1

The Beginning of the Life-Adventure

Profession as a member of a religious community "does not crown an attainment in Religion, it is but the equipment, the send-off for our life-adventure".[1] Congreve's view of life was dynamic: the adventure was the constant response to the call of God. Up to the midpoint of his life, his main visible achievement was to build, endow and beautify the church of St John the Divine at Frankby on the Wirral Peninsula. This was not without adventure, but left him unsatisfied, unsure that he had followed the call that God had for him. To his family and friends, his decision to leave his old life behind may have seemed sudden and surprising, but it was a decision long gestated and represented a continuing development of the man, rather than a break with what had gone before.

Dr Johnson said of the Congreve family that it was "of such great antiquity that it claims a place among the very few that extended their line beyond the Norman Conquest".[2] Despite being known to the wider world for William Congreve, the Restoration playwright, the family was a military one, including another William (1772–1828), a military pyrotechnician who invented an early form of striking match, a type of gun carriage and the Congreve Rocket, with the result that George's nephew Walter was known throughout his own sparkling military career as "Squibs".[3] The family held lands in Ireland, with the family seat at

---

[1] Congreve, *Christian Progress*, p. 173.

[2] Leslie H. Thornton and Pamela Fraser, *The Congreves: father and son* (London: John Murray, 1930), p. 3—though they are uncertain whether the family is of Saxon or Norman descent. The last member of the family at Congreve Hall in Ireland was Ambrose Congreve (1907–2011). He left the house to the nation.

[3] Thornton and Fraser, *The Congreves*, p. 16.

Congreve Manor in Staffordshire, but at the time of George's youth the head of the family, Richard Congreve (his grandfather), resided at Burton Hall in Cheshire. Richard had a large family of five sons and five daughters, of whom George's father Walter was the eldest. George was born in Ireland, the second of five children, on 13 September 1835 while his father was serving there with the 3rd Light Dragoons.[4] After living briefly in Portsmouth, the family moved back to Ireland when Walter became County Inspector in the Royal Irish Constabulary for County Wicklow, a post he held until his retirement on 1 January 1852.[5]

Childhood was filled with happy memories, and the family remained an important source of support and love—both given and received—throughout Congreve's life, while the rural setting of his early years imbued him with a love and knowledge of the natural world which shines out of his writing. "In the Spring the overhanging woods were full of wild cherry blossom and the meadows of marigold and cuckoo flowers. We would fish in a stream of clear gold water which flowed through the loveliest meadows and woods."[6] The family home in County Wicklow, "an old brick house in the taste of Queen Anne's reign", was a place of joy.[7] Yet he was also aware of the constant development, the "setting-off" which was so much a part of his life. In later years, in dedicating one of his books to his sister Selina he remembered that "[w]e began life together: but how soon children's souls reared in one nest find their own wings, make their own independent discoveries, and taste the incommunicable solitude of human personality."[8]

Though close to his brothers, he had a particular bond with his youngest sibling, Selina. She and George were drawn together in part by the early death of their mother, who was a crucial influence on them both, and especially on George, who nursed his mother during her last

---

[4]   Woodgate, *Father Congreve*, p. 1, says Congreve was one of four sons and a daughter. However, writing to Miss Kebbel he says, "Once we were six boys and now there is just one old boy." 8 January 1902, SSJE/6/5/2/11, f. 1.

[5]   Correspondence about Congreve family history, 1927–9, SSJE/6/5/5/7, f. 5.

[6]   Woodgate, *Father Congreve*, p. 1.

[7]   Congreve, letter to Miss Kebbel, 21 January 1904, SSJE/6/5/2/4/1, f. 4.

[8]   Congreve, *Interior Life*, dedicatory introduction.

illness and always remembered her evangelical piety and Christian commitment. Years later he wrote to Selina of her: " . . . Mother's death so gallant, and so tenderly confronted just at the last . . . ".[9] They shared memories through life, but Congreve taught a clear distinction between sterile nostalgia and remembering in thanksgiving, which leads to new things in God. For him the increasing silence in age, caused by the failure of hearing and the death of those with whom one used to converse, is:

> not the cold silence of death but the unspeakable silence of Love—Love which is life indeed. Sometimes of late perhaps one has tried to imagine oneself a little child again, in one's mother's arms, our face to her face—there is a reality corresponding to that imagination; in truth I am being withdrawn from outward solace to the very heart of God, who is Father and Mother to my being.[10]

At Eton, which he entered in 1850, Congreve's Tutor was "good old [F. E.] Durnford".[11] William Johnson Cory, latterly a controversial figure, but one of the greatest schoolmasters of his day, was also strongly influential. Cory's principle in education was the development of the whole person. It is clear that while Congreve was not among the highest-flying men of his generation, his character stood out among them. Cory's anthology *Ionica* was well known at the time, and he dedicated one of the poems, "A Study of Boyhood", to Congreve. After Congreve's death, V. S. S. Coles, the Principal of Pusey House and himself a writer of hymns, sent a copy of the verses to the community at Cowley St John. He wrote on the back:

> I had been told that this poem referred to Father Congreve and he once admitted that it was so, when I showed it to him . . . it exhibits

---

9   Congreve, letter to "N" (Selina Congreve), 11 October 1901, SSJE/6/5/2/5, f. 2. See also Congreve, letter to Br John, 9 July 1902: "I was my mother's nurse . . . in her last illness when I was a young graduate . . . ", SSJE/6/5/2/2/4. Mrs Congreve was also called Selina; the family used a confusingly narrow range of Christian names.

10   Congreve, letter to "N" (Selina Congreve), 20 May 1913, SSJE/6/5/2/5, f. 17.

11   Congreve, letter to Assheton, 12 February 1881, SSJE/6/5/5/9, f. 433.

the best side of the man who was dear to many of his Eton friends, who loved him despite what they regretted, William Cory.

In his covering note, Coles wrote:

> William Cory was not nearly all that might have been wished, but this shows him at his best. He was kind to me and I delighted to think that he appreciated Father Congreve.[12]

The verses describe a boy bereaved of his mother who is "So young, and yet so worn with pain!" The boy's "weak half-curls . . . wound / About a mother's finger long ago . . . " The poem goes on to describe the death of the mother and how the boy grew through it:

> And she has wept since then with him
> Watching together, where the ocean gave
> To her child's counted breathings wave for wave,
> Whilst the heart fluttered, and the eye grew dim.
>
> And when the sun and day-breeze fell,
> She kept with him the vigil of despair;
> Knit hands for comfort, blended sounds of prayer,
> Saw him at dawn face death, and take farewell;
>
> Saw him grow holier through his grief,
> The early grief that lined his withering brow,
> As one by one her stars were quenched. And now
> He that so mourned can play, though life is brief . . .

---

[12]   SSJE/6/5/5/10. Coles's hymns include "Ye who own the faith of Jesus" and "We pray thee, heavenly Father".

Cory was a shrewd observer, noting the Boy's interest in both art and nature, both of which would become themes of Congreve's mature teaching.[13]

At school, Congreve was close to Algernon Swinburne and to Charles Dickens, eldest son of the novelist, though Congreve was unimpressed with the famous father. In 1854, Congreve went up to Exeter College, Oxford to read Classics. Among his contemporaries at Exeter were William Morris and Edward Burne-Jones. In later life, Congreve remembered how William Morris, "himself an undergraduate, painted a piece on the library wall at the Union. Flowers mainly, but hidden in them one or two of King Arthur's knights". Congreve recollected other undergraduates mocking them as "heroic flowers".[14]

It was during his time at Exeter that Congreve determined to offer for holy orders, and preparations for ordination brought into focus the development of his religious understanding. His home was staunchly Irish Protestant Anglican. He recalled in later life that "a Roman Catholic Priest was considered a type of everything disloyal and morally dangerous".[15] Despite this the young Congreve was impressed by the seriousness of the Anglo-Catholics he met, and while at Oxford visited the newly established Cuddesdon, where Henry Parry Liddon was Principal, and found it "convincing".[16] About the time he left school Congreve had suggested at home that religious orders might be re-established in the Anglican Church. His family thought this mad, and although he was not associated with the Oxford Movement, nor with Richard Meux Benson who had become vicar of Cowley in 1850, the family had concerns about Congreve's "popish" leanings. His father would not countenance that he should go to Cuddesdon, and it was suggested that Congreve should go to read theology with a lay Evangelical Scripture reader. This the young man

---

[13]   William Johnson (Cory), "A Study of Boyhood", in *Ionica* (London: Smith Elder & Co., 1858).

[14]   Congreve, letter to Miss Kebbel, 5 July 1904, SSJE/6/5/2/4/13, f. 35. The murals in the Union were painted in 1857. See also Congreve, letter to "N" (Selina Congreve), S. Patrick [17 March] 1903, SSJE/6/5/2/5, f. 26.

[15]   Woodgate, *Father Congreve*, p. 2.

[16]   Ibid., p. 6.

rejected. The compromise was that he should train at Wells Theological College under Canon Pinder.[17]

A fellow student was a contemporary at Eton, Richard Assheton. Congreve wrote towards the end of his life, "I remember I used to notice the handsome boy at school, and did not wish to know him—the same at Oxford [Assheton went up to Christ Church]—at Wells we became acquainted personally, and have been friends ever since, ordained together in the same curacy."[18] The curacy following ordination to the diaconate in 1859 was at Warminster where they were ordained to the priesthood on the Second Sunday of Lent 1860.[19] Each then moved, Congreve in 1861 to Frankby and Assheton to his family's living at Bilton, near Rugby. There has been a church at Bilton at least since Domesday, and Assheton re-ordered the mediaeval building; but Congreve was to establish a new parish and build a church. Congreve and Assheton maintained a life-long correspondence.

Congreve had been especially sought for Frankby, which was near Burton Hall, and the Bishop had to be persuaded that he had enough experience. He was not appointed Vicar, which led him to write, "[H] urrah, I can gratify my love of abjection forever, for it is decreed by the Diocesan Lawyer and the Bishop of Chester that I am to be a Perpetual Curate."[20] Congreve later described his life at this time as being that of the English squire parson.[21] Certainly there was time and scope for reading, gardening, to travel to the Riviera and elsewhere, and to keep up with his extended family.[22] He was close to the Bartons of nearby Caldy Manor, a devout family, and Mrs Barton became for him a crucial support. "No one," he wrote, "pretends that Caldy is heaven, but some of us would never have acquired any taste of heaven but for the way heaven came to shine to us through all the every-day circumstances of life at Caldy

---

[17]   Correspondence on Congreve family history, SSJE/6/5/5/7, f. 6. See also Woodgate, *Father Congreve*, p. 7.

[18]   Congreve, letter to Br John, Palm Sunday 1909, SSJE/6/5/2/2/2–10, f. 11.

[19]   Congreve, Personal papers, SSJE/6/5/1/2.

[20]   Congreve, "Reminiscences", SSJE/6/5/5/2, f. 7.

[21]   Congreve, letter to Br John, 13 December 1912, SSJE/6/5/2/2/13, f. 28.

[22]   Woodgate, *Father Congreve*, p. 11.

Figure 2: Richard Assheton. Congreve and Assheton were regular correspondents for the whole of their adult lives.

during those years."[23] Although a bachelor, Congreve's household was full enough. His housekeeper had two teenage children and there were two cats.[24] Congreve's sister Selina lived with him and worked in the parish, working out the vocation which in time would see her join the community of St John the Baptist at Clewer.[25]

Life was not all dignified leisure. Congreve built a congregation from scratch from a population of less than three hundred. The people were often illiterate and there was a considerable problem with drinking and domestic violence which Congreve answered with large-scale temperance work.[26] He wrote on arrival:

> Like Moses from Pisgah I have had a general view of my parish. It was a dirty stormy day; muddy breakers tumbled all along the sand hills 2 miles off: everything looked lonely and sad enough, but thank God I did not despair, though the houses looked few and far between, and both land and sea unfriendly and sad,—for it is God's work.[27]

Congreve was a fine preacher, capable, for instance, of filling the church of his friend Richard Assheton on five consecutive nights of a mission in 1865. As parish priest he faced the challenges of establishing a new parish in a period of some tension between churches in the area. He wrote vividly of his early attempts at visiting. After a very good first visit, his second call was to the home of a sick man. He was about to begin teaching and devotions with the family when two men entered the house, one of whom was "wearing a white neckerchief". This was the Methodist minister, and Congreve wrote that he felt that it would have been wrong to force the family to choose between the two clerics. "Was not the opening of my pastoral work typical? No success without

---

[23] Congreve, *Christian Progress*, p. 15.

[24] Congreve, "Reminiscences", SSJE/6/5/5/2, f. 8.

[25] Correspondence on the publication of Congreve's letters, SSJE/6/5/5/8, f. 4.

[26] Congreve, "Reminiscences", SSJE/6/5/5/2, f. 6, and Woodgate, *Father Congreve*, p. 11.

[27] Congreve, "Reminiscences", SSJE/6/5/5/2, f. 1.

failure and vice versa. There is little chance of my being flattered by false encouragement here."[28]

The work of building and decorating the church went on apace. Congreve was cheered by "the great anxiety of the people to have a church". The Bartons offered strong personal support, making one who was always gregarious very much part of their family, and giving financially to the project. Congreve established classes for children in a barn and noted, "It is easy to hammer the catechism into children's heads. It is hard to teach them religion, indeed it is only at times I realise what it means myself. How earnestly we should teach if we could be living in faith all day long. Which we must try to learn."[29] A little while later he was able to write, "It is a clear spring morning, white frost melting into sparkling drops in the sun, crocuses opening, birds chattering, and a letter promising our East window in time for the consecration of the church."[30]

There was, however, a sense that he could—and should—be able to do or offer more. Part of the outlet came in the support of missionary work abroad. Assheton was also interested, and while at Oxford the two had attended meetings of the University Mission to Central Africa. Congreve became Secretary of the Chester Diocesan Missionary Society. Thomas Dover, of that Society, wrote that once Congreve took on the work, "Frankby became a second home to me."[31] At Frankby a monthly mission service was established in 1861, with a sermon about the missions, home and foreign, and a financial offering. Congreve did not take a collection but put out an alms box, and was delighted by the amounts raised in freewill offerings. He wrote to Assheton about the initiative, "[t]here is another beauty in the plan in that it unites the whole congregation (not the communicants only) on the same Sunday in an act of love to God and self-denial."[32]

This seriousness and desire for dedication stemmed, in part, from his respect for the interior "seriousness" of Anglo-Catholicism which

---

[28] Congreve, "Reminiscences", SSJE/6/5/5/2, f. 3.

[29] Ibid., f. 6.

[30] Ibid., f. 7.

[31] Correspondence on publication of Congreve's letters, SSJE/6/5/5/8, f. 4.

[32] Congreve, letter to Assheton, 3 June 1861, SSJE/6/5/5/9, f. 70.

had been growing in him for some years. Speaking of the Oxford Movement in his time at the University he said, "It was more a spiritual conversion than a change of intellectual ground that had taken place. Advance in ritual was not dreamt of; but a remarkable seriousness in depth began to be found in the lives of those who read the Oxford literature. Tractarianism was quietly making saints in those days before it made apologists and ritualists."[33] Among those who "read the Oxford literature" were two of his aunts who had given him books as a child.[34] As an undergraduate, Congreve had felt that the Oxford Movement was influencing undergraduates in "the healthiest sort of way and getting year after year the very pick of University men".[35]

In his parish, however, apart from a certain medievalism in his choice of stained glass, Congreve was by no means introducing Anglo-Catholic patterns. The Holy Communion was celebrated at Frankby only once a month, and there were no vestments, although Congreve came in for some criticism for wearing a surplice in which to preach. In 1863, there was a small local controversy over Congreve's use of a cross on the altar, flowers, and the practice of turning east during the creed. It was put to him by one of his parishioners that these innovations were an outrage and that he and others would leave the church if they were continued. Congreve wrote that he had decided "to leave them off, on the grounds that they had driven some from the church". This was hardly the response of a campaigning Anglo-Catholic. Congreve went on to reflect wisely, "[P] oor young D will learn that controversy, when successful, in religion gives us *nothing*. He will be surprised to find it just as hard now to realise his faith, live to God all day, as it was before his little victory over Popery."[36] A few years later Congreve returned home from a holiday to find the parish in uproar because he had invited a Ritualist to cover for him when he was away. In 1871 he signed the "Remonstrance" opposing the decision of the Privy Council to impose a "more Protestant" interpretation of the rubrics

---

[33]   Woodgate, *Father Congreve*, p. 4.

[34]   Ibid.

[35]   Ibid., p. 6.

[36]   Congreve, letter to Assheton, 1863, SSJE/6/5/5/9, f. 181.

of the Prayer Book.[37] There was, however, no sense in which Congreve was seeking to introduce the externals of catholic devotion, or even more frequent Communion.[38]

Congreve showed, as a young man, the same desire for "cordiality" among churchmen for which he was to call years later:

> I remember in early days showing a copy of the manual of intercession to a good clergyman in the West of Ireland. He looked it over and was pleased with the aim of the association to which it belonged, but when he caught sight of the names of those who united in the obligation of intercessory prayer and found Dr Pusey, Mr Keble, Fr Benson and others among them, he returned the book to me, saying that he could not associate with such persons for any purpose. A little later I showed the book to another Irish clergyman of the same uncompromising evangelical traditions, but he was besides a man of extraordinary self-sacrifice and sanctity. He was delighted with it; I carefully called his attention to the questionable names to be found among the members of the association; I can never forget how his answer, and the tone of it, cheered me; he said that he would join any men in the world in praying for the conversion of sinners. Some years afterwards when I went to his funeral, the little book I'd given him was shown to be worn out by his carrying it always in his pocket, and by his constant use of it.[39]

---

[37] *An Alphabetical List of the Signatures to a Remonstrance Addressed to the Archbishops and Bishops of the Church of England on Occasion of the Report of the Judicial Committee of the Privy Council in re Herbert v. Purchas* (London: James Parker & Co., 1871).

[38] Congreve, letter to Assheton, 1869, SSJE/6/5/5/9, f. 338. Later his views developed, and he noted approvingly that one of his nephews, "a Major RA fighting since the Mons retreat" had persuaded the chaplain to celebrate daily and made his own communion weekly. Congreve, Copies of letters to friends and associates, letter to Frank Thorne, 25 October 1915, SSJE/6/5/2/7.

[39] George Congreve SSJE, *The Spiritual Order, with Papers and Addresses written for the most part in South Africa* (London: Longmans, Green & Co., 1905),

While at Frankby, Congreve recalled receiving a visit from an evangelical cleric to whom he mentioned going to prayer meetings. "He was absolutely astonished at the fact of a high churchman depending upon prayer."[40] He was attracted to men of similar stamp; Dr Baylee, principal of St Aidan's School and College in Birkenhead where Congreve would make retreats, was described as one whose "chief longing is for a more structured life". Congreve went on to say "what interests me most in him is that he harmonises in his own intellect and life the high and the low notes of Christian doctrine. The individual and the catholic notes of which one longs to reach the harmony."[41]

For Congreve, the principle by which Christians should deal with disagreement is "cordiality". Writing in later life about the relations of various missionary societies, he noted that "cordiality is not the same thing as toleration; . . . between associations of self-denying men whose object is to extend the Kingdom of Christ . . . one would look for nothing less than *cordiality*—sincerest delight in each other's successes, sincerest sympathy in each other's troubles." Cordiality causes the character to grow in a way that mere courtesy cannot. "We are not created to be perfected in our individual distinctness; the man who lives for himself in himself dwindles morally; his personality grows smaller and meaner. In proportion as he lives for and in others, his personality grows rich, and large. It is not official courtesy that makes character dilate, but the giving of the heart, cordiality. No relations are fulfilled without cordiality; we give nothing if we do not give love." He goes on:

> There is often cordiality enough, and of the true sort, among its own members within each of our distinct groups; what we still wait for is the overflow of love towards persons and institutions outside our own mystic inclosure, [*sic*] who do not echo our phrases, but who do love what we love most, and live by the same Life which is also our Life.[42]

---

pp. 46–7.

[40]   Congreve, "Reminiscences", SSJE/6/5/5/2, f. 9.

[41]   Ibid., ff. 11–12.

[42]   Congreve, *Spiritual Order*, Chapter 5, "Of Cordiality", pp. 40–50.

Attracted by the seriousness he saw in Anglo-Catholicism and seeking a way to draw together what he found good in the strands of the church, Congreve was invited to preach at St James the Less, Liverpool, for Harvest Festival in October 1864. He was struck by the strangeness of the ritual and the vestments but found "nothing contrary to the teaching of the Church of England".[43] What impressed him was the sincerity of the clergy and their dedication to their poor and rough district. Writing after he had joined SSJE Congreve noted, "These Ritualists are more devoted to the conversion of souls in their mission than most of us Country Parsons are in our Parishes. For these men it seems to be praying, preaching, hearing confessions day and night, all the year round. They have no recreation that I see and are shut in the slums two miles out of the decent parts of Liverpool. The Ritual, the Processional hymns, the incense and the cross are a cheer to them and their submerged flock;—instead of the sea, the Alpes [sic], music and society for them."[44]

Congreve's sense of fun did not depart with his deepening seriousness. He sent Assheton a letter with a picture of "my new friend in Liverpool the Ritualist in beard and Biretta, an entirely novel idea to me".[45] Nevertheless, Congreve came to respect and learn from the clergy of St James. "I am much struck by the evident influence these men have for good. . . . Working men and mechanics are coming regularly to confession and Holy Communion."[46] At some point around 1870, Congreve began to make his confession, and in 1870 he first met Father Benson.[47] Shortly after this time his sister Selina entered the community at Clewer.[48] Congreve began to ask himself seriously whether his exhortations to

---

[43] Correspondence about Congreve family history, 1927–9, SSJE/6/5/5/7, f. 7.

[44] Congreve, "Reminiscences", SSJE/6/5/5/2, ff. 23b–24.

[45] Congreve, letter to Br John, 13 December 1912, SSJE/6/5/2/2/13, f. 28. (When Assheton died, his family returned Congreve's letters, "some written 50 years ago", which evoked memories he shared in his correspondence with Br John.) See also Woodgate, Father Congreve, p. 13.

[46] Congreve, "Reminiscences", SSJE/6/5/5/2, f. 24.

[47] General notebooks, SSJE/6/5/3/19, Notebook 1: "History of my own discovery of Confession".

[48] Woodgate, Father Congreve, p. 16.

missionary endeavour could or should be answered by himself. In 1870 he wrote of Frankby, "I don't believe this is a place for a man who is quite a man—a fellow who can work should go where work flourishes in quality and quantity . . . An ascetic whose work is to pray, or study, might find his refuge here, a man who can do a good deal would fret and displease himself in this 'narrow room.'"[49]

His own growing conviction that he should offer himself for more strenuous missionary work was bolstered by a direct suggestion from one of the priests in Liverpool.[50] Congreve described the moment of decision as arising from his prayer: "It was the first day of General Intercession of the Foreign Missions, December 20, 1872 that it came right into my mind that a clergyman in England, without home ties, should generally be ready to offer himself to the Church for foreign service in the mission field."[51] At the end of the month, he wrote to Assheton:

> I have for a good many years asked myself does Our Lord want more Christians to go as missionaries to the Heathens? I believe it, and have often said in sermons that those should offer themselves who are free. And then the question comes back to me, "why is it always to be someone else?" So about Christmas I wrote to Father Benson of Cowley to ask if his community would take me in and I'm going after Lent DV to see whether I can live their life, with a view to work with them in some foreign missions. Their work is missionary work in any shape that may present itself to them, at home or abroad. They are sending I believe a mission to India this year.[52]

---

[49]   Congreve, letter to Assheton, SSJE/6/5/5/9, f. 338.

[50]   Woodgate, *Father Congreve*, p. 16.

[51]   Congreve, *Christian Progress*, p. vi.

[52]   Congreve, "Reminiscences", SSJE/6/5/5/2, f. 16. The Reminiscences were never published, but are a typescript of various memories, letters and other material which Congreve seems to have gathered some time after his return from South Africa in 1905.

It was shortly after the celebration of the tenth anniversary of the dedication of the church at Frankby, on the Vigil of St Matthew (20 September) 1873, that he left to make his attempt.[53] "I feel like Samson when he was going to pull down the Palace on his own head. I am planning to leave my parish where I have been in charge 13 years."[54] It was above all for the sense of seriousness that Congreve appears to have chosen Cowley. After Bishop Jacobson of Chester gave Congreve a year of absence, he wrote to Assheton:

> I have no joyful feeling of any kind about going. I am not at all confident I can live at Cowley, that I am fit for the life. I do not particularly like anything there: I know no one there: and I do like many things here,—especially the way the larks are singing at this moment . . . I pray the grace to catch hold of the spirit of thoroughness and seriousness in regard to every detail of the work . . . My life at Frankby was not at all like the life of our Lord Jesus Christ. It is that which brings me here,—the hope of finding in this life at Cowley (God knows if I shall have pluck for it) one step at least towards realising in ever so small a degree the poverty we have revealed in Jesus Christ and in our own poor neighbours, but have not ourselves tasted.[55]

His friends supported him. Mrs Barton of Caldy Manor, who with her husband had provided Congreve with a home from home, and space and companionship, wrote to him, "How all the world can seem changed in one moment. The only bit of the day of Intercession for Foreign Missions that was of any use on my part was the few minutes in which I offered to God all who are dearest to me to be used by Him as He pleases." Her prayer had been answered in a way she had not been expecting:

---

[53] Congreve, letter to Br John, Vigil of St Matthew (20 September) 1912, SSJE/6/5/2/2/13, f. 21.

[54] Congreve, "Reminiscences", SSJE/6/5/5/2, f. 16.

[55] Ibid., ff. 16–17.

> It was not a little offering; [but] shall we offer unto the Lord of that which costs us nothing? [She went on,] [I]t is hard for you to make up your mind to go away and give up your parish. I know what it costs you by what it costs us. We will help you to "dig your grave" and will make it so flowery and tempting that you will jump into it quite merrily.

Congreve was not a man full of health, and along with others Mrs Barton was concerned that he would not be able to cope physically. She spoke of her "fear of your health getting worse, and the breaking up a pleasant daily intercourse here, and the fear of being left behind in the battle of life", but like others she had "a longing all the time to help you with cheerful encouragement every minute". She concluded:

> . . . these great turning points in our lives have to be borne so much alone as far as human friendship can avail; yet we think of you the best we can; and who can tell of all the cloud of witnesses who are helping you from above; and remember how one who chooses the straight road helps every other who desires to choose it too.[56]

This choice was to lead Congreve on the road that would make him a teacher of the faith on a much wider field and enable him to grow in stature of soul.

---

[56]   Congreve, *Christian Progress*, pp. 20–2.

CHAPTER 2

Increasing in True Religion

The Cowley Fathers came together as a "college of clergymen, living together and acting under the parochial clergy".[1] There was (at first) no Rule at Cowley beyond the "inspiration and activity of one man".[2] This was a great strength because of the greatness of the man, Richard Meux Benson, the Vicar of Cowley and founder of the Society of Saint John the Evangelist. It was also a weakness: the difficulties of the personality and thought of the Father Founder meant that the Society almost came to grief. The genesis of a Rule helped, as did the broadening of leadership. While he came to have great influence in the Society, Congreve wrote no Rule and his leadership was indirect; but he learned deeply from Benson how a life might be "lost to self and gained to Christ" and, crucially, he developed and in some ways corrected what Benson taught. He agreed that the principle of life is absolute self-sacrifice, but for Congreve the loss always implied a great gain, the gift of Christ filling the void and giving back what has been offered up. Faithful disciple as Congreve was, he saw this in Benson, and entitled his homily following the Father Founder's death, "Loss and Gain".[3] For the community as a whole, however, it was

---

[1]   Bishop Wilberforce of Oxford, quoted in Anson, *Call of the Cloister*, p. 59.

[2]   A. M. Allchin, "R. M. Benson: The Man in his Time", in Martin L. Smith SSJE (ed.), *Benson of Cowley* (Oxford: Oxford University Press, 1980), p. 11.

[3]   George Congreve SSJE, "Loss and Gain, on the Passing of Father Benson", in Anon., *Cowley Sermons: The Jubilee Volume of the Conventual Church of S. John the Evangelist, Oxford* (London: Mowbray, 1947), pp. 56–72. Also published in the Appendix of George Congreve SSJE and William Hawks Longridge SSJE (eds), *Letters of Richard Meux Benson* (London: Mowbray, 1916), pp. 363–73.

Congreve who, having learnt from Benson how to lose everything for Christ, taught them how to be filled. Where Benson taught the virtue of deadness to the world, and thought there would be no laughter in heaven, Congreve brimmed with life.[4] His loyalty to Benson lasted his long lifetime, but Congreve's different vision of the religious life permeated the Society and allowed it a second Spring.[5] In some ways, the Society of Saint John the Evangelist owed more, in its own development and in its influence on how the religious life should be lived, to Congreve than it did to Benson. The influence spread further through Congreve's writing, retreat-giving and care for other communities.[6]

When Congreve first came across Benson is not clear, though he was Vicar of Cowley while Congreve was an undergraduate. Retreats were thought of as an Anglo-Catholic practice, but influence from high churchmen in Liverpool meant that Congreve had made the practice part of his parochial ministry, leading parishioners on retreats at St Aidan's School and College in Birkenhead, whose Principal—Dr Baylee—longed for "a more structured life" and may have been an early influence on Congreve towards the religious life for himself. Baylee, wrote Congreve, "harmonises in his own intellect and life the high and low notes of Christian Doctrine, the individual and the catholic notes of which one longs to reach the harmony".[7]

---

[4]   Congreve and Longridge (eds), *Letters of R. M. Benson*, Letter 51 (Vol. 1, p. 113): "I suppose there would be nothing to laugh at if there were nothing incongruous, and there would be nothing incongruous if there were nothing wrong. Laughter is God's gift to sinful man to make life supportable. Oh, for the calm unruffled joy of the vision of Paradise!"

[5]   Congreve, *Cowley Retreats No. 1*, p. i.

[6]   Anson notes that Congreve was the first Warden of the Servants of Christ at Pleshey (*Call of the Cloister*, p. 474).

[7]   Congreve, "Reminiscences", SSJE/6/5/5/2, ff. 11 and 12b. On Retreats, see Mission Priests of S. John the Evangelist (eds), "Retreats", in *The Evangelist Library* (London: J. T. Hayes, undated).

Figure 3: The Mission House from Marston Street. The Chapel with its Rose Window is clearly visible at the top of the House.

Congreve first made a retreat at Cowley sometime around 1870.[8] The establishment of a formal Rule for the Society of Saint John the Evangelist was still fourteen years away, and Congreve had only a vague idea of the nature of the "college of clergymen". Years later, in dedicating one of his books to Benson, Congreve recalled, "So little did I understand the vocation to the Religious Life, that I supposed a desire to serve Christ as a missionary might be a proof that I was called to it. I also felt that the life at Cowley should be helpful preparation for missionary work."[9] It was therefore with missionary training in view that he wrote to Benson and came to Cowley shortly after Easter 1873.

He was given a visiting district in the parish and "a classroom of shopkeepers' daughters to whom to give a Bible class". There was, however, little to do; he had expected to learn evangelistic methods and Indian or African languages, and to undergo other preparation, but there was no sign of any training for the missions. Congreve found consolation in the beauties of Oxford and wrote to Assheton, "How lovely the fritillaries in the Iffley Meadows, 'snakes heads' the children call them. There is a [new] window in the cathedral by Morris [and] Burne-Jones with David, Timothy, Samuel."[10]

Unsure of what was happening, Congreve approached Benson for clarification. The reply was "my first lesson in the alphabet of the Dedicated life". Benson said, "I do not think the object of our association and Religious Community is to equip us to go out as missionaries. We do not come into our Community primarily in order to convert others, but rather with the desire, first of all, to be converted ourselves. Then if by God's grace we are converted to him, he may use us in missionary work, or in any other way that he pleases." Following this conversation, Congreve "awoke to the urgency of another call", and was prompted to ask, "Is there some change in myself that I need to make before God

---

8   Woodgate, *Father Congreve*, p. 15. This was possibly at the suggestion of one of the clergy at St James, Liverpool, but there is no evidence for that.

9   Congreve, *Christian Progress*, p. vi.

10   Congreve, "Reminiscences", SSJE/6/5/5/2, f. 16.

can use me in converting others?"[11] Slowly he began to understand the purpose of the community:

> To know God and to walk with God seems to its members enough to live for, out of this relation all their varied interests and activities were to grow. Their personal surrender to God was the primary end of the Institute; the work they were called to do, whatever it might be, did not add completeness to that end. If the work should fail, and leave them with God, that end would be attained nonetheless; and this personal dedication to God was the power by which they strengthened their hands to go on a mission, or to scrub the floor.[12]

The move to Cowley was a wrench from his previous life, though Assheton came to visit, and then Congreve's nephew Walter.

The community was still very new and small.[13] Congreve was clothed as a novice on 20 September 1873, but in the following May his expectations were upset.[14] He wrote to Assheton:

> Dr Jenner declares me unfit for work in India. I am in a maze as to the future . . . This is a very humbling place. It is wonderful not merely to read about holy lives but to see them and live with them . . . Each morning that I rose I remembered: there is no preaching for me today, no instructing of others, or converting the heathens; but today I have to make some advance in my own conversion to God, through whatever work you may give me to do.[15]

Holiness might be wonderful to observe, but the community life was anything but attractive. Mutuality and fellowship were deliberately

---

[11] Congreve, *Christian Progress*, p. vii.

[12] Ibid.

[13] James, *Cowley Fathers*, p. 68.

[14] Correspondence about Congreve family history, 1927–9, SSJE/6/5/5/7, f. 8.

[15] Congreve, "Reminiscences", SSJE/6/5/5/2, f. 18b.

rejected, and the Mission House was a frankly unfriendly place.[16] Some years later Congreve recalled that "no affectionate intercourse ever came to life among us". Community Recreation was an exercise neither in community nor in recreation:

> [W]e were wont to sit out the half-hour and listen with intellectual respect and expectation to anything that might fall from the Superior [Benson] but among ourselves we knew so little of one another, and were so isolated, so dead to one another that we had little enjoyment of recreation and were glad when it was over.[17]

Congreve's naturally gregarious personality reached out to others in the novitiate and particularly to another Irishman, Basil Maturin, with whom he formed a friendship which was life-long. Congreve said of Maturin, "[H]e makes me understand that curious Celtic missionary force which converted the northern and central parts of Britain and many parts of the continent in early days. I feel if I were a Heathen, I should be able to understand Christianity with him to teach me. The House always seems more cheery when he is in it."[18] It was only to Maturin that Congreve confided his loneliness asking, as he later recalled, when off guard one day, "[I]t is very strange that our Brethren come and go, and we never know anything about them; are we never to know one another?"[19]

There was one other whom Congreve came to know. Father Simeon Wilberforce O'Neill was one of the very first of Benson's brethren, and in him Congreve found support and a fellowship which he always recalled thankfully.[20] "It did one good just to be near him. His rare character and life of sacrifice grew out of his close union with God." Benson's

---

[16] Woodgate, *Father Congreve*, p. 19.

[17] George Congreve SSJE, "On Correspondence Between Fathers", SSJE/6/5/5/1, f. 12.

[18] Woodgate, *Father Congreve*, p. 21–2.

[19] Congreve, "On Correspondence Between Fathers", f. 10.

[20] Anson, *Call of the Cloister*, p. 74 and James, *Cowley Fathers*, pp. 37–40, show that in some ways O'Neill was the beginning of the Society even before Benson.

Figure 4: Simeon Wilberforce O'Neill. One of Benson's
first collaborators, O'Neill showed Congreve kindness and
sympathy in the first difficult months of his time at Cowley.

explanation of the purpose of the religious life needed also O'Neill's warm example of how to live:

> When I came as a Postulant long ago, [wrote Congreve] I remember how the silence and the real simplicity of the life impressed me; but a Postulant has "long, long thoughts", grave questions to face, and doubts to settle with himself; and I think it was not the genuine austerity of the small family that satisfied my last doubt, but the frank and cheerful kindness of one professed Father who sought me out in the strangeness of the first silent days, and took me for a walk in the country; he brought me back to my cell convinced. I had doubted whether a life all at a low temperature (so to speak), all in the shade (as ours might seem possibly at first to a Postulant), could be a truly Christian life; in Father O'Neill's friendship I found the unquestionable argument of light: where such joyous generous charity shone, I recognised the indwelling Christ, and there it was good for me to be.[21]

In January 1874, O'Neill left for India, but not before coming to say farewell: "[H]e left a little kiss on the top of my unworthy head—that was the first touch of nature I had received at Cowley—and I felt from that moment that perhaps the true aim of Religion was to sanctify brotherly love, not to kill it, as the novitiate seemed to do."[22] But with O'Neill's departure, Congreve was left to "drop into the unbroken loneliness of our novitiate".[23]

The austerity of the Father Founder was personal and emotional as well as physical. Benson taught personal distance as part of his vision for the Society and for all Christians.[24] Years later Congreve wrote, "[W]e

---

[21]   Congreve, *Christian Progress*, p. 204.

[22]   Congreve, "On Correspondence Between Fathers", f. 10. On O'Neill, see James, *Cowley Fathers*, pp. 65–6.

[23]   Congreve, "On Correspondence Between Fathers", f. 15.

[24]   Benson wrote, "[W]e need to die to all our own visions that we may be pure in heart and see God." Congreve and Longridge (eds), *Letters of R. M. Benson*, Letter 50 (Vol. 1, pp. 111–12).

all felt that this individual solitude was Fr Benson's ideal of religious deadness." Benson did not make friends, nor did he seek colleagues in his work. He once spent months cataloguing the thousands of books in the Mission House library, working at night without telling anyone, for "he preferred to work alone, to rule alone, to be alone, to think alone".[25] Congreve remembered that:

> When he returned to the Mission House after some work or distant journey, we never expected to hear him speak to us of anything that had happened while away, whether of failure or success. All that we knew was that, as he had gone out to each work armed with prayer and self-discipline, so on his return he reverently left with God in silent prayer and thanksgiving the results of the work.[26]

After Benson died, another Father noted:

> Those of us who lived with him knew really very little about him, except that he lived a very hard and secluded life.... Even amongst his own immediate associates he was not an easy person to talk to. I knew him perhaps as intimately as any of my contemporaries, but I always found an interview somewhat alarming. As he once said, "I never knew anyone intimately." His natural shyness and reserve, intensified by his theory of detachment, held him aloof from those who could gladly have given and received from him far more than he would allow. And yet he had a very tender heart, which on rare occasions showed how he really thirsted for human friendship and sympathy.[27]

---

[25] Woodgate, *Father Benson*, p. 91.

[26] Congreve and Longridge (eds), *Letters of R. M. Benson*, Preface, p. v.

[27] Ibid., Appendix, p. 359. Page noted on the front page of Congreve's paper that Page once asked Benson if he was ever intimate with Charles Marriott, and Benson replied "I never was intimate with anyone." Congreve "On Correspondence Between Fathers", f. 1.

Others felt the same: "[T]here was always a certain aloofness which made it difficult for others to approach him, or to live on intimate terms with him. He seemed to live habitually in a world where ordinary human sympathies were transcended, and only supernatural relationships counted."[28] Congreve noted the capacity of the Superior for sympathy, but also its limits:

> I never knew a man with so deep a capacity of sympathy as Fr Benson and we learned to wonder at the generosity with which he gave his time, his care, his tenderness, his whole heart to us undoubtedly as Shepherd, but I do not think he would ever allow himself to receive the least grain of comfort or reverential affection from us, and somehow inspired us with the idea that while we were free to open up all our difficulties and sorrows and joys to him, we ought to grow very independent of one another's sympathies and affections among ourselves in the Society and never to be very intimate with our brethren.[29]

In this, Congreve fundamentally disagreed with Benson:

> [M]y conscience rises up against it as contrary to the whole spirit of Catholic religion—to die to the wish to know about my brother's life seems to me to be an approach to the spirit of the Hindu ascetic but to be an explicit contradiction of the Spirit of the Sacrifice of the Church.[30]

In establishing a religious community, Benson did not see himself as establishing an institution so much as ordering a dedicated but ordinary Christian way of life. Congreve agreed. The foundation of the religious life is prayer, whatever outward works might be undertaken. The vocation is "not to work, but firstly to God himself". The Religious has a "double consecration; baptism and the vocation". Like Benson,

---

28   Congreve and Longridge (eds), *Letters of R. M. Benson*, Appendix, p. 360.

29   Congreve, "On Correspondence Between Fathers", f. 10.

30   Congreve, "On Correspondence Between Fathers", f. 8.

Congreve emphasized communion with God, but he understood each community to be "a school of prayer founded on intimacy with God". Thus "Communion with God is itself a great work, than which none is more invigorating to the whole community or more influential in the advance of Christ's kingdom."[31] By contrast, Benson emphasized the transcendent awefulness of God and his sovereign demands on the soul. It would not seem possible for Benson, so focussed on the otherness and glory of God, to make a statement like Congreve's—"God is kind, and makes Himself, who is beyond us, approachable to us in the incarnation."[32]

The concept of "deadness" in "mortified" relationships was not simply something Congreve found difficult, or disapproved of, but was a mistake which he was in time largely responsible for correcting.[33] He analysed the problem as one of a misunderstanding of how relationships in the religious community should be ordered. As a mature religious he noted with disapproval that the view of the community at the time of his novitiate had been that engagement with others in the parish was not matched with good relationships within the Society:

> As Religious we were to live in continual union of heart with Christ and that would of course involve union with our brethren: but we should learn to be dead to the comfort of fraternal affection and support within the community. Love of *neighbour* yes, outside the community, but *within* separate from all mutual love and support.[34]

---

[31] Congreve, "Sisters, their Vocation and Special Work", in *Pan-Anglican Papers, being problems for consideration at the Pan-Anglican Congress 1908;* SC Group 5, *The Church and its Ministry: The Ministry of Women, Section 2: Organised Associations* (London: SPCK, 1908), pp. 1, 7.

[32] Congreve, *Cowley Retreats No. 1,* p. 7.

[33] It is ironic therefore that, as James notes (*Cowley Fathers,* p. 57), it was following a sermon Congreve preached in 1876 on mortification that SSJE was accused in the *Plymouth and Cornish Advertiser* of practising flagellation.

[34] Congreve, "On Correspondence Between Fathers", f. 11. (Emphasis in the original.)

Congreve rejected the idea that mortification should simply empty a person; rather, mortification clears a space which God may fill and from which the love of God may overflow: "Christian mortification helps us betimes to lay aside every weight, and so leave little for death to do . . . Some are so holy that almost everything that can die had slipped away from them before death came."[35] Congreve saw the prime example of this in Father O'Neill:

> I remember how the gladness of one mortified Religious brought light of heart into our Novitiate, how his spirit would come out of his long fast and severe penance like a bird's song into our silence or dullness. He did not give to his community what our coldness gave to him, but he shared with us all that Christ Risen from the dead was to him; and how joyfully that splendour shone for us out of a mortified life![36]

Congreve taught that friendship, properly ordered, can become a means by which a life can be orientated to God:

> We must only love anybody with God's love, and whom God loves, and as He loves them. Thus our affections, instead of becoming a means of developing our own self-will as they are in the world with worldly men, become even a means of suppressing and killing our own world and developing the will of God.[37]

To Benson renunciation was the foretaste of glory, the preparation of the soldier for the victory. Even if the glory was clear to him in the midst of the spiritual battle, it was not obvious to others, and the practical working out of this renunciation was difficult for many. Chastity became an inhibition of community, and poverty became deliberate discomfort. Although he did counsel care as to "the bodies of our workers", and wrote

[35]   George Congreve SSJE, *The Parable of the Ten Virgins: Addresses Given in Retreat* (London: Mowbray, 1904), p. 59.

[36]   Ibid., p. 60.

[37]   Congreve, *Cowley Retreats No. 1*, p. 89.

No. 851.A FATHER CONGREVE. J. BEAGLES & CO. E.C

Figure 5: George Congreve. This undated photograph must
have been taken in the first years of Congreve's religious life.

"as you would take care of a piano or any handsome school furniture, or a chasuble, so you must take care of a priest",[38] Benson was able to say, "The poorer one's place of lodgement the better,"[39] and few could see with him past the austerity to the glory. In 1899, speaking to the Community at the annual retreat, on "Fraternal Charity in Religious Communities", Congreve told the story of his own novitiate and offered a very different model of the religious life. The profession of the religious:

> is not their death to that faculty of human sympathy and fellowship with which they were born, but on the contrary it will show them that faculty raised to a higher life and power, enriched with new depth, tenderness and courage, and inspired to discover and win new fields for love, through the grace of the vows by which they died for ever to all that could chill or impoverish the love of the Brotherhood, the sympathies of the Body of Christ.[40]

It was almost an explicit repudiation of Benson's method and thought. With a strikingly Victorian turn of phrase, he continued, "A Religious Order where we should find affectionate cordiality among the members banished or disapproved, would be a portent . . . "

Friendships were important and valuable to Congreve, and while they seemed so alien to the method and desires of the Founder, Congreve asserted that friendship is part of the vocation of the religious, and by implication that of all Christians, not something that works against it. On a day on which three new members of the Society had been professed, he spoke of "all those dear people whom they leave in order to join us". He asked whether the newly professed Fathers had now parted with "treasures of home fellowship and tender spiritual associations in parish or mission in order to be separated to the sympathies of Christ alone, dead to all other sympathies for ever?" His answer was that they had emphatically not done so:

---

[38] Congreve and Longridge (eds), *Letters of R. M. Benson,* p. 38.

[39] Congreve and Longridge (eds), *Letters of R. M. Benson,* p. 171.

[40] Congreve, *Christian Progress,* p. 202.

That kind of phrase, delivered with appropriate coolness, strikes us as a bullet from a rifle strikes. Whatever grain of truth may be hidden in it, to us it sounds like blank untruths, flat contradiction to Christ. If I have not quite misunderstood the Gospel, and the lives of saints who served God in the cloister, I see Christ calling Religious Brethren to Himself, not in order to purge them of natural affection, and so to absorb their faculty of sympathy, as to leave none for any created object; but I see Him calling them in order to purify and ennoble their natural facility of loving, and to invigorate and enrich it by adding to it the gift of His Own Heart, so as to send them forth more in sympathy than ever with all saints and sinners . . . [41]

Not for Congreve the transcending of all human relationships, but rather their fulfilment. Friendships within and beyond the community were, for him, necessary for the proper ordering of that community to God.

There was an attempt in the first years of Father Page's time as Superior in the 1890s to use Benson's commentary on the Rule as a justification for forbidding personal correspondence between the Fathers of the Society. Congreve wrote a lengthy paper in which he categorically rejected the idea, describing again the emotional coldness of the period of his novitiate.[42] After noting how community life is bound together by mutual knowledge of work and circumstances, particularly between those who are separated by great distances, he went on to point out that if suppressed in community life:

---

[41] Ibid., pp. 201–2. These professions in 1899 included H. P. Bull and G. S. Maxwell, both of whom were to become Superior General: James, *Cowley Fathers*, p. 460.

[42] Though Congreve was careful not to reject Benson himself: "I cannot help regarding this phrase as one of those paradoxes which sometimes startle one's conscience in Fr Benson's teaching and which the whole Catholic Context as it were of his theology, and the intentions of his own heart—and his own practice—contradict." Congreve, "On Correspondence Between Fathers", f. 7.

> [T]he social side of the soul which you cannot extinguish . . . will find relief in more or less secular interests instead of in the Religious Community from which it has been broken off by the doctrine of pseudo-deadness. The soul will seek common sympathies in the houses of the aristocracy; in literature; science; morbid developments of exaggerated and excessively systematised works.[43]

He was uncharacteristically sharp in his tone, noting that St Paul was pleased to be uplifted by news from afar, and asking, "[W]as this a weakness of S Paul and his disciples which they ought to have mortified?"[44]

Congreve looked back to the early days of the Society and went on, "I believe most of our great disappointments and failures of vocation may be traced mainly to this cause. It is true we were left too few at home, but the deeper mistake was that we had never been taught how to live together, few or many, in cordial, brotherly intimacy and affection."

Here once again is Congreve teaching cordiality. He noted that to offer cordiality is good for the giver even when there is no mutual response. Speaking to his brethren in their retreat, Congreve said:

> Consider, too, the generosity of giving sympathy to unsympathetic people. Christ gave not simply material service, but His Heart's tenderness besides to persons separated far from Him by pride or despair . . . We may learn to give with all our service of the brethren something that is worth more than service,—sympathy. Proud and weak spirits cannot submit to accept our service, if it is given merely on an abstract principle of duty without cordiality. The service which conscience offers while the heart stays behind, is not like Christ's service, does not reach far into our needs; but you might, perhaps, break an unsympathetic spirit if you could master generosity enough to accept your brother's cold service cordially. Then you become the benefactor by graciously accepting an ungracious gift; and your kindness in receiving

---

[43]   Ibid., f. 13.

[44]   Ibid., f. 8.

kindly what was not in itself worth having, transforms the gift itself, and may, perhaps, awaken the life of grace where it is keeping its winter underground. In that way you may make a man feel that service has a double life, and implies the meeting of the love of two persons. It can never be perfected by the mere superiority of one meeting the indigence of another; it requires the meeting of the love of two persons,—yes, and more; it requires a Third Person to come between the two, our Lord Jesus Christ, Who is the Life of both, Who takes away by a touch the pride of indigence from the one, and the sense of superiority from the other, and imparts to both the grace of love, which enriches both, by giving and receiving, and so makes them equal.[45]

In July 1896 Congreve preached at the Profession of the first Novices to the Sisterhood of the Holy Childhood in Oxford.[46] He began by noting that "our Profession as Religious is that act by which our weakness and unworthiness are cast completely upon God". The religious life is not a question of being strong or heroic but "my life given to God to keep it safe, rescued in His love from self, and the corruption of the world, and from all chance desires". Those making their profession are not acting independently, though they are acting freely. Their dedication is itself a "result already attained" such that the question of success or outcome passes away. In this, there is the echo of Benson's assertion that a religious order is not a foundation for the future or something whose success can be measured. It is, however, Congreve went on to say, "an act which brings new results; it brings us, as every act of faith does, into closer relation to Christ".[47]

---

[45] Congreve, *Christian Progress*, p. 204.

[46] George Congreve SSJE, *Increase in us True Religion: An Address by Father Congreve SSJE preached at the profession of the first novices to the Sisterhood of the Holy Childhood, St Margaret's Day, July 20th 1896* (Oxford: Mowbray, 1896). Reprinted in Congreve, *Parable of the Ten Virgins*, pp. 129–45. For the Sisterhood, see Anson, *Call of the Cloister*, p. 530.

[47] Congreve, *Parable of the Ten Virgins*, p. 131.

Congreve went on to consider the religious vows. In seeking his original permission to establish his "college of clergymen" Benson had conducted an interesting correspondence on the matter of vows with Bishop Wilberforce of Oxford.[48] Responding to Wilberforce's initial refusal to allow the new Society vows, Benson wrote, "[T]he blessedness of a vow consists in the faith that God will give special gifts as a covenant to those who thus definitely give up some possible future of earthly enjoyment for him." Naturally, it would be "mischievous to make a thing accidentally sinful to ourselves which would not be sinful naturally". Faith, however, "seeks to give up natural possibilities for divine promises".[49] For Congreve, "[T]he Religious vows renew all the old vows: Baptism; Confirmation; Confession; Communion . . . The whole meaning of this Religion of three vows is something done to bind me more personally to Christ than I ever realised before while I kept my independence." This is a grace from Christ, who is the only perfectly consecrated human, given in his human nature body and soul to God. "And so Jesus in Heaven is the Fountain of all consecration of all holy vocations."[50]

Duty must be thoroughly carried out: "[W]e cannot love laxity under Rule because we cannot honour it; it means the failure of sacrifice, the failure of love." Congreve therefore enjoined religious to embrace keeping the rule as "that particular work which will bring no credit to us. Dull and uninteresting work being careful in every detail of it . . . Let it be said 'she was always faithful, always true.'"[51] This path was for Congreve no dry legalism, nor negative asceticism. Speaking to his own brethren, he gave one of his arresting exemplars, contrasting the obedience of the religious with the obedience of the sentry at Pompeii, whose blind obedience to orders led to a needless death. Through obedience the religious is in a "perpetual relationship with Christ", and accepting things that go against

---

[48] James, *Cowley Fathers*, pp. 41–6.

[49] Woodgate quotes the correspondence at length in *Father Benson*, pp. 64–72. The passage about vows is on pp. 69–70.

[50] Congreve, *Parable of the Ten Virgins*, p. 135.

[51] Ibid., p. 139.

personal judgement for love of Christ deepens that relationship and is therefore "sacramental".[52]

Congreve agreed with Benson that it is not the work that is the focus of the religious life but rather the conversion of the soul into God. "If I have learned to pray my work, when I can work no longer I shall be able to pray. I shall still be increasing in true Religion."[53] In the end, the purpose of the religious life is the development of true charity over the course of life. "The object of growing old is to grow in love—to learn at last to exercise that gift of Christ's love which in youth we had hardly discovered. And our interest in one another, young or old, is Jesus Christ's interest in each."[54] This, once more, is cordiality, which will make a community's secular work flourish through their religious life. So, speaking to the teaching Sisters of the Holy Childhood, he said:

> [Y]our influence of personal character on children and young teachers will be in proportion to the soundness of your Community life, that is to its solidarity and love, the joy of unity, which does not mean only abstaining from quarrels, but the cordial and generous love of Christ through us touching all who belong to us.[55]

So Congreve drew for the Society of the Holy Childhood a distinction between a religious Community, which is the "family, the Home of Jesus Christ", and "a boarding house for church workers". He concluded:

> You will never be too austere, too self-denying to accept kindness, *benignitas*—that is, kindness elevated and purified by piety. *Simplicitas*—a simple character that loves One only and sees all things in the clear daylight of that love. *Hilaritas*—gladness; the

---

[52]   SSJE Summer Retreat 1899, Day XI, Meditation I, SSJE/6/5/4/5.

[53]   Congreve, *Parable of the Ten Virgins*, p. 144.

[54]   Ibid., p. 141.

[55]   Ibid., p. 142.

open "Merry heart" which "has a continual feast" and "doeth good like a medicine".[56]

In time, it was through George Congreve that this medicine would be brought to his own Community.

---

[56] Ibid., p. 143. Cf. Proverbs 17:22.

CHAPTER 3

Glimpses of the Beauty of God

In July 1874, two months after his disappointment in being passed unfit for the missions, Congreve attended a Community Retreat, given by Benson. The Community held retreats regularly, and these were significant times for teaching and reflection. For instance, the Advent retreat for 1875 comprised fifty-eight meditations given by Benson and recorded in notes taken by Congreve and the other novices, Basil Maturin, William Black and George Sheppard.[1] Congreve was professed after this retreat on the feast of Saint John the Evangelist, 27 December 1875.[2] O'Neill had left for India more than a year previously. Then in 1876 Maturin departed for the United States, and Congreve was left at Cowley to live the dedicated life. Congreve's quality was evident, if not perhaps to himself, certainly to the community, and following his profession he was quickly given responsibility, being put in charge of the Lay Brothers, with whom he forged good relations.[3] He was also sought after beyond his own community. Just eighteen months after his own profession, he was giving a woman preparing to enter on the religious life guidance and help. He wrote that the substance of the religious life is Christ himself, and nothing else, so the postulant should be ready to see all her anticipations fail her, and "all you naturally fancied about it fading very soon, everything about it changing and fading except . . . Christ Himself". Congreve continued:

---

[1]   Richard Meux Benson SSJE, "Advent Retreat 1875", in Retreats, Vol. 15, SSJE/8/1/15.

[2]   Woodgate, *Father Congreve*, p. 26, gives this date which is entirely probable. However, Correspondence about Congreve family history, 1927–9, SSJE/6/5/5/7, f. 8 gives the date as 30 December 1875.

[3]   Bull, "George Congreve", p. 98.

> Though everything in the world should lose its joy for me, and every hope should fail me, it makes no difference, for I have nothing to lose, nothing to hope but what I have in my Master and King who loved me and gave Himself for me. If He remains faithful to His promise, I can lose nothing, I can never be disappointed of my Hope.[4]

Renunciation of the things of this world by the Christian, secular or religious, is rewarded with a gift in return, which is Christ himself. In this, Congreve reflected the guidance he himself was receiving at Cowley. While he resiled from the lack of human contact, he embraced the physical austerities of the Mission House. In a world in which gentlemen had servants to undertake manual tasks, and even the professed Fathers had Lay Brothers to take on elements of work, when Walter came to visit, Congreve "girded his nephew with a sack-cloth apron and gave him broom and dust pan and tea leaves with which to sweep out Fr O'Neill's cell".[5]

Benson taught not only mortification of relationships, but also "deadness" to this world and its pleasures. It was not utterly negative, as Congreve recollected after Benson's death: "While keeping up his own stern self-sacrifice, [Benson] would help to make our life possible to us, and lead us on gently if he could, and step-by-step . . . It is this tender consideration of others which distinguishes Christ's austerity from the self-regarding contemptuous austerity of the pagan ascetic."[6] Nevertheless, Congreve's understanding of mortification grew to differ from Benson's, and took a form more sustainable and more attainable for souls. His view was to have a profound influence on the Society,

---

[4]   Longridge (ed.), *Spiritual Letters of Fr Congreve*, p. 4.

[5]   Even Benson had help with his tidying: "[T]he Father who tidied the rooms next morning sometimes discovered signs that the Superior had found no time at all to use his bed the previous night." Congreve, "Loss and Gain", p. 61. Used tea leaves were scattered on hard floors; they would gather the dust to themselves which was then not simply swept back into the air by the broom. Woodgate, *Father Congreve*, p. 24.

[6]   Congreve, "Loss and Gain", p. 61.

developing and nuancing the teaching of the Father Founder. Linked with this, Congreve articulated an understanding of the material world and its beauty which similarly had great influence.

For Benson, the Christian life is based on the utter transcendence and incomprehensibility of God. There is nothing that the individual can bring of value: "[A]ll gifts, eloquence, learning, health, etc become useful only when they are burnt up by the fire of the Holy Ghost." Life itself is exile, at the end of which:

> contemptuously shall we look back on many things which, as time went on, we fancied to be important for God's glory, and we shall see how we measured things by our own self-love, rather than by devotion to Him. If we had been more dead to this world while living in it, we should not have set so much store by them; we should have seen how everything was nothing, except what came from Him, that wherein He Himself came. Oh, that we could know our only purpose in life to be the identification of ourselves with His Passion, while the world takes a religious form in honour of Him. To rise out of His Passion, by passing through it, is the stern reality of loving fellowship wherein He calls us to be associated with Himself—a real passing through it, and so away from the present world, and right onward into the glory of His throne and God's right hand.[7]

Benson recognized that this was hard teaching. Congreve recalled how the Father Founder, in giving instructions to the Brethren on the Rule, "showed the greatest consideration for others who are less strong in body ... He said to us, 'if we cannot fast as our forefathers did, at least let us take our food as befits the penitent; that is take food with thankfulness that God does still give us a life in which we have done so little that is profitable to him.' So he used to bear with us and strengthen our weakness."[8] Congreve quoted to one of his correspondents the advice of Father Benson on the Eucharistic Fast for those who are ill—to have

---

[7] Congreve and Longridge (eds), *Letters of R. M. Benson*, Letter 51, p. 154.

[8] Congreve, "Loss and Gain", p. 61.

a cup of tea and some plain bread to make it possible to communicate, for "the Church's recent tradition is designed to secure devotion not to excommunicate".[9] This from one who into his nineties observed a strict fasting regime.[10] Again Benson taught, "[I]f we cannot live up to the mortification of the saints at least let us find mortification in our own weakness a real mortification, a real humiliation of spirit, a real avowal of how little we have of God since we are so sensitive to the life of the world."[11] Thus failure itself can become a source of self-surrender.

There are points at which Benson makes an almost platonic separation of body and soul:

> The more our body is brought under control the more we shall be able to bring it under. We cannot now wound body without injuring our spiritual life because our body and soul are so closely united together and the soul is so much the slave of the impulses of the body, but as the soul becomes more and more filled with the spirit of God it becomes more disassociated from the movements of the body, and the body will be to the soul as an encumbrance, a deadweight, a weight well-nigh dead; so we shall be able to beat it down. As St Paul says "I browbeat my body and bring it into slavery."[12]

Despite this, Benson was not simply a dualist. For him, the glory of God suffuses all human life and fills us with joy so that in the resurrection our lives are transfigured. He said that "the real test of the monastic community is not its 'otherworldliness' but its faithfulness in love".[13] Nevertheless, despite his emphasis on the taking up of our lives in the divine victory, "to Benson the world is still the enemy to be died

---

9   Congreve, letter to Miss Kebbel, Shrove Tuesday 1897, SSJE/6/5/2/4/1, f. 6.

10   Congreve, "Loss and Gain", p. 58.

11   Richard Meux Benson SSJE, "Instructions upon the Rule of Life", On Mortification. SSJE/1/1/1–2, p. 248.

12   Ibid., pp. 251–2.

13   R. Kemsley SLG, "The Religious Life: Aspects of Father Benson's Teaching", in Smith (ed.), *Benson of Cowley*, pp. 106–107.

to".[14] In his ordering of the Society he preached, therefore, a "ruthless detachment".[15] The Rule called the brethren to die to the world:

> Deadness to the world must henceforth be complete. Any conscious violation of such deadness becomes a grievous sin. Earthly hopes and fears are to be entirely put away . . . The professed who gives himself wholly to Christ should long, if it were possible, to be admitted to the crown of martyrdom. He must not look forward to such a possibility as an idle dream. He must gather strength for his daily life, to meet the difficulties of his ordinary duty, by the consideration of the martyr's fortitude. The deadness of the religious is not dull apathy, but triumph and joy in the consciousness of possessing a true eternal life, from which nothing but the lingering love of the world holds us back.[16]

If renunciation was for Benson triumph and joy, it was not obviously so to others, and the practical working out of his doctrine of deadness was difficult for many. Holy poverty became deliberate discomfort, and not all could see past the austerity to the glory.

Between 28 December 1879 and 4 January 1880, Congreve gave the Christmas Retreat at Cowley. Three addresses were given on each of the six days, and these were published in 1929 as *The Incarnation and the Religious Life*, the first of Congreve's works to be written, but the last to come to press. Containing many seeds of his developed teaching, he nevertheless at this point reflected Benson's austerity more clearly than he later would:

> Earthly means are really hindrances . . . If man is to give himself up to the power of the Spirit it must be by tearing himself free from the power of the flesh, by dying to it . . . Weakness and continual disappointment [are] the very material of victory . . .

---

[14] A. M. Ramsey, "Bruising the Serpent's Head: Father Benson and the Atonement", in Smith (ed.), *Benson of Cowley*, p. 59.

[15] Kemsley, "The Religious Life", p. 101.

[16] SSJE Rule vii, Of Profession, quoted in Kemsley, "The Religious Life", p. 107.

> What we want is not the power to work miracles but to have the
> helplessness and hopelessness of our own position brought home
> to us . . . What we want is more disappointment in the flesh,
> greater weakness, sadder pains to break down completely that self
> which we are still so clinging to . . . because into that emptiness
> Christ can flow with all His strength.[17]

Congreve brought his own thought to these themes in his emphasis on
what it means to be empty, that Christ fills our emptiness. While he
continued to teach Religious that "you are in yourself nothing", for him,
"your very existence is nothing less than a glorious purpose of God".[18]
This means that the renunciation is the means by which to re-apprehend
the things of this world, now made glorious in all their material beauty:

> What a master passion it is, the life of Christ in us! To an artist
> beauty is his life, his Passion. Think of the enthusiasm of an
> artist for the lovely forms which he creates in his mind. Think
> of the grace and wondrous discoveries, how they are life to bold,
> original genius. But to the Religious soul, not created beauty, not
> discoveries, not wealth, not the glories of literature, but Christ is
> his life. Oh, what an infinitely more glorious world the Religious
> has! What a world of eternal progressive discovery of beauty he
> has in Jesus Christ! That which absorbs him, really stirs his heart,
> kindles and devours him, is the love of Christ.[19]

With Christ as the "master-passion", created things take on a new and
greater meaning, and attain their "noble destiny". Drawing on St Paul,
Congreve looked to the beauty and the purpose of nature, which is not a
distraction to be overcome, but the very place of the revelation of God:

> We may see nature and all created things in the light of Jesus, and
> realise the Spirit of Jesus in all creation around us, in that it has

---

[17] Congreve, *Cowley Retreats No. 1*, p. 98.

[18] Congreve, *Parable of the Ten Virgins*, pp. 22–3.

[19] Congreve, *Cowley Retreats No. 1*, p. 123–4.

Figure 6: The Mission House Chapel. Congreve gave many of his retreats and addresses here. This is in effect the view from his stall.

so noble a destiny, in which also we are so closely linked. "For the earnest expectation of the creature waits for the manifestation of the sons of God. For the creature was made subject to vanity, not willingly, but by reason of him who has subjected the same in hope, because the creature itself also shall be delivered from the bondage of corruption into the glorious liberty of the sons of God." [Romans 8:19–21] We may have no artistic sense of beauty, but still we may look upon the world as the Saints looked upon it, and see heaven through it, and see God's beauty through it. If we cannot form a very artistic conception as we look upon nature around us, yet we can, if we will exercise the faith given us in our baptism, see God's loveliness underneath it, and God's purpose for it.[20]

As his thought matured, Congreve more and more emphasized not the emptiness, but that with which God fills the mortified soul. Meditating for Sisters on the parable of the ten virgins (Matthew 25:1–13), Congreve wrote that the virgins represent human nature created in essential incompleteness.

It is supposed to be the misery of man that in himself he is essentially incomplete, but it certainly is also his glory, for it means he was not created for himself or any limited good but for the perfect love, for God. It is a great help to remember that this imperfection of man himself, this need of God, is *essential*, that when God created man and woman very good, the acme of their goodness was that they never could be sufficient to themselves, or to one another, but at every moment they needed God absolutely, and were to help one another to reach God and to abide in God.[21]

For Congreve, our essential incompleteness is part of God's gift, the prerequisite of his fulfilment of our being with his love. "Man", he wrote, "is never great in his attainment; the moment he begins to be satisfied

---

[20] Ibid., p. 55.

[21] Congreve, *Parable of the Ten Virgins*, pp. 22–3. (Emphasis in the original.)

with anything, he begins to drop below himself. He is always greatest in his want, and in his striving after that which is above himself."[22] Things of earthly beauty, both of the human intellect and of Nature, can therefore be means by which we may come to God, thus in the atonement the cross was not the focus, but Christ, "who was not made for the tortures of the cross, but for the sacrifice, the love, the victory of the cross".[23]

In a letter to Benson, Congreve describes an evening on a visit to Wales on which he had read the first part of *Hamlet* to members of his family:

> It was quite dark by that time, and an extraordinary sky scene, a scene of immense cloud forms, perfectly still; standing above them the open heavens in their clearness full of stars—a sight that would make anyone stand still. It seems to me to have exactly the same sort of power as Hamlet—power to break the crust of earthiness and habit of living absorbed in things of the moment, which for the most part hides the eternal and infinite from us. Nature (in the material or literary world) may hide God, but how often—at least several times—have I felt the power of Nature to set one's mind free from the prison of time and earthiness and rise up to rejoice in the Eternal Beauty and praise of God.[24]

Nature can reveal God because of the solidarity of God and the whole of creation in Jesus who is God made man:

> The solidarity of mankind with the whole creation is real. It is simply a fact that we are dust and return to dust. But St Paul does not find our oneness with nature in the doom of the common death; he finds it in Christ the Conqueror of death, and bids us

---

[22] Congreve, "The Need of God", in The Cowley Evangelist, February 1904, p. 58.

[23] Ibid., p. 55. In this Congreve echoed Benson, see Ramsey, "Bruising the Serpent's Head", pp. 58–9.

[24] Congreve, Correspondence with Fr Benson, SSJE/6/5/2/1, f. 36.

look up to the throne of God to find the Eternal Son there, sharing in His glorified manhood the solidarity of created things.[25]

This is the very source of art for "so deeply is our Fellowship with nature rooted" that it is "a main source of the poetry of all the ages . . . To the poet and the saint this Fellowship of man with nature in the Word Made Flesh is no figure of speech, but the very ground of all reality, and the source of all their inspiration. They see the bush in the desert aflame with God."[26]

The material world therefore provides a means to come into contact with "the most real and substantial thing in the world". Encouraging retreatants that they can continue to know God when their Retreat is over and they are back to commonplace living, Congreve points to "the fact of the sense of beauty" which reveals God by "glimpses":

> God flashes revelations every day, by which He makes you aware of a mystery,—of something you call beauty, which passes from some external object you look upon into your intelligence, by which you become assured that love, and not mechanical necessity, governs the world. There was something just now in the play of the waves that for an instant arrested you, you could not tell what it was, you could not trace or analyse it; while your eye followed and sought to seize it, it was gone, but for the instant it filled your whole being with joy and desire. Desire for what?— There was something in the light touching the rocks yonder, the flowering shrubs, and the waters, which awakened a feeling of a beauty which human nature could not bear if it were completely unveiled. It was but a glimpse, but it was as much as you could well stand under. But though it has gone now, and you could not tell anyone what you saw or felt, yet you know that that moment's glimpse of an immaterial perfection was one of the most real impressions of your life. That glimpse revealed to you, with an assurance that could not be questioned, what is the true basis

---

25 Congreve, *Christian Progress*, p. 259.

26 Congreve, *Christian Progress*, pp. 260–1. The reference to the burning bush is to Exodus 3:3.

of your own and of all created being. Now though you have to live among common and commonplace things which never rise to perfection, and where there is nothing lovely, yet you have learned by this hint of the joyful mystery of beauty in created nature something of what God is, and what His purpose is for yourself and all the other imperfect people amongst whom you live.[27]

This idea of "the moment's glimpse of an immaterial perfection" and "half unveilings" as signs of God's presence was one which Congreve developed in a meditation made at the end of his life on memories of a trip to the Alps:

> One day long ago two old friends who could not climb far ...
> spent long hours of a Spring day there together alone with the
> Beauty of God. The depths of the blue overhead were without
> a cloud, views opened below full of sunshine, leading down
> to the shore of the Lake of Geneva; the green of the mountain
> pastures was dappled with the light shadow of Chestnut trees
> just unfolding their young leaves, or with patches of white, where
> acres of Narcissus Poeticus filled the morning air with sweetness.
> Every cranny among the rocks nursed some new treasure for their
> delight, wonders of Primula, Auricula, Violas, Gentian, Alpine
> Rose, Tiarella, St Bruno Lilies, and crimson cushions of Saxifrage.
> One of the two friends passed on long ago to discover the eternal
> reality that these wonders symbolised,—the Beauty of God. The
> other, while he waits below, still tries to learn the alphabet of the
> mystery. One moment's recollection brings that May morning
> back to him, and now the outward and visible sign of an inward
> and spiritual grace is at work in him, half unveiling the eternal
> and unseen Beauty of God. He is no idle dreamer of dreams, he
> goes to his business to-day with the keenness of a soul newly
> bathed in joy and charity. No bad news, no discourtesy suffered,
> no ugliness of surroundings can depress him to-day, or make him

---

[27] Congreve, *Christian Life*, pp. 267–8.

reflect unkindness or gloom. The Beauty of God that he saw in the Swiss valley has touched his soul in his prayer, and his heart will be full of thanksgiving, and all day reflect something of the fair beauty of the Lord that has been revealed to him in His Temple.[28]

Beauty is furthermore the wellspring of thanksgiving. Remembering Frankby, he wrote:

> If you know the estuary of the Dee on winter nights when a gale of wind rises with the rising tide, or on a spring morning when you have heaven overhead and heaven underfoot reflected in the wet sands, and the air flooded with sunshine and ringing with larks' songs, what you have seen has left a vision which turns to thanksgiving as a relief from too much beauty.[29]

This is an illustration of the fact that while Congreve loved nature and the beauty of plants and scenery, the focus is always on humanity and our need of God. Writing from Iona later in life, he remarked that:

> the *human* life of the blessed island is mostly I should think that of the missionary monks and hermits of S Columba and his family. All that is gathered up safe in heaven long ago; the life today, after the trippers visit between 11 and 12, is the life and conversation of the Seagulls, Terns, Cormorants etc which are always awake and voluble in matters which concern them and the harvest of the sea. I look out across the sound on the long low hills and cliffs and bays of Mull—green wherever there is room for a blade of grass to grow—for the red red [sic] granite toned by lichens and seaweed, scarred and rent and caverned by time and the wrath of the sea and the wind. The sound, about a

---

[28] George Congreve SSJE, "The Beauty of God", in *The Cowley Evangelist*, August 1916, pp. 170–1. Cf. Psalm 27:4. Congreve does not say who his fellow-traveller was, but we may surmise this was a trip made with Assheton before his entry into the religious life.

[29] Congreve, *Christian Progress*, p. 16.

mile wide, runs between; no waves today, but the sea is all alive, in motion, the tide running fast, though quite smoothly. There is life everywhere, in every cranny of the rocks, rock flowers, cranesbills, saxifrages, cilla, wild rose (not out yet), honeysuckle, primroses, bluebells (hyacinth), marsh marigolds—eyebright etc. It is the human life that hides itself in the little stone cottages with thatch tied on to prevent the gales blowing it into the sea—or do they burrow underground?[30]

This teaching on beauty was influential on another young visitor to the Mission House in the early days of Congreve's life there, Ninian Comper. Comper's father, John, was Rector of St Margaret's Brae in Aberdeen and a leader of the Anglo-Catholic movement in Scotland. John Comper was a friend of Benson's, and Congreve also became close to him and to the family. Ninian Comper first came to the Mission House in 1874 when he was about ten, to spend the end of the school holiday there. Congreve reported to Assheton, "I believe his father cannot afford to keep him all the vacation. He reads nearly all day, and helped by being in charge of the door now and then and is very well-behaved and obliging." Later in the same month Congreve reported a visit with Comper to the church at North Moreton where "they showed us the vestments and the Parsonage which are fine enough and nearly fit to please Kempe".[31]

At Frankby, Congreve had commissioned glass from the great stained-glass artist Charles Eamer Kempe and from Congreve's Oxford contemporary, Edward Burne-Jones. The commission from Burne-Jones was not merely loyalty to an old friend, but based on a robust assessment of the quality of work. Congreve criticized with a shrewd eye the work of Clayton & Bell, who had also placed windows in Frankby church: "[T]here is an utter weariness in C and B's designs—a feeling that the designer had done it so often that he did it in his sleep now, as well as in his waking hours—there is not one grain or momentary flash of passion

---

[30] Congreve, letter to Miss Kebbel, St Columba's Day [9 June] 1906, SSJE/6/5/2/4/17, f. 7. (The punctuation in this quotation has been amended for clarity.)

[31] Letters to Assheton, SSJE/6/5/5/9, ff. 385, 387.

of genius, or delight in any part of the cartoon—such as makes you glad in every piece of first rate work."[32] He even went so far as to have a "very poor" Clayton & Bell window of St John removed from the church and replaced with one by Albert Moore, whom Congreve had seen painting the frescoes in St Alban's Rochdale.[33] As late as 1904, three years before Kempe's death, Congreve's sister-in-law commissioned a church window from him in memory of her husband William, Congreve's older brother.[34]

It was Congreve who persuaded John Comper to allow his son to train as an artist and introduced him to the artists who were to form him. In 1880, Congreve took the young Ninian to St Michael's, Camden Town to see G. F. Bodley's unfinished church, an experience which convinced Comper he should become an architect. In 1881, Congreve consulted with W. B. Richmond, Slade Professor of Fine Art, about Comper joining the Ruskin School of Drawing in Oxford, and arranged that he would stay at the Mission House while studying there. Then on 11 January 1882 Comper recorded in his diary, "introduction from Fr Congreve to see Mr Kempe and then Oxford". The meeting with Kempe took place at the Mission House. In April 1883, Congreve arranged a further meeting between the two. It did not start well. Comper wrote to his mother:

> Kempe took it for granted that I was going to be a monk and even that I had an ambition to form a brotherhood of artists, and for a long time talked on this, showing in what way he could not agree with "Congreve" and me about it. It was not until he had exhausted his arguments against it that he allowed me to speak and to explain that I have never had any such intention.

---

[32]   Letter to Assheton, February 1863, SSJE/6/5/5/9, f. 153.

[33]   Letter to Assheton, November 1865, SSJE/6/5/5/9, f. 225: "[H]e is also about another window for Caldy which I look forward to with great interest. He has done a great deal of fresco painting lately . . . I hope he will be a great painter. I think he has it in him."

[34]   Congreve, letter to Miss Kebbel, 5 January 1904, SSJE/6/5/2/4/13, f. 1. In the church of S Nicholas Burton; the subjects were "Christ on the Cross with S Nicholas and S George".

Finally Kempe advised that following his time at the Ruskin, Comper should serve a year of apprenticeship to learn figure drawing.[35] When it arose, Comper seized the opportunity to study with Kempe in London. It seems he found the community at the Mission House difficult. He wrote, "[S]orry as I shall be to leave Oxford yet to leave Cowley I shall be delighted. I had such a nice letter from Father Congreve this morning—him I like more and more but Father Benson and the others—!—!"[36]

Congreve's influence continued after Comper had moved to London. In May of the same year, Comper wrote to his sister that Kempe had taken him to Bodley's Church of the Holy Angels at Hoar Cross in Staffordshire, where Kempe was installing windows, and that they had also visited the private chapel of Caldy Manor, the home of the Bartons, "which Kempe was painting all over" and where Congreve continued to be a regular celebrant.[37]

Congreve's connection was not simply with Ninian Comper. Sometime in the mid-1880s he visited John Comper in Aberdeen to try to deal with some difficulties which had arisen in the Community of St Margaret, where one of Ninian's six siblings—Mary Ellen—was one of the Sisters.[38] Congreve contributed a preface to an edition of some mediaeval texts on death by Frances, another of Comper's sisters.[39] At the time Congreve was introducing Ninian to Kempe, a younger brother, Leonard Comper was

---

[35] Anthony Symondson SJ, "'An Ass or a Devil'? Sir Ninian Comper and Charles Eamer Kempe", *Journal of Stained Glass* Vol. 34 (2010), pp. 53–78; Anthony Symondson and Stephen Bucknall, *Sir Ninian Comper: An Introduction to his Life and Work, with complete Gazetteer* (Reading: Spire Books, 2006), pp. 21–24.

[36] Symondson, "'An Ass or a Devil'?", p. 56.

[37] Albert Moore had installed glass at Caldy; Congreve, letter to Assheton, 21 December 1865, SSJE/6/5/5/9 f. 231: "[Moore] is also about another window for Caldy which I look forward to with great interest."

[38] Congreve, Correspondence with Fr Benson, SSJE/6/5/2/1, f. 76: " . . . the difficulties between the mother and the novice mistress belong to the situation and can only be partly remedied."

[39] Frances M. M. Comper, *The Book of the Craft of Dying and other Early English Tracts Concerning Death* (London: Longmans, Green & Co., 1917).

an undergraduate at Aberdeen University. When, following his visitation to the Convent, Congreve extended his stay in Scotland preaching retreats and covering parishes in Braemar, Leonard travelled with him.[40]

If Ninian grew to be the most well-known of the family, it was on him that Congreve had perhaps the greatest influence. He became an architect because of the visit to Camden Town which Congreve arranged, and it was Congreve who effected the introduction to Kempe, who "activated Comper's latent talents and opened the vista to a vocation".[41] When Ninian considered becoming a Roman Catholic in 1897 (influenced by the conversion of Basil Maturin), it was Congreve who dissuaded him and his sister Frances from doing so. Congreve may have been responsible for winning Comper the commission to work on the Hospital Chapel for St John's Home in Cowley, not far from the Mission House: he had introduced Comper to the All Saints Sisters of the Poor who ran the Home in 1889, and the commission came in 1902. In December 1903 Congreve wrote home from South Africa, "I am grateful to you for thinking of what I happened to say about good Ninian Comper. He is an enthusiast and true artist and poet in stonework and all kinds of cunning handcraft, but wife and children cannot live on his enthusiasm."[42]

Congreve was back from South Africa in time for the first Mass in the Sisters' new church, which he travelled from London to celebrate, a fact which Sister Mary Teresa, the Mother Superior reported to Comper:

> We had the proper Assumption office at [Fr Congreve's] dear hands and all went without a hitch . . . [F]or my own part having just returned from Southwold, Walberswick, Blythbrough and Dunwich and having seen what had been exceeding magnifical, sitting in sackcloth and ashes, when I behold our church I had a vision of those old churches in all their former glory; the spirit in

---

[40]   Congreve, Correspondence with Fr Benson, SSJE/6/5/2/1, f. 54.

[41]   Symondson, "'An Ass or a Devil'?", p. 74.

[42]   General correspondence, 14 December 1903, SSJE/6/5/2/3, f. 45. The addressee is not recorded, but Serenhedd James suggested to me that this was possibly one of the "letters of the day" from brethren who were away which were laid out in the library.

ours recalls all that, and Fr Congreve I think was intensely happy in it all, and proud of you.[43]

As Comper came into contact with classical as well as Gothic models he developed his concept of "Unity by Inclusion" based not only on the conviction that a cosmopolitan style drew on much that is good, but also a conviction—echoing that of Congreve—that "beauty inspired by the Creator Spirit is one, as all goodness is one and all truth is one",[44] and that the church is above all the place in which the people of God gather to celebrate baptism, hear the Word and worship at the Altar. While these were lessons Comper learned from his study of architecture,[45] Congreve would not have disagreed.

---

[43]   Symondson and Bucknall, *Sir Ninian Comper*, pp. 97–9.

[44]   Ibid., p. 106.

[45]   Ibid., pp. 212–13.

CHAPTER 4

Even Superiors Must Keep the Rule

In the period after giving the retreat on "The Incarnation and the Religious Life", Congreve became established as a master in the field of how men and women might live together in community.[1] His care as Master of the Lay Brothers had given him further experience within the Society, and he had a personal capacity to help people get along.[2] He was not, however, an administrator. Congreve's method of teaching was similar to Benson's in that, "If he speaks of anything that is going on in the world, it is almost always to pass on to its bearings upon the kingdom of God."[3] In contrast with the leaders of the next generation, there is little in the writing of either Congreve or Benson of the practicalities of managing a community.[4] Constitutionally the Society was still developing, partly because Benson was slow to allow any source of authority beyond his own.[5] Benson wrote to Fr Grafton after the latter's withdrawal from the Society in 1882, in the context of their strong disagreement about the establishment or not of an American Province, that:

> [A] constitution cannot really come into force until the Society has passed out of the founder's hands. There may be in some cases a longer and in others a shorter time, but the founder through whom God gives life to a Society must always be in a position different from his successor, who will act as a constitutional head.

---

[1] Woodgate, *Father Congreve*, p. 27.

[2] Congreve, letter to Assheton, 29 October 1899, SSJE/6/5/5/9, f. 769.

[3] Congreve and Longridge (eds), *Letters of R. M. Benson*, Preface, p. vii.

[4] See, for instance, the correspondence of Waggett and Page, SSJE/6/16/1/1.

[5] Woodgate, *Father Benson*, p. 151; Pendleton, *Press On, the Kingdom*, p. 76.

> God has called our Society to so vast a work for its small numbers
> that it is plainly impossible to have that complete constitution
> which might have been contemplated ere now . . . I have striven
> to exercise my authority with the greatest possible elasticity, so as
> to give the heads of the branches all the power I could, sustaining,
> not crippling them. If I have erred, I have erred on the side of
> leniency.[6]

No wonder Congreve described the process of obtaining a Rule as a "strain".[7] That the Father Founder was not acting as a "constitutional head" but rather as "the autocrat he was at heart",[8] and that he could neither take advice nor share authority, was beginning to be a serious problem rather than a help to the development of the Society, and by the 1880s things were coming to a head.[9]

From 1884, when the written Rule was at last signed, Congreve was Assistant Superior, named in the Chapter lists after Benson and before Hodge and Page, the Provincial Superiors in America and India. The signing of the Rule did not completely remove the tensions in the Society over the way that authority was exercised and the religious life led. All the more it became clear that Benson himself and the obedience he demanded lay at the heart of the difficulties. Congreve was never the Superior, and he was not one to make a Rule or revise what had been done, but he was the key person in the coming crisis. His understanding and theology of the religious life was developing, at once influential in the Society and subtly different from Benson's. Congreve's ability to see the human and personal aspects of the difficulties was key, as was his courage in acting decisively at the denouement.

This had a wider importance than merely the specific events of 1890 when Benson resigned as Superior. Congreve maintained love for

---

[6]   Pendleton, *Press On, the Kingdom*, p. 74, quoting Benson to Charles Grafton, 14 August 1882, Grafton Collection, SSJE Archives, Boston, MA.

[7]   Congreve, Correspondence with Fr Benson, 21 January 1890, SSJE/6/5/2/1, f. 111.

[8]   Woodgate, *Father Benson*, p. 91.

[9]   Ibid., p. 151.

Figure 7: SSJE in 1887. Standing, L to R: Br James; Frs Convers; Osborne; Golding Bird; Black; Br John. Seated L to R: Frs Longridge; Maturin; Congreve; Benson; Wyon; Br Beale; Fr Puller.

Benson and loyalty to him all his life, but his different vision permeated the community and allowed it a second spring in which its influence in the Church, and through the Church in society at large, increased.[10] Congreve's gentler and more sustainable vision was thus carried to the Church and beyond, spreading further through his writing, the retreats he gave and his care for other communities. His influence on his brethren— many of them great spiritual figures in their own right with their own spheres of influence—was considerable.[11] It is noteworthy that the first of the proposed series of published "Cowley Retreats" was Congreve's *The Incarnation and the Religious Life*, rather than any of Benson's many retreats. Father Callaway said that if he were sent to a desert island and allowed only one devotional book it would be *The Incarnation and the Religious Life*.[12] In some ways, SSJE owed more in its future life and impact to Congreve than it did to Benson.

The roots of the crisis of 1890 lay in the beginnings of the Society. In June 1865, Bishop Wilberforce of Oxford received two proposals for the establishment of the religious life for men in the Church of England. He gave them very different replies. Brother Ignatius (Joseph Leycester Lyne) was attempting to establish a Benedictine community. A gifted mission preacher, "born with a dramatic temperament", his work in the end came to nothing. "From the human point of view he was the worst possible man for this difficult task."[13] Dom Cyprian Alston, one of those who was part of the experiment for a time, wrote of this extraordinary man:

> As in matters of doctrine, so also in management of his monastery, he acknowledged no superior or higher authority over himself. Though professing to follow the Rule of S Benedict, it was his own interpretation of it, coloured by his own whims and fancies . . . Men with real vocations and true ideals felt that the real monastic

---

[10] Congreve, *Cowley Retreats No. 1*, p. 1. Fr Bull in his Preface speaks of Congreve as a voice from the "Springtime of the Society".

[11] James, *Cowley Fathers*, p. 455.

[12] Woodgate, *Father Congreve*, p. 27.

[13] Anson, *Call of the Cloister*, p. 59.

life needed some firmer basis than the changing will of one man and so left . . . [I]n spite of his claims to be a Benedictine, the Rule at Llanthony was in fact an eclectic one devised by the Superior himself. Parts of the Holy Rule that did not appeal to him were unhesitatingly set aside or ignored, whilst, on the other hand, customs and traditions from elsewhere, however un-Benedictine, that he had read of or heard of, but which took his fancy, he incorporated without scruple.[14]

Wilberforce refused to give his approbation to Brother Ignatius and criticized the romantic exteriority of the attempt. Benedictines of old, he said, "took the dress to help the work. You mar the work to have the dress." He went on, however, "I believe that colleges of clergymen, living together and acting under the parochial clergy, might meet many of our great spiritual wants; further, I believe that brotherhoods of unordained men not in Holy Orders might be of most excellent use."[15]

When Benson proposed The Society of Saint John the Evangelist a few weeks later, Wilberforce wrote, "I like your idea of a *College* very much indeed."[16] On the face of it, the experiment at Cowley—with all the personal reservation and austerity which Congreve found there—was very different from the exuberances of Ignatius; but as at Llanthony, there was at first no Rule at Cowley beyond the "inspiration and activity of one man".[17]

Although keen to hold the direction of the Society in his own hands, Benson recognized the need for structure. Grafton recalled that when, at the foundation of the Society of Saint John the Evangelist, he and O'Neill

---

[14]   *Ibid.*, p. 63.

[15]   *Ibid.*, p. 59. The letter, which Anson describes as "brutal", was the antithesis of episcopal soft soap: "You are sacrificing everywhere the great reality for which you have sacrificed yourself to the puerile imitation of a past phase of service which it is just as impossible for you to revive in England as it would be for you to resuscitate an Egyptian mummy and set it upon the throne of the Pharaohs."

[16]   Woodgate, *Father Benson*, p. 65.

[17]   Allchin, "The Man in his Time", p. 11.

had "elected him Acting Superior", Benson had agreed that when the number of professed reached twelve he would grant a Rule,[18] and as early as 1874 was giving verbal Instructions on a rule of life in a form which was very similar in scope and outline to the Statutes and Rule eventually signed at Cuddesdon in 1884.[19]

The Instructions began to shape the "College of Clergymen" into a religious community, and they showed all the strengths and weaknesses of their author. Benson was clear that the object of the devoted life is not any specific work outcome, and we see that Congreve was Benson's true disciple when he said vows in religion are already an object attained.[20] The rule stated: "It is the Object of the Society of St John the Evangelist in adoration of the Divine Majesty to seek that sanctification to which God in his Mercy calls us."[21] The Instruction explained: "The purpose of our work is to do the work of the Incarnate Lord." On the other hand, the "Instructions upon the Rule of Life"—given verbally and recorded in notebooks—and the Rule of 1884 itself, lacked a thorough structure in detail and reflected—sometimes bizarrely—the Father Founder's emphasis on austerity: "The brethren should avoid sitting on sofas."[22]

The Rule provided regulations for the day: "They will rise at 5am and the gas must be out by 10pm."[23] Towards the end of his life Congreve described one of his days. He got up at 5 a.m. as the Rule prescribed and wrote a sermon for the clothing of a Novice at Iffley. (He does not say of which order.) A cab came for him at 7 a.m. for the clothing service which was "long— it was nearly 10 when we came back". He then said Matins for

---

[18] Pendleton, *Press On, the Kingdom*, p. 75, quoting Grafton to O'Neill, 6 September 1882; Grafton Collection, SSJE Archives, Boston, MA.

[19] Richard Meux Benson SSJE, "Instructions upon the Rule of Life", SSJE/1/1/1–2; Statutes and Rule of Life of the Society of Mission Priests of St John the Evangelist, 1884, SSJE/1/1/3. On the development of the Rule, see James, *Cowley Fathers*, pp. 76–84.

[20] Above, see p. ??? [insert after typesetting].

[21] Statutes and Rule, f. 1. This echoes one of the objects set out in the Rule of the Society of the Holy Cross of which Benson had been a member.

[22] James, *Cowley Fathers*, p. 80.

[23] Statutes and Rule, f. 2.

Fr Benson, too ill to join the community in church, in the library before lunch, followed by General Recreation when he read letters from brethren working in India and Africa to the community. A rest period followed in which he wrote letters followed by "a little walk". Solemn Evensong was sung in the community church, but that day Congreve went to the Convent of the Holy Name "to hear the Candlemas Nunc Dimittis, which always moves me". This was followed by "tea and talk" and Vespers, after which Congreve went to say Evensong with Fr Benson.[24] He then read to "the young and the Lay Brothers" before another period of recreation and letter writing. "Then Compline with Fr Benson as I do daily when he is in bed." Congreve ended his letter by noting that he had forgotten to record his "morning attempt at meditation".[25]

Benson had set his understanding of his foundation of the Society of Saint John the Evangelist in the framework of a response to a call of God, not as a matter of Rule or law. His view was that no institution should survive beyond the second generation, for it would lose sight of its original purpose.[26] The future lay entirely in the hands of God:

> He . . . has been pleased to call our little Society to varied works far beyond our strength, but in so doing we may be sure that He desires to sanctify us and prepare us for greater works to come. Then, if we will yield ourselves up to Him, how wonderful is the future, as we see it stretching out with continual expanse to the fullness of the infinite love with which He is calling us.[27]

---

[24] In the early years of the Society, the priests fulfilled their Anglican duty to Matins and Evensong and added parts of the Roman Office. This was debated at the turn of the century; General Chapter Minute Book, 1884–1905, SSJE/2/1.

[25] Congreve, letter to Br John, 13 December 1912, SSJE/6/5/2/2/13, f. 6.

[26] Kemsley, "The Religious Life", p. 99; see also Allchin, "The Man in his Time", p. 11.

[27] William Hawks Longridge SSJE (ed.), *Further Letters of Richard Meux Benson* (London: Mowbray, 1920), p. 208.

As he had told the postulant Congreve, the purpose of the "institute" was that members should first be converted themselves so that they could be missionaries to others.[28] At its heart, therefore, the religious community was simply the outworking of ordinary Christian life. He wrote, "As missionaries we have just to carry the burning torch and kindle hearts with the fire of the Holy Ghost. The simpler the way of doing this the better. But the primary need is to have our own hearts burning brightly. The less we think about *how* we live the better. The great matter is to see that we *do* live, by constant prayerful communion with Christ."[29] Congreve agreed. The foundation of the religious life is prayer, whatever outward works might be undertaken. The vocation is "not to work, but firstly to God himself".[30] For them both, the great example of this life was O'Neill, who had written of the missionary power of the example of the religious life and who lived that out in Indore, in a solitary life of prayer and austerity from 1875 until he died of cholera in 1882, mourned by the poor among whom he had lived but whom this missionary had, in fact, not converted.[31]

Agreeing with Benson in much, Congreve offered a corrective in the way in which the community was to live together under the Rule. Just as Congreve understood the need for "cordiality" in relations within the community rather than the "deadness" espoused by Benson, so he also approached the matter of obedience to the Superior differently. The Rule of 1884 allowed for a General Chapter of the Society every three years, but day-to-day governance of the Society was firmly in the hands of the Superior General. The Superiors of the Branch Houses ruled their communities, and they kept in close touch (by letter) with the Superior General at Cowley. A great emphasis was placed on obedience, not merely on a human level, but, along with poverty and chastity as one of the great pillars of the religious life. Benson's instructions taught that "as pride is

---

[28]   Congreve, *Christian Progress*, p. vi.

[29]   William Hawks Longridge SSJE (ed.), *Spiritual Letters of Richard Meux Benson* (London: Mowbray, 1924), p. 60.

[30]   Congreve, "Sisters, their Vocation and Special Work", pp. 1, 7.

[31]   James, *Cowley Fathers*, pp. 38–42 (O'Neill's theory of mission), p. 84 (the grief of the people at his death).

the principle root of all sin, so is humility the foundation of all virtues, and this foundation is laid in the secure stronghold of holy obedience". Obedience was due even when the Superior seemed to be in the wrong:

> Sometimes the very outward defects of authority may lead to the greater virtue of obedience and when we have to surrender our judgements to that which seems to us to be less fitting, we may be exercising a spiritual virtue which will be to us of the greatest profit.[32]

This was not simply about submission to human authority but was to be a key to the establishment of community. Obedience leads to the "entire setting aside of self, the losing of self in the Society such that the Society lives in our persons . . . " Because Christ "dwells in the Society", this loss of self is "a loss of self in Christ: 'I live yet not I, but Christ within me.'"[33] Benson continued: "obedience must be no mere servile acquiescence in that which is enjoined but the heartfelt self-surrender of trustful love accepting the Voice of God in those who are set in authority over us." The Superior did not have to be explicit about his wishes:

> [N]ot only the express commands, but the known wishes of the Superior must be carefully complied with in all matters which do not involve the violation of conscience, and where there is any conscientious difficulty in carrying out the wishes of the Superior such difficulty must be respectfully communicated . . . So the blindness of obedience must pass on to the vision of God. We shall see God more and more in proportion to the blindness with which we obey.[34]

Even as early as his retreat addresses on "The Incarnation and the Religious Life" of 1879, Congreve was offering a carefully different view. In the addresses, he considers the religious vows as exemplified in

---

[32]   Benson, "Instructions", Chapter 8, "Of Obedience".

[33]   Galatians 2:20.

[34]   Benson, "Instructions", Chapter 8, "Of Obedience".

Christ. In his poverty, Jesus surrenders all outward goods, the things of this world, though he is the maker of all things and owns them all. His chastity surrenders his body to the Father with all that implies on the cross. The vow of obedience is, however, "the crowning sacrifice", because in it Christ gives up his will: "which is the life of His life in our nature, He gave to God in His vow of obedience: Lo I come to do your will O God."[35] Obedience is "the very life" of Christ. It is not that he was "obedient one moment and free the next", he was always the servant of God:

> He became by his perfect obedience the principle of restoration, by which the whole creation is to be brought out of the discord and disorganisation of sin into the obedience and harmony of holiness, that is into obedience to God's will . . . Let us think therefore of the human will of Jesus perfected in obedience and love, and communicated to us by the sacraments to be the means of our restoration in God, not merely to awaken a better impulse in our own independent will, but to enable us to give our whole will to God so as to have no other impulse but His will in any movement of our life, to become the servants of the Lord Jesus. "I live; yet not I, but Christ liveth in me"[36]

It seems at first as if Congreve is simply teaching as Benson. The religious is called by special vocation to "a life of subjection to Jesus Christ". His "life is valuable and holy, not as we do good things but as we bring ourselves, our whole will, into subjection to Jesus Christ". Obedience needs to go beyond being simply external and become "really sacramental". In a passage which poignantly speaks of the would-be missionary who must stay seemingly useless at home, Congreve says:

> We feel perhaps at some time or other: I can do nothing, I am very little use, God has set me aside. And then we may answer: yes, but I can keep the Rule as God's will, and that fills my doing or not doing with infinite glory. So we must practice keeping the Rule

---

[35]   Congreve, *Cowley Retreats No. 1*, p. 85; the scripture passage is Hebrews 10:9.

[36]   *Ibid.*, p. 86; Galatians 2:20.

when its inconvenience is felt; it is intended to be inconvenient, intended to check and kill our own impulsiveness and make us responsive to grace. And so we are not to be disappointed when we find the Rule hindering and checking us in some work. If it develops the surrender of our will it develops God's glory in us, and that is worth more than the work would have been.[37]

Here is the warning to those who allowed the busy work of parishes and missions to divert them from religious observance, and a call to the Society to come back to its fundamental work, which is not that of external activity but of dedicated life.

Yet the disciple was not simply echoing the master. Typically, for Congreve the offering of obedience is "joyous because it is so complete". Furthermore, obedience, far from separating one from another, forges relationships:

Obedience does not give the external act of obedience merely, but it gives our heart along with the act. And the Christian, the Religious, cannot say, I will keep the rule and I will obey the authority of the community life, but my heart, my inmost heart, my mind, my sorrows, my joys, what are they to the community? . . . Oh no, obedience keeps nothing to itself, no sphere of nature in which self is to remain . . . Obedience to our Religious Rule in spirit and in heart develops great simplicity and sincerity and openness of character. I wish to have no thought, no delight, no sorrow, no hope which I cannot share with all my brothers in Christ Jesus, if I really love him . . . And so by choosing His will all day long we are taken up into His self, and we go forward with Him in the glorious progress of the life of God. His wisdom, His power, His love act in us as we live in loving obedience. It is this perfect union with God which obedience means. "I live, yet not I, Christ lives in me."[38]

---

[37] Congreve, *Cowley Retreats No. 1*, p. 87.

[38] Congreve, *Cowley Retreats No. 1*, p. 90; Galatians 2:20.

Congreve at once demands that the self is mortified and calls for a lively mutuality in community; indeed, to be mortified is precisely to be loving others whom God loves with God's love. Given the context in which the brethren were living such separated lives, his meditation was an electrifying criticism of the community "deadness" he had found.

Congreve taught always to turn away from external things and to be focussed on God. This gave him the framework to deal with conflicts which could arise when the direction of the Superior seemed to be unreasonable. To Benson the answer would be clear: here is an opportunity for humiliation and emptiness. Congreve is more nuanced. Congreve was always close to Brother John, one of the Lay Brothers who spent most of his ministry in South Africa, and who was a steadying and wise influence in a community there which was not without its difficulties.[39] He had a "sprightly pen",[40] and the local Superior seems to have upset Brother John by telling him that he should write less.[41] This may have been in the context of the questioning in the Society in the early 1890s of the extent and nature of correspondence between brethren.[42] Congreve's focus on God allows him to take a line which is both loyal to the local Superior and helpful to John. Congreve says that the withdrawal of permission to write should be accepted "assuming this is a rule for everyone in the House and not about getting more work from one who has never been lazy", and that the direction would be proper if it is "about the quietness and retirement of life proper to Religious". He goes on, however, to remark that even "Superiors must keep the Rule", and that the Rule allows correspondence between brethren. He advises John to clarify the motives by asking permission to write. This questioning of the Superior's decision is for Congreve quite proper. Authority must be exercised within the framework of helping the brethren to grow in holiness, not simply in an arbitrary fashion because the Superior has power.

---

[39] For a pen portrait of Brother John, see Woodgate, *Father Benson*, pp. 99–101.

[40] Woodgate, *Father Benson*, p. 100.

[41] Congreve, letters to Br John, 18 July 1895, SSJE/6/5/2/2/1, f. 8. The superior was Fr Osborne.

[42] See above, p. xxx

This view of the nature of obedience gave Congreve the ability to be able to raise with Benson the problems which threatened to wreck the life of the Society in 1890. In January that year Basil Maturin, who had recently returned from America, came to Congreve.[43] Maturin opened his heart about the lack of community at the Mother House and the widespread sense of alienation and disappointment among the brethren.[44] The situation at Cowley was concerning. Men came and went, unable or unwilling to live in what was a dysfunctional society in which, Maturin said:

> hardly any community existed, and each one seemed to live by himself . . . The House seemed thoroughly unattractive in every way . . . though some came to us from time to time none stayed . . . [Benson] would say "the sepulchres cannot be attractive"—but if we were to survive as a community we must have recruits and the tone of the Mission House was impractical—the monastic side of the life alone was presented, the community side—that side of the work was left out.[45]

Maturin went on to set out two equal and opposite problems of "deadness" and distraction. At the Mother House in Oxford new men were not ready to accept the "Cowley deadness" which Congreve had found when he had arrived,[46] and which had only intensified with the departure of O'Neill and Maturin to the missions. On his return, Maturin had spoken of how he found it "so dull and gloomy here . . . I don't find much difference between the Silence Day and any others—sometimes in Recreation times nobody comes into the Common Room—Holland said to me it

---

[43] On Maturin's work in America, see Woodgate, *Father Benson*, p. 113, and Steven Haws CR, *The Cowley Fathers in Philadelphia* (Bloomington, IN: Author House, 2019), pp. 90–119.

[44] Congreve, Correspondence with Fr Benson, 21 January 1890, SSJE/6/5/2/1, ff. 111–15.

[45] Benson often likened the religious life to sharing the tomb of Christ; Kemsley, "The Religious Life", p. 109.

[46] Congreve, "On Correspondence Between Fathers", f. 15.

seemed impossible at the Mission House to get to know anybody. There is especially a dead time after Evensong on Sundays.[47] Then the food is so poor."[48] Congreve himself described the situation some years later: "[W] here each goes his own way there is not really any community at all but a collection of lonely and selfish individuals who have nothing to make them one except the accident of living under one roof."[49] Congreve said that this had the effect of scaring away vocations.

It was not just Maturin. Others coming home from America for the Triennial Chapter found the same thing, and it seems clear that a head of steam was brewing to challenge the situation. There was an attempt to use the provision in the Rule for a "fortnightly walk" to encourage the Brethren to engage with one another. Congreve recalled, "[A]fter many years of this mutual deadness I remember some Fathers coming home from America and opening their minds to me very frankly. 'You are like dead people,' one said, and so indeed we had become in a sense. They took up the idea of the walk once, was it or twice, in 15 or 20 years. Nothing came of it; cordial brotherly love was dead amongst us."[50] Such society as the Fathers enjoyed came from those with whom they worked in parishes and elsewhere: "[W]e retreated from deadness within into the little comfort of the welcome of the people amongst whom we worked."[51]

In the branch houses, there was certainly more fraternity, but conditions could be very hard: the house in Cape Town was verminous and flea-infested. In addition, there were significant difficulties maintaining the

---

[47]   Congreve, Correspondence with Fr Benson, 21 January 1890, SSJE/6/5/2/1, f. 111. The visitor, identified only by a surname in the letter, may have been Henry Scott Holland, who at the time was at St Paul's Cathedral but may have visited Cowley.

[48]   On the food, see Woodgate, *Father Benson*, p. 100: "[O]ne Good Friday the whole community had ninepence worth of sprats for dinner; one of the priest novices wrote a poem: 'I smell a rat—it is sprat / For our Good Friday dinner / please give me one that is well done, / or else I shall be thinner'; but most of the time it was no joke to those who came to Cowley."

[49]   Congreve, "On Correspondence Between Fathers", f. 16.

[50]   *Ibid.*, f. 12.

[51]   *Ibid.*, f. 15.

SAMUEL A. WALKER. (COPYRIGHT)

230, REGENT STREET, W.

Figure 8: Fr Maturin. Congreve's fellow novice whose concerns
about the direction of the Society sparked Congreve's action
in suggesting to the Fr Founder that he should step down.

religious life in the face of busy parochial and other commitments and without the guiding hand of the Superior General. Benson was clear that such commitments were not contradictory to the life of a community, but others were not so sure. Congreve reported Maturin saying that:

> in America[52] they looked upon their work as a failure—the Religious Life was lost for the sake of Parish Work which having been begun they could not get rid of—he gathered from others that the Religious element had failed equally in Bombay.

Maturin summed up by saying that "at the Mission House there was this solitude, gloom and austerity,—at all the branch houses—secularity."[53]

Looking back around the turn of the century on the situation in the 1880s, Congreve reflected that the Father Founder was personally ill-equipped to help the situation. Despite his austerity, Benson was able to reach out to others and maintained many connexions with the result that he could not see that the conditions he was creating prevented a healthy community from developing among others. Congreve wrote that "the deadness in the house never chilled nor narrowed Fr Benson's heartiness and natural affection. For him sympathies were experienced in a wide space. He kept a thousand links of affection." Moreover, Benson was not confined in the House as the others were:

> [H]e could never purge us of our disastrous community deadness because he practically lived outside the vault in the open sunshine. He did not need "comfort of love" in community life because he had another life, into which he could slip two or three times a day, his pastoral and public life which was full of sympathy and the most worthy Christian interests.[54]

---

52 Pendleton, in *Press On, the Kingdom*, Chapters 4 and 5, describes the busy parochial work in America and Benson's refusal to allow autonomy to Grafton as either Superior of a branch of the Community or as Parish Priest.

53 Congreve, Correspondence with Fr Benson, 21 January 1890, SSJE/6/5/2/1, f. 112.

54 Congreve, "On Correspondence Between Fathers", f. 15.

Others, however, did not find warmth and love in Benson's character.[55] Even Congreve remained in awe of the Father Founder and the power of his personality: "[H]e had a rarely convincing way of pulverising our self-indulgent subterfuges, and sending the Gospel home to our hearts."[56] Benson's perceived personal coldness had a deleterious effect on the ability of the Superior to lead. Coupled with his theological insistence on total and unquestioning obedience, the life of the Mission House— physically and emotionally austere—became intolerable to many, and few who came to try the life stayed with it.

Maturin's conversations with Congreve in January 1890 convinced the Assistant Superior that he had to act. The immediate context was the conflict about the status and constitution of the American Branch of the Society. Benson's desire for control and refusal to compromise had led to the breakdown, during the 1870s, of his relations with his original companion (with O'Neill) in the Society, Father

Grafton, who was by then Superior in America, and to a crisis in the work in Boston in 1881, precipitated by Benson's withdrawal of confidence in Grafton and the latter's resignation from the Society.[57] Arthur Hall was now the Superior in Boston. He had stayed loyal to Benson when Grafton had withdrawn, but was shortly himself to take up the call for the American Branch to be allowed autonomy from the Superior at Cowley.[58] Congreve's coup was conducted by letter—which reflects on the personal distance even between Congreve and Benson, but which means its course can be followed in detail.

The correspondence begins with a note from Congreve on Sunday 12 January written from the Mission House in Cowley, advising Benson not to force Father Duncan Convers to come to England from Boston, since, says Congreve, an order to do so would make Convers leave the Society. In writing to Benson, Congreve not only challenged the absolute rule of the Society over its members, but by implication that of the Superior over the Branches. "It seems to me," he wrote, "open to question whether the

---

[55]   Congreve and Longridge (eds), *Letters of R. M. Benson*, Appendix, p. 359.

[56]   Congreve, "Loss and Gain", p. 57.

[57]   Pendleton, *Press On, the Kingdom*, pp. 47–8 & Chapter 5.

[58]   Pendleton, *Press On, the Kingdom*, p. 79.

Society has a right to require him [Convers] to spend a year in England against his will."[59] Congreve's conversation with Maturin took place before the following Thursday, 16 January, when Congreve wrote to Benson again, now from the Community of All Hallows in Ditchingham, Suffolk. Congreve told Benson of the conversation he had had with Maturin, making clear not only his own sympathy for Maturin's concerns, but also that what he said was felt by many others in America: "[Maturin] gave me the impression that all the members of his community had the same feeling that he had—the impression he gave me was a very serious one, I gather that most everyone in the community was more or less alienated from the Mother House, and disappointed." In theory the members of the Society in America were all simply on deployment from Cowley, but Maturin had said that some members of the community "shrink from the Mother House and will do anything rather than come to it. This was not merely because of external discomfort—though he said that 'some always get ill here directly they come'—but from a feeling of difficulty in talking about community matters with you [i.e. Benson]."[60]

Maturin had told Congreve that he was going to speak to Benson, and that he hoped that a full discussion could be had at the forthcoming Triennial Chapter of the Society, but Congreve had replied that he would write to the Superior himself. Having reported the conversation, Congreve drew a line across his letter to mark that what followed was "absolutely my own solitary impression and suggestion". He continued by saying that after the strain of settling the constitution, he had himself "felt something of this chilling of heart of the members of our community for some years". Despite the giving of the Rule, Congreve felt that members were not hopeful or happy. "I have after each Chapter for several years had the thought in my mind, and discussed with myself whether I should mention it to you, what I am going to mention now." He then continued starkly:

59   Congreve, Correspondence with Fr Benson, 12 January 1890, SSJE/6/5/2/1, f.
      111. This was a different situation from that of Fr Puller on his election to the
      Bishopric of Zululand, since Puller was happy to be obedient to the Society
      and the Superior in the matter. See below, pp. XXXX.
60   *Ibid.*, 16 January 1890 f. 112.

[I]t has several times occurred to me, and now it seems to be a settled thought, that just now your best way of helping and directing the community would be to stand apart from the centre for a time, I do not mean merely to resign allowing yourself to be re-elected,—but to insist upon the community putting the charge for three years at any rate—in the hands of some member whom you might indicate to them. (I feel fully the responsibility of suggesting this to you;—it has never as far as I know been hinted in the Society, nor have I ever hinted it to any until now that I say it to you.) I have a good hope that if you did this, no harm would come of it, but that a certain hope and interest would revive in the members of the Community who are dissatisfied and disappointed with the way things are going among us. I think it would be worth even a great risk—(I don't think this need be a risk) to return heart to the community, if it is disheartened and disaffected—I should personally not delight in changes,—but I wish to be absolutely indifferent except to what is of Religious Principle,—and the sticking to our Rule and Constitution—I shall always heartily accept whatever you may decide;—but my pre-judgement (entirely without consulting anyone) is as I have said.[61]

Congreve went on to suggest names of a possible new Superior: "I think you might make Father Hall superior (the community would doubtless elect anyone you wished). I believe the community would thoroughly trust Father Hall or Father Page for Superior and perhaps Father Rivington—I speak with certainty of the two whom I know best."[62] By including Hall among them Congreve perhaps attempted to make the point that he was not simply seeking from Benson a resolution of the issue of autonomy for the American Branch. He went on to suggest that Benson might "be able to do what is much-needed—viz to inspect and encourage the several works of the Branch Houses". Congreve concluded vigorously:

---

[61]   *Ibid.* ff. 115–18.

[62]   *Ibid.*, Hall was later Bishop of Vermont.

> I think it would awaken some life in the Society—now nobody
> speaks, nobody hopes—and we seem to hold together only
> because nothing happens to shake us—such a change for a time
> would bring circulation of consciousness between the centre
> and the extremities—I pray God that my own faults may not
> hinder God's good purposes in beginning our Society. I will not
> apologise for saying what I have said; having thought of it more
> or less for two or three years, it would have been unfaithful not
> to say—if I am wrong you will put it aside and God will show
> you what is right.

Letters at this period were answered almost immediately. It is notable, therefore, that when Congreve wrote again five days later (on Tuesday, 21 January), it seems Benson had not replied. Congreve opened: "I have not had a moment's doubt whether I ought to write as I did to you; I could not have kept it back without a sense of coldness and strained conscience." He was, however, anxious that he might have caused "pain and worry". He also pointed to himself as being partly at fault in the "dissatisfaction of the Community with the Mother House".[63] He remained adamant, however, that in his view Benson should step aside as Superior, suggesting now that he and Benson might go to establish a Branch House in London.

Benson laid down his office at the General Chapter on 4 August 1890.[64] In doing so, this most authoritarian of men demonstrated a new teaching in humility. Speaking to the Chapter just before his formal resignation he said, "[H]ad I had more divine wisdom, had I been more true to God, we might have been in a very different position now." Congreve had suggested that the Father Founder might arrange with any Superior who was selected to keep the disposal of money in his own hands as Founder of the Community (and donor of many of the funds).[65] Instead Benson

---

[63]   *Ibid.*, 21 January 1890, f. 119.

[64]   General Chapter Minute Book, 1884–1905, SSJE/2/1, p. 94.

[65]   Congreve, Correspondence with Fr Benson, 16 January 1890, SSJE/6/5/2/1,
       f. 112. Pendleton, *Press On, the Kingdom*, p. 30, notes that Benson's personal
       fortune was held in trust for the Society and was the foundation of its wealth.

stood completely aside, and a finance committee was set up.[66] Shortly after the Chapter he left England to take Congreve's suggestion of travelling to visit the work of the Society in India before going to America.[67] There Benson worked for nine years; because of the independence of the church in America he was ineligible to be granted a preacher's licence and therefore, while he was able to celebrate and write, as far as teaching was concerned this giant of the spiritual life served simply as a Sunday School teacher, delighting in catechizing African-American children in Boston.[68]

There was much more to the resignation than mere age, though it is true that Benson was now "sixty-six and had carried for nearly twenty-five years the whole burden of the Society".[69] The period leading up to the resignation was difficult not only because of the desire of the American Branch for autonomy, and the bleakness of life at Cowley, but because of the difficulties—caused by his inability to delegate authority— Benson found in administering the Society.[70] As Father Hall wrote in his Introductory Memoir for Congreve's edition of Benson's letters:

> [He] probably attempted to carry alone a greater burden than any one could bear, combining the charge of a large parish with the rule of a religious community, without the aid for many years of subordinate officers, with continual ministerial engagements in London and elsewhere, and an overwhelming correspondence. If the giving of a constitution to the Society and its more complete organization had not been so long delayed, some serious troubles and losses might have been avoided.[71]

It was a situation in which vocations were drying up, many were discontented, the American Branch was fracturing, and community life

---

[66]   General Chapter Minute Book, 1884–1905, SSJE/2/1, p. 94.

[67]   Woodgate, *Father Benson*, p. 153.

[68]   I am indebted to Serenhedd James for this insight. See James, *Cowley Fathers*, pp. 126–7 and photo no. 17.

[69]   Woodgate, *Father Benson*, p. 151.

[70]   Allchin, "The Man in his Time", p. 11.

[71]   Congreve and Longridge (eds), *Letters of R. M. Benson*, pp. 17–18.

was breaking down. Though he was Assistant Superior it is noteworthy that it was to Congreve that Maturin turned, partly based on their old friendship, but also on Congreve's more open personality. It remains a measure of Congreve's growth in the religious life that he was able to write to Benson so directly in the way he did; and it is a measure of Benson's humility that he was prepared to listen. Congreve believed Benson to have acted with saintly humility and saw in Benson's decision to resign none of the struggle which had characterized the agreement of the Rule. Reflecting at the end of his life on Benson's example, he wrote of the Father Founder, "[T]here were naturally a good many things in the changes that followed his retirement that were not to his taste according to his judgement; about such things he probably spoke to the Superior to let him know his thoughts but was never heard speak of any such matters afterwards. He was no longer responsible, he looked away from what he disliked *to God* and was at peace."[72]

The Chapter elected Father Page as Superior General. Congreve remained Assistant Superior and continued to develop his thought and teaching about the religious life in sermons, letters and retreats, and prefaces to books, and to help communities to live it. From Benson he learned the self-surrender that is necessary, and he always pointed to Benson as the source of all his teaching. He wrote to him, "[I]f I have grace to persevere, and improve, and overcome evil I shall owe it to God's mercy through the Society and your charity."[73] Despite this, even Congreve at the beginning had been convinced to remain at Cowley only when Father O'Neill offered friendship. He corrected Benson, "never intimate with anyone", and taught that surrender to God alone is the path to better human relationships:

> Sacrifice, emptiness, what a cruel sound the words have for nature
> ... what a heaven it means for the Sister who perseveres in prayer,
> gives all to God, and keeps nothing for herself ... She sees old

---

[72] Congreve, letter to "N" (Selina Congreve), 1 August 1915, SSJE/6/5/2/5, f. 49, emphasis in the original.

[73] Congreve, Correspondence with Fr Benson, 21 January 1890, SSJE/6/5/2/1, f. 119.

times, old faces, but sees them now where they really are, in the love of God; and so they no longer rival or dispossess God, but become at once more dear than ever, and at the same time a subtile [*sic*] and all-pervading joy, like light, that takes no room that is wanted for other things, but irradiates them all.[74]

He went on, "In a life that becomes sacrifice, something given as a means of union with God, one observes that nothing remains trivial. A life given to God can only bring God into everything." For Congreve, beyond the self-surrender lies the joy of the soul who rejoices in personal relationship with God, and who in and through that prime relationship can come to a deeper love of others than is possible without him.

---

[74] Congreve, *Interior Life*, pp. 283–4.

CHAPTER 5

The Protest of the Spirit of Christ

When Congreve came to Cowley in 1873, he expected to receive—from missionary priests—training for the mission field. He was mistaken; in the first months of his novitiate Benson taught him the grammar of the religious life and he swiftly came to understand the Society of Saint John the Evangelist to be a religious community, and the call he had received as a vocation to the religious life. This was, however, not to eschew the work of the missionary which had first attracted him to Cowley. Benson was a missionary at heart, who had himself packed for India when the express request of the bishop to remain in his parish arrived, and whose consolation in resigning as Superior General was at last to be able to go abroad himself.[1] Despite Benson's teaching that external works of whatever kind are entirely secondary to the primary vocation of a life offered to God in love, there remained a persistent temptation in the Society to abandon the religious life in favour of living and working wholly as a society of mission priests.

This temptation was felt especially in the busy life of the branch houses. While many of the Fathers indeed wished to live as religious, Superiors were charged with organizing missionary activity, building churches, establishing schools, managing finances and engaging with ecclesiastical and secular authorities. Those charged with these responsibilities were often less able or willing to establish and protect the regular routines of the religious community. This tension was inherent in Benson's dual

---

[1]   William Braithwaite O'Brien SSJE, "Some Anglican Forms of the Religious Life for Men", *Holy Cross Magazine*, July 1937, p. 203 (SSJE/6/24/2/1). Woodgate, *Father Benson*, p. 152.

vision for the Society of Saint John the Evangelist.[2] O'Neill worked it out by withdrawing from the busy work and becoming a "Christian *sadhu*".[3] Others let the religious life fall away in the face of busy parochial and missional activity. Around 1890 this happened in the Society's Mission in Cape Town. Congreve, the would-be missionary who had become a religious, was charged twice over the following fifteen years with helping the South African mission retain its equilibrium as a religious community engaged in mission. He was remarkably successful, and when the Society as a whole debated its nature, Congreve's voice and experience weighed strongly to ensure the Society held fast to its vocation as a religious order.

Cowley Fathers went to parishes all over the British Isles—sometimes singly, sometimes in pairs—to preach missions in parishes for a week or a fortnight at a time, giving addresses each day, leading devotions and raising the profile of churches in their community. In addition, SSJE had opened Houses in the United States in 1870, India in 1874, and South Africa in 1883. In all these centres the Society was committed to an active missionary life conducted by religious. Benson was suspicious of purely contemplative religious life, and Congreve agreed: "[T]he great monasteries were centres of industries. Christianity does not tolerate dreams. 'If a man will not work, neither shall he eat.'"[4] Congreve wrote that mystics like St John of the Cross and St Teresa of Avila were "not dreamers" and pointed to their active lives. He remarked tartly that "[w]e make no step towards the truth by renouncing the world's unreality to clothe ourselves with religious unreality".[5] Benson thought the modern world unfitted for contemplation. In contrast to past generations, "[T]he nervous system is so much fretted by the excitement of life . . . We have neither the same logical subtlety nor the same simple childlike gaze in

---

[2]   Kemsley, "The Religious Life", p. 99.

[3]   James, *Cowley Fathers*, p. 176; see also James, p. 84. A *sadhu* is a religious ascetic or holy person, usually Hindu.

[4]   Congreve, letter to Assheton, July 1881, SSJE/6/5/5/9, f. 454. The reference is to 2 Thessalonians 3:10.

[5]   Congreve, *Christian Progress*, p. 164.

which former generations might live."[6] He taught that contemplation was something that would flow from active work, and indeed active work was required for contemplation to be pure. Early in Congreve's life as a Religious, Benson wrote to him about a Sister who wished to join a contemplative order:

> I have no confidence in that Society. I think there would be great self-will in going there. Probably the attraction for a contemplative life is only a form of Pride. If she has such an attraction there will be no danger of work luring her away from prayer, but if the attraction is out of the fancy of pride then in fact it is a work of her intellect leading her away from God.[7]

Congreve agreed. In 1902 he wrote:

> I can never fit in the mystic's view of God, the Infinite the Eternal, with my own daily sensations, interests, cares, the weather, my health, cooking of my dinner, politics, religious controversy, and 100 other things which are important. It is the universal difficulty of bringing the finite into relation with the Infinite—dealing with these two different worlds, one seems to be two different persons.[8]

Because in Jesus, the Word made flesh, the Infinite has been "brought into our finite", Congreve taught, we are able to be united with Christ in everyday things: "Christ sweeps the room, Christ suffers, Christ bears burdens—the deadweight of my humanity and years and infirmity." These very things are the means by which a soul can rise to God: "My sweeping, my burden-bearing lift me up into the fellowship of the

---

[6]   Kemsley, "The Religious Life", p. 118.

[7]   Benson, Correspondence from Cowley, 4 September 1878, SSJE/6/1/2/7/11, f. 1. See also Peta Dunstan, *The Labour of Obedience: The Benedictines of Pershore, Nashdom and Elmore, A History* (Norwich: Canterbury Press, 2009), p. 27.

[8]   Longridge (ed.), *Spiritual Letters of Fr Congreve*, p. 82.

Infinite."[9] Moreover, the mystic impulse and faculty is a "universal human faculty, quickened by an illuminating gift of grace which belongs to every Christian"[10] and implies activity. Unlike the Hindu ascetic, who "accumulates merit for himself alone by his labours and sacrifices, the Christian ascetic on the contrary suffers for the glory of God and for the salvation of souls . . . " This activity is missional:

> It is much to be noticed how many of the great missionaries to whom Europe owes its Christianity, issued from the Benedictine cloister, which was the great school of the mystical life, of contemplative prayer in the West.

Rather than being a specialism of certain souls, the contemplative calling is for all.[11]

This was just the period when the SSJE were becoming less friendly with Father Aelred Carlyle and his Benedictine experiment which led to the founding of an Anglican Benedictine community on Caldey Island (off the coast of Wales). In 1899, Father Aelred and Brother Henry had lived at Cowley for a while and then, at Father Page's invitation, at the SSJE House in London. As Aelred became more contemplative (and was drawn to Roman Catholicism), the division with SSJE deepened. Notably, when Carlyle did become a Roman Catholic—with most of his monks—the Abbot of the successor Anglican community at Pershore, Brother Denys (who as a parish priest in Liverpool had received SSJE missions) taught that contemplation must arise out of activity, and that to misunderstand this had been Carlyle's failing.[12]

---

9   Ibid. See also Luke Miller, *The Sorrow of Nature: The Way of the Cross with George Congreve and Thérèse of Lisieux* (Oxford: The Catholic League, 2014), pp. 5–7. Congreve is careful to say that the external work leads one deeper; Congreve, *Interior Life*, pp. 1–9.

10   Congreve, *Interior Life*, p. 182.

11   *Ibid.*, pp. 172–94.

12   Dunstan, *Labour of Obedience*, pp. 26–7. Pershore is in Worcestershire. Dunstan records that before entering the religious life, Denys had been a curate at St Margaret's, Liverpool.

There were those in SSJE who took a more positive view of the enclosed contemplative life. In 1906, Father Hollings was, with the support of Father Page, actively engaged in the work which would lead to the establishment of the Sisters of the Love of God.[13] When Congreve preached to the SLG, he offered a model for the enclosed Religious which emphasized "the things we are doing all day in the active side of life". God is found and contemplated through inviting Him into day-to-day activity, in what Congreve called the "Sacrament of the Present Moment". He warned against any artificial separation of what is holy from the mundane. He spoke of "Blessed Mary's work at her wheel" and went on:

> So we will try to learn to think of the details of everyday life as shadows bringing a hidden great thing into every day, *God's will.* But God's will is no *abstraction* . . . it is God Himself willing, having a glorious will as to *all* that we are to do . . . God's will is sought and found by the Saints and welcomed because it is to welcome God himself.[14]

Congreve was, however, no activist. Writing about the vocation and work of Sisters for the Pan-Anglican Congress in 1908, he reiterated that the end of the religious life is not any achievement or specific success, and it is by death to the world that the things of the world are made truly useful: "[T]he sacrifice of the virgin life makes it *more* not *less* useful to others . . . People know that the ring of a Sister is not the token of a passing phase of philanthropic sentiment but of a whole life given to Christ in their service". For Congreve, this is a good not only for others, but for the Religious and her or his community: "[T]otal dedication to God nothing held back means no anxiety . . . Her community is solidly based on mutual self-sacrifice". He contrasts a convent characterized by this dedication with a "mere hostel of temporary 'good women'".[15]

---

[13]   Peter F. Anson, *Building up the Waste Places: The revival of monastic life on medieval lines in the post-Reformation Church of England* (London: Faith Press, 1973), p. 188.

[14]   Congreve, Sermon notes, SSJE/6/5/3/18. Emphasis in the original.

[15]   Congreve, "Sisters, their Vocation and Special Work", p. 3.

Also to be avoided is "an obstinate keeping of myself needlessly busy. Fussing about many things in the outer court, the court of the Gentiles, to save myself the surrender which it costs to enter within to escape the absorbing claim of the divine presence."[16]

"God will take care of the work, He is more honoured by your obedience than by any work succeeding."[17] The principle of active obedience was the basis on which Congreve built his own understanding of the religious life. Benson, he wrote, "practised this himself when at last he was not re-elected Superior—No one saw a touch of anxiety or depression in him. He just went on as a subject under obedience instead of as Superior. Went under obedience to America filling minor offices as he was able, or as help was wanted here or there: and all the time keeping not merely obedience to his junior who was now his Superior but giving him loyal and cordial support and help and affectionate sympathy."[18] Here once more is Congreve's principle of cordiality: not simply the external acceptance of authority, but the joyful reception by both the will and the heart of what is required by God's commanding love.

Following Benson's resignation, Congreve remained Assistant Superior and took his part alongside the new Superior General, Robert Page, in seeking to excise the "deadness" which had so characterized the Mother House and had driven postulants away. It was necessary to ensure that those who came to test the life were properly cared for and trained. Frederick Puller, who since 1883 had been serving as the chaplain to the All Saints Sisters of the Poor Hostel for Girls in Cape Town, was recalled to Cowley to become novice master. Before he had an opportunity to leave, he was elected Bishop of Zululand. Puller wrote to Page to inform him of the election and to place the decision as to whether he should accept entirely in the Superior's hands.[19]

---

[16]   Congreve, General correspondence, undated, around 1903, SSJE/6/5/2/3, f. 11.

[17]   Congreve, letter to "N" (Selina Congreve), 1 August 1915, SSJE/6/5/2/5, f. 49.

[18]   See also Woodgate, *Father Benson*, pp. 158–9.

[19]   Correspondence regarding the election to the Bishopric of Zululand, 11 February (Ash Wednesday) 1891, SSJE/9/2/3/7.

Congreve's letter to Page on the subject could not have been clearer. In his view, the Society had grave needs safeguarding its character as a religious community. Congreve was sure, therefore, that the Superior must ask one of its members to forego preferment for himself and turn down the opportunity for the Society to lead what was clearly a significant piece of mission work. He quoted Maturin, whose "comment on this news was blunt: 'Well, if he is to go we may as well pack up, and leave Cowley altogether.'" Congreve emphasized that he felt the Society to be at an existential crossroads:

> I think our last General Chapter and election was as far as one can see the supreme effort of our Society to right itself, and recover discipline and hope—The Church in South Africa may have strong claims and great needs—but has to set against them the needs of the English Church at home and throughout the world ... Unless we have a Master of Novices we cannot have a Novice and without Novices as a Society—we come to an end—there is a risque [sic] of course in letting go an important opening in Africa like the Zulu work. For the sake of raising up the dedicated life in England one has to consider what God has called us for; there will be risques and losses in every course and they don't matter if they are sustained in the way of duty—one cannot be sure what duty is without knowing the circumstances—but my prejudice is to stick to the call to build up the Religious Life in England and decline other kinds of work on any side. The sense of loss which this line may bring will be a loss to us, and rouse us out of the natural tendency to take things easy—one must rouse oneself to a vocation which involves declining a call to lead a mission in the heart of Africa.[20]

---

[20]   Zululand correspondence, Lent 1891, SSJE/9/2/3/7. The very tone of Congreve's letter (written from Burton Hall) and his willingness to quote Maturin by name in these forthright remarks show how much and how quickly the atmosphere at Cowley was changing with the new Superior.

Page agreed with Congreve. He wrote to the Bishop of Carlisle, to whom the election had been delegated by the South African bishops as Chairman of the Zululand Mission Association, "[T]he mind of the community is that we should not part from Fr Puller even though called so unanimously . . . it would be simply ruinous to our community for Fr Puller to leave . . . It is not too much to say that the future of our Society as a Religious Community very largely depends on him." The Superior went on to say that Father Benson had founded the Society to be "a Community in the English Church in which souls called by God to consecrate themselves to him under the vows of Religion may find their home. We stand almost alone and are few in number, but I think we may believe that if we are faithful to our trust God will multiply us and use us for his glory."[21] The decision was not without criticism. The election had been unanimously accepted by the South African Synod, and *Southern Cross* (the paper of the Church in South Africa) deplored the Society's decision in an editorial of 15 May 1891 entitled "Cowley and Zululand".

The decision was based on a theology of mission which Congreve articulated to his friend Richard Assheton. A nephew of Assheton's had criticized the members of the Society as being introspective and more interested in the salvation of their own souls than of others. Congreve replied that "to save my own soul is not to get something good for myself—but to give myself soul and body absolutely to the Creator for His love's sake to dispose of as He pleases".[22] The result of this self-giving to God is a missionary desire to share this first love with others. Far from being selfish, therefore, self-offering leads out into mission. "It is participation in the Divine Nature that makes every consideration necessarily secondary to the soul's personal relation to God. But this is the opposite of selfishness and is the only thing that actually turns us away from selfishness." The personal relationship of the soul with God is what enables the soul to lead others to conversion. Congreve said that without the absorbing enthusiasm for God which comes from this personal relationship, mission is reduced to "picking out" from among the "value

---

[21]   Zululand correspondence, Page to the Bishop of Carlisle, 21 March 1891, SSJE/9/2/3/7.

[22]   Congreve, Letters to friends and associates, SSJE/6/5/2/6, f. 98.

systems" of religion "the one best suited to improve the moral condition of the Heathens". There is then no specifically Christian mission, and any religion becomes an "equally dead machine", while mission is reduced to "a matter of tactics". To lose the focus on God, he wrote elsewhere, is "to stiffen into a machine for work", while by contrast the "living touch of grace will awaken neglected, forgotten graces in those to whom [the Christian] ministers. This strikes one irresistibly in our missions to the heathen abroad, the influence that the Sisters of Mercy unconsciously exercise over the idolaters, an influence which awakens in them a desire for that moral beauty which even wild human nature recognises in a life given in their service for the love of God."[23]

Mission without sacrifice is, says Congreve, "secular". Its source is "the neglect of sacraments in our church".[24] Since true mission requires an entire focus on God, it must be sacramental because in the sacraments Christ himself is ministered, not simply ideas about him. Congreve wrote, "Christ did not leave only a 'view', a 'philosophy'. If so it is worth little more than any other philosophy. If He gives himself in the sacraments of grace His religion is Himself and is worth living and dying for." This in turn means that results may not be visible or measurable. Congreve adduces the examples of O'Neill who died having converted "no one", but who was loved and respected by the people among whom he had lived, and Henry Martyn whose life ("[N]ow let me burn out for God"). Congreve saw as a great example, but whose visible successes were meagre.[25] Nevertheless, Congreve asserts that results will come, and souls will be brought to Christ if the missionary brings Christ himself sacramentally and not simply ideas and "propaganda". "We can trust results, for in spite of European vices . . . [w]hat we bring is God himself and the results will be worthy of God."[26]

Congreve understood the work of mission to be at the heart of what it means to be a Christian, and therefore saw no conflict between the

---

[23]   Congreve, *Interior Life*, p. 286.

[24]   Congreve, Letters to friends and associates, SSJE/6/5/2/6, f. 98

[25]   The words were written in Henry Martyn's journal on 17 May 1806 as he began his ministry in North India.

[26]   Congreve, Letters to friends and associates, SSJE/6/5/2/6, ff. 99–100.

religious life and missionary activity. In an address given towards the end of his life, Congreve explained that mission is not simply obedience to the Great Commission (Matthew 28:18–20) but a response to the fact that "Christ has taken human nature and made all one." To help in the salvation of souls is therefore not "accidental, but vital for every Christian". This might be "parents at home, or missionaries abroad".[27] Moreover, the mission is not motivated by a desire to increase numbers of Christians, but springs from what it is to *be* a Christian, for to turn from mission is to turn away from Christ. "When a church loses its missionary enthusiasm and allows indifference as to the conversion of heathen nations, their own Christianity begins to die out, as it happened to the British Church refusing to join in the conversion of the hated Saxons."[28] To bring the Good News is not "a favour that we do for the heathen, but a necessary instinctive action in our new nature of Christ in us". Because of this union in Christ between those who evangelize and those who receive the message, "in turn we ourselves receive help and grace from those who are won to him". The Church "without them is incomplete, and all the members share in the enrichment of life in virtue which the conversion of each new member brings".[29]

The religious have a special duty to call the church out of complacency and back to her work of active mission. Speaking in 1897 to the Sisters of Bethany, Congreve said that the religious orders are to be a "perpetual protest of the Spirit of Christ against hidden worldliness in the church". Commenting on the Oxford Movement he said, "[N]ow, when the first humility and depth of the Movement has passed away, and we are grown a little pleased with all that the Movement has affected, we think we belong to the Movement because we still build churches, and know better how to paint them than 50 years ago." In contrast with this, the religious are "the Reformers of religion in our own times, always returning to first principles". That is, the principles of "prayer and self-discipline". Thus it is:

---

[27] Congreve, Address to the East and West Missionary Society at St Mary Magdalene's Oxford, 1913, SSJE/6/5/3/18.

[28] Congreve, Sermon notes, Maundy Thursday 1904, SSJE/6/5/3/10.

[29] *Ibid.*

> . . . not for our own souls only but to help others, not by talking or
> writing about it, but by practising it, by showing how the commands
> of Christ are practicable still, just as practicable today as 1800 years
> ago. What you have seen in the Religious movement in our own
> time is not its improvement in ceremonial but its dedication to
> Christ and the change of heart and life which it has shown us.

This dedicated life is "a protest against unreal religion where religion has
become a department of sentiment".[30]

If Congreve was clear about the relation between the religious life and
missionary activity, difficulties remained for those who tried to work out
the life in practice. In the early 1890s, the expanding mission work of
the Society in Cape Town brought on a press of secular business while
"things with regard to the Religious Life were not much developed".[31] The
tension between the religious life and the busy work of mission priests
became acute. The same pressures were felt by the All Saints Sisters of the
Poor who worked closely with SSJE in Cape Town, one Sister noting the
difficulty of remaining in union with God in "a life so externally secular
as this".[32] Other difficulties appear to have exacerbated the situation. The
Provincial Superior, Father Edward Osborne, was a man of large character
and great energy. In Boston, where he had been Grafton's assistant, he
had been described in the local paper as one who "knows what to do in
every emergency, stands faithfully with the poor through thick and thin,
and has not more the courage of conviction than the audacity of duty".[33]

In 1891, there was a disagreement between Osborne, supported by
the archdeacon and the bishop, and Mother Caroline Mary, who had
worked in Cape Town and was now back in England as Superior, over

[30] Congreve, Sermon notes, SSJE/6/5/3/8.

[31] George Herbert Hodge SSJE, Correspondence with Fr Page, 22 November
1898, referring to the situation in 1892; SSJE/6/17/1, f. 12.

[32] Correspondence of All Saints Sisters of the Poor, November 1897,
SSJE/9/2/3/5, f. 25.

[33] Quoted by Pendleton in *Press On, the Kingdom*, p. 61. Osborne was later
Bishop of Springfield, Illinois.

the rebuilding of the unsuitable All Saints Sisters Home.[34] Mother Caroline Mary objected to the great cost and thought the new site less advantageous.[35] The sums involved were astronomical, a total of £30,000. Mother Mary was adamant that her community would not contribute the £2,000 sought from them, nor could they raise £10,000. The following March Sister Eileen wrote to Page, "I once heard Fr Osborne say he could easily raise money in America 'by means of a magic lantern.' Perhaps he might be asked to do so."[36] The local Superior, Sister Clementina, had clearly felt under pressure to agree, and in the end, Mother Caroline Mary conceded that if everyone locally felt it right, then Sister Clementina "must be entirely guided by Fr Osborne".[37] Then, in 1892, the amount of money coming from England to support the Fathers was reduced, and there was a threat to cut the wages of those working for the Mission.[38]

This was the context in the spring of 1893 when Page decided that someone senior from Cowley had to go to Cape Town. Congreve was sent.[39] Publicly the trip was described as a "Missionary Journey", but at the same time Osborne returned to England for a while.[40] The money for the Sisters' Home was largely given, in the end, by Cecil Rhodes.[41] Congreve retained a respect and liking for the great Imperialist, and it is possible that his wide contacts in the upper reaches of English society made him a good person to be on hand during the discussions about the gift.[42]

---

[34]   Anson, *Building up the Waste Places*, p. 324. Anson suggests that a typhoid outbreak was linked to the insanitary conditions of the old Home.

[35]   Correspondence of All Saints Sisters, undated, 1891, SSJE/9/2/3/5, f. 14.

[36]   *Ibid.*, 20 March 1891, f. 18.

[37]   *Ibid.*, 29 October 1891, ff. 14–15.

[38]   William West Jones, Correspondence with SSJE, undated, 1891, SSJE/9/2/3/1.

[39]   Woodgate, *Father Congreve*, p. 40.

[40]   Scrapbook of mission notices, 23 April 1894, SSJE/10/1.

[41]   Anson, *Building up the Waste Places*, p. 324.

[42]   Congreve, "The Need of God", in *The Church Chronicle of South Africa* (reprinted in *The Cowley Evangelist*, February 1904, pp. 55–60), contains a vivid description of Rhodes' estate and asserts that the statesman has as much need of God as Moses Runene, a young African teacher who was dying, equating the two, and offering both as examples, in many ways with more sympathy for Runene.

Figure 9: Fr Page. After Congreve encouraged Benson to resign, Robert Lay Page was elected Superior General. In 1893, he sent Congreve on his first journey to South Africa and India.

Congreve was no sailor; Fr Waggett described him as, "a lost man physically, an agonized man mentally, so long as his death-in-life was on the deep",[43] but from the outset the journey was one of natural wonders. He described his joy at seeing the peak of the island of Tenerife, and the fear of evil he felt on seeing a shark in the water. His nephew Walter, now in the Army, paid for him to travel first class, but the tropical heat was enervating.[44] He was sea-sick all the way, and when he arrived he found the mission buildings flea-ridden and extremely uncomfortable.[45] The new Cowley House was not to be built until the following year. While it is fairly certain that he helped with the sore relationships and practical business surrounding the Sisters, and that he brought to the life of the Fathers the regularity of Cowley, the specific problems which he came to deal with do not feature in his correspondence.[46] Instead, his letters shine with delight in South Africa, its people and the "New botanical wonders" he found there. In some scrubland he found:

> bind weed twisting itself around one plant bush after another, till the whole place was a web of yellow thread, good stout pack-thread which strengthens the plant it touches. You can imagine the delightful excitement which a walk alone among these wildernesses awakens . . . One feels almost crazy with delight and wonder to find in every place new wonders.

He was fascinated by everything. He continued, "I am sure that if I were not a missionary I should become an artist and an ornithologist."[47] The natural world was a source of profound meditations. In a hastily scrawled letter with poor grammar, he arrestingly described how beauty brings us to the divine presence:

---

[43] Philip Napier Waggett SSJE, "Father Congreve", in *The Cowley Evangelist*, May 1918, p. 129.

[44] Copies of letters to friends and associates, SSJE/6/5/2/7.

[45] Woodgate, *Father Congreve*, pp. 41–2. Woodgate writes "bug" where Congreve has "cockroach": Congreve, letter to Assheton, SSJE/6/5/5/9, f. 619.

[46] Woodgate, *Father Congreve*, pp. 44–5.

[47] Congreve, letters to Miss Kebbel, 1894 SSJE/6/5/2/4/3, ff. 8, 9.

> As I looked all round I caught sight of a bush a good way below, a
> burning bush aflame with a gold light and thought I recognised a
> Hostia I had not found before—scrambled down, and found the
> bush burning with gold fire (amber flowers etc) I can only give
> you dead words, if you had seen it you would have shouted with
> joy—I could not take off my shoes—I took off my hat; it was a
> beauty which made one feel the beauty and joy of God with great
> reverence ... God has given us all things richly to enjoy and
> he will not come short of it notwithstanding the sadness often
> apparently on the surface.[48]

He delighted also in the people: "I had taken my office book but the
children gave quite a different character to the morning to what I had
intended, and I brought my office book back full of squeezed wild flowers
and ferns." He loved the adults as well: "[T]hese men are more intelligent
than our countrymen, have more humour I should think and yet more
seriousness and manliness."[49]

Congreve was in Cape Town for a few months before continuing
his "missionary tour" to Ceylon and then India, visiting the Mission in
Poona where in 1903 Ninian Comper would build the Society's church,
St Crispin's.[50] After some weeks, Congreve travelled on to Calcutta and
Bombay to take a ship home. O'Neill had died more than ten years
previously, and Congreve did not go to Indore to see his mission there.
When he returned from his travels in the spring of 1895, now nearly sixty,
Page relieved him of his duties as Assistant Superior and he approached a
more retired life, though Africa remained in his heart, and in the summer
he reminisced in a note to Brother John, who was in South Africa, "I can
see the stars, and the black mass of the mountains and by day the sea, and
the odd wild plants and the dear human faces and the patient ocean."[51]
Assheton was making preparations to travel to Cape Town, and Congreve
wrote to Brother John asking him to "forget stories of [Assheton] I may

---

[48]   Congreve, letter to Miss Kebbel, 1894, SSJE/6/5/2/4/3, f. 12.

[49]   Congreve, letters to Assheton, SSJE/6/5/5/9, ff. 619, 621.

[50]   Lesley Walton, "St Crispin's Home for Girls" (2007), SSJE/10/5.

[51]   Letter to Br John, 18 July 1895, SSJE/6/5/2/2/2, f. 1.

have garrulously told you, as he is a man of great reserve". This is an indication of the openness in relationships which Congreve espoused during his religious life, and which was different both from the "deadness" that Benson had encouraged at Cowley before 1890 and the reserve of wider Victorian society, particularly between those of different social status.[52]

In South Africa, Congreve had his first experience of what was to him the "strange weird music" of Africa which he found "full of sadness and sweetness; sometimes there was wild and lofty aspiration in it, sometimes a horror of the gloom of lost souls". The dancing was an "extravagant exhibition" of:

> the wildest freedom; the whole thing tender and grotesque, and
> was proportionally painful; what was edifying in it was as it might
> be edifying to look into hell, and feel the contrast of the sweet
> order and grace of Christian life.[53]

In all probability, Congreve approved the formal dancing of his own culture, though there is no evidence for that, and as one who lived a rule of life which forbade theatregoing he may well have thought an English dance just as "hellish".[54] His point was not a cultural but a spiritual one: that the self-discipline of God's law in Christ enables true pleasure. A Christian culture is superior to a "heathen" culture, not because of any racial superiority, but because only Christ gives the discipline in which enjoyment of any cultural expression can be found. In the same letter to his sister, describing African dance, he expresses the opposite of cultural imperialism:

---

[52]   Congreve's correspondence with John, in addition to the business of the Society and religious reflection, gives many snippets of family news and remarks about current affairs. James, *Cowley Fathers*, pp. 79, 83, discusses the issues of class within SSJE.

[53]   Congreve, Copies of letters to friends and associates; 30 August 1893, letter to "N" (Selina Congreve), SSJE/6/5/2/7.

[54]   James, *Cowley Fathers*, p. 80.

> I never knew how beautiful and to be loved the human soul is, as
> human soul. Before I somehow fancied it was lovable because it is
> English: there are men here with faces as black as midnight with
> souls that reflect all the light of God with just the same joy as any
> saint in England, and that capacity of reflecting the beauty and
> goodness of God in the soul is I feel the essence of humanity.[55]

The religious rule, and the wider duties of Christian discipline, open the
way to enjoyment:

> No department of life and no human relationship is left without
> that sober brightness and that joyous persistence in all good
> which only religion can insure. So use everything, but do it well.
> Do not hold aloof from amusements but try to free them from
> the extraneous influences by which they are too often diverted
> from their proper use.[56]

Self-discipline does not inhibit but consecrates pleasure, enhancing it
for good:

> [T]he world we forsake is not the *pleasure* which belongs to
> healthy humanity—pleasure in society, friendship, in art, in
> nature, in food. It will be *worldliness* in lawful pleasure: pleasure
> we rest in selfishly. Pleasure we fail to consecrate, by making it a
> means of union with God, by our thanksgiving, and by making
> it conduce to the good of our fellow Christian.

It is self-discipline which "leads us more from worldliness every day".[57]

---

[55] Congreve, Copies of letters to friends and associates; 30 August 1893, letter
to "N" (Selina Congreve), SSJE/6/5/2/7.

[56] Congreve, Sermon notes, "What Is the World We Give up?", SSJE/6/5/3/18.

[57] *Ibid.* This sermon is written in an untidy notebook and is difficult to decipher.
The emphasis is given by Congreve who underlined the words given in italics
and the punctuation has been altered for clarity.

While Congreve was defending the Rule but attempting to show how it could be structured in a way that made it possible to live as a proper community, the new Superior General himself was questioning whether the Society could or should continue as a religious community. In 1891, just after succeeding Benson, Page had faced a renewed crisis of relations with the American brethren of SSJE. The context was wider, but the issues included the controversial decision to recall the Superior in America, Father Hall. Many outside the Society tried to advise Hall to refuse, but he was obedient to the summons and came to Cowley, though he returned to America in 1893 on his election as Bishop of Vermont.[58] Defending the decision to require Hall to return to Cowley, Page unequivocally characterized the Cowley Fathers as religious:

> SSJE must be able to move people, or whenever a strong character is sent to a distant country he will practically be lost to the Society. We are not a mere training college for missionaries, we are a society of Religious under vows of obedience.[59]

Three years later, however, in July 1896, Page decided that it was time for SSJE to give up the vow of poverty because "postulants are likely not to be Religious, but missionaries". Page felt he had support for this view: it

---

[58]   These events are narrated in Woodgate, *Father Benson*, pp. 157–61. Hall had not voted for the election of Bishop Phillips Brooks, but as a member of the Synod certified his orthodoxy and fitness for office. At the induction of Brooks as vicar of his parish he had allowed non-conformist ministers to communicate. Most of the SSJE Fathers in England saw this as an abandonment of the catholic faith. Hall's support for Brooks in the controversy (though not for his action in opening Holy Communion to those who were not confirmed) was the cause of his recall. Hall was also in favour of the separation of the English and American Provinces of SSJE, and it was hoped that his recall would allow the attempt to be made to keep them united. After he was released from the Society to become Bishop of Vermont, Hall continued to live by the Rule and was a welcome visitor to Cowley.

[59]   Frederick William Puller SSJE, Correspondence with friends and associates, Letter of Fr Page to Fr Puller, 7 November 1891, SSJE/6/9/1/23, f. 58.

was "what Maturin has always said", and, he noted, Benson himself had "despaired of the Society maintaining his ideal".[60] He opened his mind to Puller and said that he intended to mark the shift with outward changes: the choir offices at Cowley would no longer be sung in the Mission Chapel but in the new church of St John. Furthermore, because the Society was no longer vowed to poverty it would now accept for the church gifts of expensive stained glass and other fine fittings previously refused because the Statutes specifically forbade acceptance on the grounds that "the chapels of the Fathers should reflect the Spirit of Poverty".[61]

Puller objected vigorously, contesting the right of the Superior to make such a change on his own and questioning the ability of the Society, even were a Greater Chapter to be called, to alter "the fundamentals". Congreve was asked his view. He wrote to Puller to say that if the Superior did not withdraw his suggestion, then it should be taken to the Chapter (which was due to meet that August directly the forthcoming retreat was completed), and concurred with the view that if the change were to take place it would represent such a significant departure from the fundamentals that he and Puller "would have to ask for release", since SSJE would no longer be the Society into which they had been professed. Page withdrew his suggestion. Congreve was by no means a lone voice, but he was a senior and respected figure whose intervention was crucial in ensuring that—at least in theory—the Society maintained its self-understanding as an active religious community and not as "merely a society of mission priests".[62]

None of this prevented Congreve appreciating the grand new church of St John built by Bodley, with glass by Kempe and decorated by Brother Maynard, the SSJE Lay Brother whose skills as an architect and decorator underpinned Bodley's practice in many ways. On 16 March 1895, it was

---

[60] Frederick William Puller SSJE, Letters on proposals to change the Society, July 1896, SSJE/6/9/1/2, f. 6.

[61] *Ibid.*, f. 1. The Statutes are found at SSJE/1/1/1–2, Benson, "Instructions", 1890–1907.

[62] Puller, Letters on proposals, July 1896, SSJE/6/9/1/2, ff. 1–11.

Congreve who climbed to the apex of the new building to fix the finial stone cross.[63]

The character of the Cowley Fathers as religious was underlined in the late 1890s when the Bishop of Argyll and the Isles, Alexander Chinnery-Haldane, gave SSJE care of the Bishop's House on Iona, the island off the west coast of Scotland where St Columba had developed monasticism in the sixth century as a deliberate attempt to restart the religious life in western Scotland.[64] The Society maintained a presence on Iona for thirteen years.[65] Congreve echoed Columba in describing Iona as "the beautiful desert".[66] He loved the island, which he visited in 1897 and 1898. He was moved by the association with Columba and his monks. They provided a template for the religious life in which the loss of all worldly things led to the great gain of life in God: it was "the mystery of the cross accepted inwardly".[67] He wrote:

> It was through Columba's heroic self-sacrifice, his lifelong penitence, that his eyes were opened to see wonderful things where others saw only what is trivial and perishing. There is a wild, unregenerate love of nature which is almost physical; a passion which belongs to our early years, and has no perception yet of the true heights and depths of human life. To this the dedicated man will die; and that death is expressed in Columba's life-exile and missionary sacrifice. The little hill of the Angels where he

---

[63]   Photographs, SSJE/11, record the event of Congreve placing the cross. On the church, see James, *Cowley Fathers*, pp. 98–103.

[64]   James, *Ibid.*, p. 106. On Chinnery-Haldane's links with Cowley, see also James, pp. 92–3.

[65]   1896–1909. During this period SSJE Fathers made frequent visits, and a permanent presence was maintained from 1906–8. In addition to the inclusion of Columba in Kempe's east window of the church at Cowley, mentioned by James (*Cowley Fathers*, p. 106), Columba was carved on the cross of the Benson memorial in the churchyard of SS Mary & John.

[66]   Congreve, letter to Br John, 17 March 1908, SSJE/6/5/2/2/9, f. 10.

[67]   Woodgate, *Father Congreve*, p. 48. Longridge (ed.), *Spiritual Letters of Fr Congreve*, p. 120.

was wont to sleep, might be soft with the short mountain turf and sweet with wild thyme and euphrasy, the fitter for angels to visit him in his night-long prayer; but when the hour of his sleep came, a stone was his pillow. He never relaxed in the observance of the sacred services and died in his place in the choir, just as he came to say the night Office at the first stroke of the bell. The pride and impatience of an imperious nature died daily to make way for the brave patience of the cross.[68]

Congreve meditated on Iona's natural beauty:

[T]he blue overhead is transparent, and full of sunshine. A fair linen cloth, as it were, of fine, white cloud is stretched across the lower part down to the horizon.[69] The little green meadows, and sandy bays between the bluffs of red granite in Mull, and the boats drawn up on the shingle over there, suggest rest. The tide is running in fast, and full of movement and sparkle, but without waves, and suggests life and joy. The whole scene represents the festival of the Repose of the Blessed Mary ever-Virgin; it makes one draw in one's breath, and desire the eternal rest.[70]

Despite the idyllic scene he drew, conditions were not always comfortable. On his last visit to Iona in 1908, Congreve wrote that "our personal washing is done in a small crofter cottage and what we had white comes back yellow and ragged and shapeless by what process I cannot imagine".[71] To him, "Celtic spirituality" was the joy of God coming through what was often hard and austere. "Today the sound is white with rage, storm and rain, and the wind rushing in the windows, high and low, sorrowful

---

68 Woodgate, *Father Congreve*, p. 49, citing Congreve.

69 The reference is to the "fair linen cloth" which the Prayer Book rubric stipulates should cover the altar in church.

70 Longridge (ed.), *Spiritual Letters of Fr Congreve*, 15 August 1898, p. 121. Congreve was keeping the day as the Feast of the Repose of the Virgin rather than the Assumption.

71 Congreve, letter to Br John, 17 March 1908, SSJE/6/5/2/2/9, f. 10.

enough. But not too sorrowful for those who pray seven times a day."[72] Speaking of St Patrick's Celtic way he said that "[W]e recognise to this day among the Celtic people whom he brought to Christ some special feeling of our Lord *as the light*".[73] The route to the light of the presence of Christ was through darkness and difficulty. He described the boy Patrick seized and taken into slavery:

> Christian by profession, but in behaviour denying Christ, drudge to a half savage heathen . . . Into the heart of this darkness and hopeless desolation the light followed, and found him . . . Pining for home in this exile, he remembered Jerusalem, his home—the religion that he had hitherto neglected; and now he began to pray . . . This new light, which he calls the love and fear of God, so filled his soul that he who had never prayed in earnest before when living at home among Christians, now among heathen strangers was often in prayer . . . It was a long way that light led him from the drudgery of the herd boy on the mountains of pagan Ireland to become the founder of the church of Christ there, the great apostle and shepherd of souls . . . The light which changed everything for him was no mere new and higher view of things . . . This was a light which was immediate, self-attesting, personal, the light which is Christ himself, shining by the power of the Holy Spirit in the heart of a Christian as he prayed.[74]

While Congreve the Irishman was drawn to the "Celtic", his Irish friend and brother, Basil Maturin, was more and more drawn to Rome, and in 1897 he became a Roman Catholic.[75] In the process Maturin's relationship with Benson was irrevocably broken.[76] For his part, Maturin remained friendly towards those he had left behind:

---

[72]   Congreve, letter to Br John, 16 July 1908, SSJE/6/5/2/2/9, f. 11.

[73]   Congreve, *Interior Life*, p. 33. Emphasis in the original.

[74]   *Ibid.*, pp. 30–31.

[75]   Basil Maturin [SSJE], *The Price of Unity* (London: Longmans, Green & Co., 1912).

[76]   Woodgate, *Father Benson*, p. 149; James, *Cowley Fathers*, p. 133.

I think I may say that I have had exceptional opportunities of observing the [Oxford] movement and knowing the men who are taking part in it. I have seen it at work all over England and the United States, and in South Africa, and I cannot say that I ever came across a clergyman whose sincerity in good faith I could for a moment doubt.[77]

The breach was costly, and he wrote of himself:

[T]he thought of the friendships of a lifetime cling around him with endearing memories, what will they think of him, a deserter from their ranks, a traitor to the cause they had championed together? One more gone over to those who do not understand them and so bitterly oppose them.[78]

Congreve maintained his friendship to the end of Maturin's life. A few years later, Maturin was appointed Roman Catholic chaplain to the University of Oxford, and he and Congreve "were often to be seen walking arm in arm down the High".[79] After tea with Maturin one St Patrick's Day, Congreve wrote to Brother John: "[H]e has a larger collection of very best qualities possessed together than most of the best people—moral enthusiasm, intellectual brightness, humour, sympathy, generosity besides the something which his native land gives him and which could never be caught to be named."[80]

By 1899, Congreve, now nearing sixty-five, was an old man by the standards of the day and might have expected his work to be done. However, the troubles that had arisen in Cape Town at the beginning of the decade resurfaced, and at the General Chapter of 1899 it was decided that he should go to South Africa once more. His expectation was that his time abroad would amount to a year or so, but in fact he was to spend five extremely fertile years in South Africa—years from which some of his most influential and interesting writing was to flow.

---

[77] Maturin, *Price of Unity*, p. 205.

[78] *Ibid.*, p. 281.

[79] Woodgate, *Father Congreve*, p. 49.

[80] Congreve, letter to Br John, 17 March 1908, SSJE/6/5/2/2/9, f. 8.

CHAPTER 6

The Need of God

"I am hoping to hear that May brings you sunshine and soft weather as well as large chestnut leaves, and spires of white and pink blossom,—how beautiful Oxford is in May and June." Congreve's correspondent was Miss Kebbel, the former secretary of Edward Pusey, who after doing so much for the Oxford Movement had died in 1882.[1] The formalities of the time mean that in hundreds of letters, Congreve never mentioned Miss Kebbel's Christian name, but he visited her in Oxford for many years, and now in the English spring of 1900 he wrote from South Africa where the season was inverted. "Here—we have the very reverse—we have midwinter—most solemn skies and the mountain looking awful, the clouds majestical." Congreve gave Miss Kebbel, who had been housebound, a wonderful description of his early morning walk to the women's home run by the All Saints Sisters:[2]

> When I go to celebrate at Lillebloem on the mountainside, I walk with my face to the East—as I start the world is still asleep, wrapped in folds of sea mists and distant low grey clouds—and presently the grey roof of cloud begins to let out the secret of the hidden sun rising, and changes all to pure rose coloured fire—and there appear serene rents in the cloud roof—lakes of what will be the blue sky later in the day, but now is a pale green, as luminous and full of light as the fiery clouds—the splendid

---

[1] Congreve's correspondence with Miss Kebbel runs from 1892 to 1917; SSJE/6/5/2/4/1–24.

[2] "I am hoping that you are downstairs again and perhaps gardening, or driving in your carriage."

Blueberg mountain range shows all its peaks and crags in deep violet against the orange sunrise—and then there appears a flash as the sun circle springs up between two tall mountains perhaps 60 miles away, and then at once the topmost crag of our mountain is all lit with the rosy light.

It is like a great drama unfolding for me at every step as I leave our door in the grey of the edge of night, and reach Lillebloem in the splendour of morning, the sky alive with the light of all the precious stones of the Heavenly City: And when I come back about nine the drama is over, has faded 'into the light of the common day'—but our 'common day' in midwinter is like yours in July—sunshine that makes everything beautiful: and by this time in the morning the veld flowers have had time to come out—jewels of all colours, oxalis, sparaxis, geranium, protea, roses, pinks, gold, sky blue, and all the colours—their leaves still grey with dew. It is a country brim-full of light from God, and makes you sing for joy at its beauty inwardly.[3]

It was beautiful, but as Congreve wrote elsewhere, "[T]here is no missionary romance here. The neighbourhood of a cosmopolitan city kills that."[4] The Society's mission church of St Philip stood in District 6, "where Cape Town has its worst slums and is a hotbed for plague".[5] Father George Sheppard SSJE had died of typhoid in Cape Town in 1888,[6] and before the completion of their new House the All Saints Sisters had suffered ten outbreaks of the disease caused by "bad drainage affecting constitutions

---

[3]   Congreve, letter to Miss Kebbel, 22 May 1900, SSJE/6/5/2/4/9, f. 11. "Lillebloem" is today Leliebloem, and "Blueberg" is Blaauwberg.

[4]   Lillian Rousby, *Under Table Mountain* (London: Mowbray, 1906), p. 6.

[5]   Report on St Philip's Mission, Cape Town, 1902, SSJE/9/2/4/5, p. 30.

[6]   Richard Meux Benson SSJE, *A Short Account of the Life and Work of George Edmund Sheppard* (London: J. T. Hayes, 1889). Copies of letters to friends and associates: letter to Mrs Torr, 3 May 1888, SSJE/6/5/2/7.

weakened by over work".[7] When Congreve arrived at the end of 1899, the
Boer War was starting to add to the significant social problems.

Despite all this, Congreve consistently looked through the veneer of
human ugliness to the beauty in things, beauty which reveals the Creator.
For Congreve, this revelation was to a purpose—that human beings who
are the cause and victims of so much suffering can know and love God.
However lovely the natural world, people were his focus, and his letter to
Miss Kebbel continued with a request for prayer for St Columba's Home,
a hostel run by the Fathers for men who came in from the country to
seek work in the city, men who were much more important than plants:

> Humanity, not that which Holland or England imported, but
> what the Creator put here, is as full of natural graces of mind
> and heart as the wild plants are of graces of their own humbler
> sort, graces of plants, that reach and touch God from whom they
> come. It is wonderful—we need not pray for the wild plants on
> the veld—there is never a break in their link to the creator—but
> I ask you to remember S Columba's and the native wild men and
> women of South Africa—who have such a dear image of God
> left in their fallen nature, and are so capable of becoming saints.[8]

Congreve had come to the Society's mission in Cape Town because the
demands placed upon previous Superiors by wide and complex work
had caused great difficulties. Since their arrival in 1883 led by Frederick
Puller the Fathers had developed four main areas of work.[9] Puller began
with the chaplaincy to the All Saints Sisters of the Poor, and their home
for women. To this was added the care of the parish of St Philip, which
by 1899 had grown from "a handful of houses" to become a large mission
district. In addition, the Society had responsibility for evangelization of

---

7   Copies of letters to friends and associates: letter to Miss Sharman, 1 July 1893,
     SSJE/6/5/2/7. See also Anson, *Building up the Waste Places*, p. 324. Anson
     writes that "several children and all the sisters" were struck with typhoid;
     Congreve says, "[S]ix sisters were ill at one time and one nearly died."

8   Congreve, letter to Miss Kebbel, 22 May 1900, SSJE/6/5/2/4/9, f. 11.

9   James, *Cowley Fathers*, pp. 115–25. See also Report on St Philip's Mission, p. 7.

the men constantly arriving in Cape Town from the country seeking work, for whom St Columba's Home was established. This house became "the centre of nearly all the work that is done in the whole Peninsula for natives, and its influence extends to all the Native districts of South Africa".[10] Finally there was a work of support to a number of mission stations, chaplaincy to the leper colony on Robben Island, and a mission to the Muslim immigrants in the city, who were known collectively as "Malays".[11] In addition to maintaining wide activity, practical issues of buildings and finance arose, and there were sometimes problematic relations between personalities.[12] In the face of these many pressures, community life came under great strain in just the ways on which Congreve had been reflecting over the previous decade. By keeping focussed on God, whom he found through the things of nature and the souls of those among whom he lived, Congreve was able to help his community to come through the immediate difficulties and to flourish.

These fertile years brought forth some of Congreve's most attractive and lovely writing: correspondence, sermons and other material flowed from his pen. His first major publication, *Christian Life, a Response*, had been published in 1899, and through it he had already begun to be known in a wider circle.[13] On his return from South Africa, he published a second collection of sermons and addresses, *The Spiritual Order*, "written for the most part in South Africa", further extending his reputation and reach.[14] Cape Town and it surrounds opened doors to God rich in evocative beauty. Though for Congreve beauty in itself was not enough:

> Yesterday I was on Table Mountain on a spring morning. All the
> slopes and rock-terraces were flushed with fresh green after the

---

[10] Report on St Philip's Mission, p. 8.

[11] "Malay" was the generic term used for all Muslims in the Cape at this period, despite the fact that many came from North Africa and India.

[12] Report on St Philip's Mission, p. 8.

[13] George Congreve SSJE, *Christian Life, a Response, with other Retreat Addresses and Sermons* (London: Longmans, Green & Co., 1899).

[14] George Congreve SSJE, *The Spiritual Order, with Papers and Addresses written for the most part in South Africa* (London: Longmans, Green & Co., 1905).

rain, the sky was blue without a cloud. The pine trees were alive with the purring of the little grey doves and the African sunshine filled the world with beauty and delight. . . . I looked all round me slowly, across the flats, to the distant mountain ranges eastward, that I might measure the extent of my happiness: I drew a long breath, as if to take into my soul all the delight of the loveliest place in the world, on the freshest spring morning. Hungry for joy I wanted to make sure of so much bliss. I looked into my soul, but it was empty and uncheered. I could not enhale [*sic*] peace of mind along with the warm sunshine and the scent of the veld flowers . . . I seem to possess for my own enjoyment the beauty of the whole world; and still I find that all put together, it is not enough to make me happy. Then the truth comes back to me, and I know that it is the *need of God* which leaves my spirit in perpetual hunger. Lord thou hast made me for Thyself, and my heart is not at rest until it rest in Thee.[15]

Part of the reason for Congreve's visit to South Africa in 1893 had been the disputed rebuilding of the Sisters' house.[16] Following Congreve's intervention and Osborne's return from furlough the house had been completed, but though healthier than the old building it was considered by some a "fatal mistake", and the quality of work was poor.[17] Osborne had next begun the very necessary building of a Mission House for the Fathers and a church in the parish of St Philip. Problems arose, partly because the colony was governed by an unfamiliar legal system.[18] The landholdings for the buildings were placed in the name of Fathers (including Congreve) in a personal rather than joint or corporate capacity; some of the funding

---

[15] Congreve, "The Need of God", p. 55, quoting S Augustine *Confessions 1:1*. Emphasis in the original.

[16] See above, p.xxx?

[17] Correspondence of All Saints Sisters of the Poor, Sr Frances Bernard, 2 October 1898, SSJE/9/2/3/5. "[I]t is already cracking and falling to pieces, it would cost £800 to put it in thorough repair."

[18] Hodge, Correspondence with Fr Page, 1899, SSJE/6/17/1. Fr Hodge explained that Dutch Law was based on Roman Law and not the English Common Law.

was managed through a syndicate of shareholders.[19] As with the Sisters' house, the quality of the building work was poor. It was years before the complications were finally sorted out.

The press of business was deleterious to maintaining the regularity of the religious life. Father Hodge had spent a period at Cowley in 1896. He wrote that he had had "no first-hand experience of life at home since '92. What does community now mean?" His answer to that question throws light on the situation as it was in Cape Town: "[T]he old ways according to the Letter of the Rule are the right ones—Poverty, Chastity, Obedience, mortification, regularity, industry, retirement."[20] The "old ways" seem to have been missing among the community in South Africa. Osborne's personality was not helpful. The Bishop of Cape Town's view was that "Fr Osborne's natural tendency is to enforce unduly his own personality and to leave too little liberty of thought and action to the Sisters"—and by implication the Fathers. While the Bishop recognized significant achievements, he had reservations: "[N]o doubt what has happened at the time has to a great extent told in his [Osborne's] favour; but at the same time I still believe that if his personality had not been so vigorous, things would not have come to the climax which they reached."[21]

The Superior General, Robert Page, visited South Africa in 1896, and Osborne was recalled. Father Philip Waggett, newly professed, sailed with Page to Cape Town to take charge. An active man and a strong character, Waggett was a former Oxford scientist who had a reputation—before he came to Cowley—as a slum priest, and who had bonded swiftly with Congreve.[22] He at once began trying to sort out the difficulties, but there were continuing problems. The congregations in the Mission District

---

19 Cape Town Mission Accounts, 1884–5, SSJE/9/2/2. On the syndicate, see Hodge, Correspondence with Fr Page, 1898, f. 12.

20 Hodge, correspondence with Fr Page, 1898, SSJE/6/17/1, f. 12.

21 William West Jones (Bishop of Cape Town [Archbishop from 1897]), correspondence with SSJE, 25 February 1896, SSJE/9/2/3/1. Osborne was also an indefatigable worker for the poor and those in need, and had established SSJE's work with African Americans in Boston. See Pendleton, *Press On, the Kingdom*, p. 61.

22 Woodgate, *Father Congreve*, p. 39.

Figure 10: St Philip's Mission, Cape Town. The new Mission House in Cape Town under Table Mountain; problems with the buildings were part of the reason for Congreve's recall to South Africa.

were outgrowing the church of St Philip, which was the chapel of the SSJE Mission School, and Osborne had begun plans for a new and enlarged building. Waggett was energetic, but when the Mission House was served with an enforcement notice to build effective drainage (which would have helped to combat typhoid), funds for the work were lacking, because the new church of St Philip's had "seriously crippled our finances".[23] Page arranged for the money to be sent, but financial management was poor. Writing to Page to thank him, Waggett reported that he could not give time to the 1899 accounts for St Columba's School (for which SPCK, the Society for Promoting Christian Knowledge, had given £200) because the secretary at Lillebloem had left the accounts for that part of the work in a "complete state", and £80 was "hopelessly lost".[24] It turned out that the quality of the building work at St Columba's, as at the Sisters' House, was terrible, with poor foundations and windows falling out. Waggett's failure to consult on the design exacerbated the problems: "St Columba's House has been handed over, but there are no windows, no handles on any of the doors, doors badly made, a class for 65 men with no urinal, walls and plaster already falling down."[25] Waggett also failed to consult on the design and contracting for the new church of St Philip, causing strains among the Fathers. Hodge wrote in exasperation that Waggett "seems at times to have almost a craze for spending money recklessly and lavishly".[26]

People were as difficult as buildings. A new lay schoolteacher came but was immediately unhappy. Waggett's management of her was hardly calculated to be effective: "I intend to smile at her and put the poor woman at her ease."[27] After a short time, she began deliberately to behave badly, which Waggett believed was because dismissal would

---

[23] Hodge, Correspondence with Fr Page, Advent 1898, SSJE/6/17/1, ff. 12, 27.

[24] Philip Napier Waggett SSJE, Correspondence with Fr Page, 22 March 1899, SSJE/6/16/1/1, f. 74.

[25] Frederick Cecil Powell SSJE, letter to Fr Page, 6 January (Epiphany) 1899, SSJE/6/18/1, f. 1.

[26] Hodge, Correspondence with Fr Page, 3 and 25 January 1899, SSJE/6/17/1, f. 12, ff. 35, 42.

[27] Waggett, Correspondence with Fr Page, 20 February 1899, SSJE/6/16/1/1, f. 68.

92.R.
BEAGLES' POSTCARDS

REV. FATHER WAGGETT.

COPYRIGHT.
ELLIOTT & FRY.

Figure 11: Fr Waggett. Philip Napier Waggett was gifted,
learned, vigorous and highly strung. His inability to manage
others and to regulate his own energy led to breakdown
but he recovered and was a close friend of Congreve's.

be financially better for her than a voluntary resignation.[28] A caretaker was caught running a private loan scheme from which money had gone missing.[29] More difficult were the letters which it was discovered Osborne was sending from America to his former parishioners, which Waggett found undermining and deeply upsetting.[30] Meanwhile Father Powell was behaving in a way which betrayed a "fatal want of perception and judgement", becoming too close to the young women at the Mission.[31] Waggett did not believe there was any actual wrongdoing, but though "the dear man is guileless", there was clearly a significant problem which required careful management, at which Waggett was not skilled.[32] "I spoke to him yesterday and as usual did all the apologising myself."[33]

All this took a toll on Waggett, who had a "highly strung nervous constitution".[34] Relations between Waggett and Powell broke down and the Superior began to be very difficult with the other brethren.[35] "Very often he is kindness and love itself, and again for days at a stretch he will have us all in a perpetual ferment of hurry and bother and huge fuss about something."[36] It was all the sadder that Waggett recognized some of this himself, sharing a prayer with the Superior General in a letter home on Ash Wednesday 1899: "I become a monster unto many—and to myself.

---

[28]   Waggett, *ibid.*, 20 February and 22 March 1899, SSJE/6/16/1/1, ff. 64, 87.

[29]   Waggett, *ibid.*, Ash Wednesday 1899, SSJE/6/16/1/1, f. 72.

[30]   Br John SSJE, letter to Fr Page, 6 September 1897, SSJE/9/2/3/6, ff. 3–4. "[B]ut still the letters come to school teachers—pupil teachers—coloured servant girls—half coloured servant girls—asking them to continue writing to him in America."

[31]   Waggett, correspondence with Fr Page, 22 March 1899, SSJE/6/16/1/1, f. 86.

[32]   *Ibid.*, f. 84. Reviewing the correspondence, it might be suggested that it was Waggett rather than Powell who was "guileless"; see also ff. 44, 54, 84.

[33]   *Ibid.*, f. 85.

[34]   Hodge, Correspondence with Fr Page, 14 March 1899, SSJE/6/17/1, f. 44.

[35]   Powell, letter to Fr Page, 6 January (Epiphany) 1899, SSJE/6/18/1, f. 3. "If I speak to Fr Waggett on any important subject he gets angry. He cannot accept questions or suggestions." See also Br John, letter to Fr Page, 27 July 1898, SSJE/9/2/3/6, f. 8.

[36]   Powell, *ibid.*, f. 4.

But my trust is in Thee."[37] Nevertheless, community life was now worse than it had been under Osborne.[38]

In the spring of 1899, it became clear that Waggett was undergoing a nervous breakdown. The Fathers in Cape Town were slow to seek help from the Superior General as they felt inhibited from criticizing their Superior. Eventually Brother John wrote bluntly:

> If I had another year with Fr Waggett like this one just passed there might be a probability of my dying at Robben Island but as a lunatic not as a leper. At times he really drives me off my head although there is so much that is loveable about him still.[39]

Page with difficulty obtained a view from Waggett's doctor,[40] and the Chapter of 1899 was told of the decision to bring Waggett home to recover, and to send Father Congreve in his place.[41] Shortly after arriving Congreve asked Miss Kebbel to show Waggett the letter about his "walk to Lillebloem", for "it might for a moment refresh his love for Africa which however does not need refreshing".[42] In doing so, Congreve was reaching out to a friend and brother who was recovering from the pressures of a situation he had been unable to manage. Being asked to manage it himself was not something Congreve relished: "I have for 25 years, perhaps all my life, been a buffer—mitigating the daily collisions of life for other people

---

[37] Waggett, Correspondence with Fr Page, Ash Wednesday 1899, SSJE/6/16/1/1, f. 66.

[38] Hodge, Correspondence with Fr Page, 1 March 1899, SSJE/6/17/1, f. 43: "I take it that you understand how very grave and critical the position here is—not so much I should say in regard to the work (that could be gathered up and put in order with a little trouble and diligence)—but in regard to community life."

[39] Br John, letter to Fr Page, 25 February 1899, SSJE/9/2/3/6, f. 18.

[40] *Ibid.*, f. 12. Also, Hodge, Correspondence with Fr Page, 14 March 1899, SSJE/6/17/1, f. 44.

[41] General Chapter Minute Book, 1884–1905, SSJE/2/1, pp. 293–4. Hodge was placed in temporary charge until Congreve arrived.

[42] Congreve, letter to Miss Kebbel, 22 May 1900, SSJE/6/5/2/4/9, f. 12.

in my little sphere.—And a buffer is the most hopeless sort of superior. To thump people and keep order is not me."[43]

Buffer or not, after the difficult history of the preceding years it is remarkable how Congreve brought calm. He perhaps benefited from work already done by Waggett. For all their faults, the buildings were going up. Father Hodge was already bringing the finances under control, and Congreve seems not to have interfered as Waggett had done.[44] Above all, Congreve re-focussed the community on the Religious Life. Where members had been "harassed and dissatisfied", Congreve brought order to the community.[45] He preached hope and happiness. Happiness, he taught, comes from being "single hearted" and thorough in "surrender to the leading of Christ". This thoroughness:

> is like the pattern woven into some textile, that is not merely stamped upon the surface, but goes through and through it ... [T]he aim of the Priest and of the Religious means taking seriously for our own practice the religion which we profess and teach to others; it means our purpose actually to become what we were made by power and privilege in Holy Baptism.[46]

Congreve did not look, as perhaps both Waggett and Osborne had done, to complete the tasks which were set out for him, but to be faithful in the Way:

> The worldly heart is like the traveller who has been following the road all day, and, footsore and tired, sees nightfall, and he has gained nothing. There goes the road on and on into the shadow; he sees it miles ahead, just as he saw it in the morning; he takes

---

[43]   Congreve, letter to Assheton, 29 October 1899, SSJE/6/5/5/9, f. 769.

[44]   Hodge, Correspondence with Fr Page, 22 November 1898, and Ember Wednesday (mid-December) 1898, and 3 January 1899, SSJE/6/17/1, ff. 1, 27, 23, 35: "The debt on the church is much reduced and may be paid off by the end of the year."

[45]   Hodge, *ibid.*, Ember Wednesday (mid-December) 1898, f. 27.

[46]   Congreve, *Spiritual Order*, pp. 121–2.

one step after another but never overtakes the road; he sees it still vanishing before him in the distance, and he seems as far from the end as ever, and to gain nothing by going on. Ah, but the Christian heart sees something else besides all this; he sees the mystery of the Way. The Way in which he journeys is a new and living Way. It is Christ. And every weary step, every day's journey, though it seems as vain as all the others, is a real advance into the new world of the eternal love ... Perhaps he never has anything great to do, never any great success; but he is always making way spiritually by everything that he does or bears,—because he does it and bears it *in the Lord*, Who is the living Way.[47]

After years of building and business, Congreve called the Society back to its focus on saving souls for Christ. This was a process in which individual conversions mattered. In 1901, Congreve preached on the feast of the patron of the Society's parish, Philip, the "missionary deacon", who took such pains for the conversion of the Ethiopian Eunuch in whom began the evangelization of Africa.[48] Philip, said Congreve, recognized that "any one soul is worth more than all the treasures of Earth". He rejoiced that the Fathers worked alongside lay preachers, "not men of learning nor power but who have Christ in their hearts, such men as our Brother Bernard who gave his life—only a layman, but a martyr". This was a reference to Bernard Mizeki, the catechist and former worker at St Columba's who was martyred in 1896. Congreve continued:

We will never allow S Philip's or S Cyprian's to be respectable churches where people come to worship for their own comfort only.[49] We shall ask God to kindle hearts with the fire of love and with missionary spirit, the spirit of S Philip and S Cyprian and

---

[47] Ibid., pp. 126–7. Emphasis in the original.

[48] Congreve, Sermons at St Columba's and St Cyprian's, Cape Town, Sunday in the Octave of St Philip (17 November 1901), SSJE/6/5/3/15, ff. 1–6. See Acts 8:26–40.

[49] St Cyprian's was the "Iron Church" built at the Ndabeni Location in 1901—see below, p. xxx.

> Bernard. God never reveals his love to any soul to make only that
> one soul happy—he gives you the joy of grace in order that this
> joy may overflow your heart and multiply greatly.[50]

This and other sermons to Africans were translated both into Xhosa and
the "Taal" or Dutch patois. Congreve remarked wryly that "the interpreter
evidently improves on the sermon greatly, often leaving the preacher
far behind, and travelling into regions of thought which are all his own,
returning at last safe to earth again and the scarcely necessary preacher,
when his flight is spent."[51]

Some of these sermons took place in a little cottage behind Zonnebloem
on the edge of Table Mountain, where the first Mission services had been
held. The cottage belonged to Lydia Williams, who had been key to the
beginnings of the work of SSJE in Cape Town. She was described around
the time of Congreve's arrival as:

> an aged and devout coloured woman, who, it is said, bears yet
> the marks of the sjambok of the Dutch master whose slave she
> was in her youth. She still calls the people to worship there with
> her hand bell.[52]

In describing the pictures in her cottage (St Theresa; King Edward VII
when Prince of Wales, in the scarlet uniform of a Colonel of the Guards;
and Christ of the Sacred Heart), the Report of St Philip's Mission gives an
insight into the piety of this important supporter of the mission's work.
Each year, on the first day of December, she celebrated her Emancipation
Day, when she would hold a service of thanksgiving followed by a feast.
The Fathers called this "Lydia's Day".[53] When the time came, shortly

---

50   Congreve, Sermons at St Columba's and St Cyprian's, SSJE/6/5/3/15, f. 6.
51   Report on St Philip's Mission, p. 11.
52   Ibid. On Lydia, see also Rousby, *Under Table Mountain*, pp. 15–17. A sjambok
      is a heavy leather whip. Lydia Williams died in 1910.
53   Michael Ian Weeder, *The Palaces Of Memory: A reconstruction of District
      One, Cape Town, before and after the Group Areas Act* (MA mini-thesis,
      University of the Western Cape, 2006), p. 26; <https://core.ac.uk/download/

Figure 12: Lydia Williams sits in the centre of the group of "working women" of the Cape Town Mission— which was in many ways as much her work as it was that of the Fathers.

after Congreve's arrival, to petition formally for the consecration of the new St Philip's church, Lydia Williams—as the senior member of the congregation—signed with the Fathers and the churchwardens.[54]

There were others whom the mission honoured. Preeminent was Bernard Mizeki, "our saint"; some less prominent were no less cherished. Mercy Ndilele was snatched as a child, escaped and came to the mission; she returned home and converted her family. Also remembered was Julia, a girl who died young, but in holiness.[55] In an article for the *Church Chronicle* of the South African Province, Congreve considered what makes a person important. He began in a way that seemed comfortable enough for the assumptions of imperial society, meditating on the beauty of the gardens of Cecil Rhodes on the slopes of Table Mountain. But he was "uncheered" at heart by "the loveliest place in the world on the freshest spring morning". He writes of Rhodes's great political and commercial aspirations, but goes on to observe, drawing possibly on personal knowledge, that "his far seeing spirit would fail and refused to spring with his soaring plans", because all achievement is empty and unsatisfying "which yet fails to reach what the beauty of nature only symbolises and never can give, the peace which comes to a heart that rests upon God". Congreve then shifts the scene to the "rows of iron houses at the Kafir Location", where he had been kneeling at the bedside of Moses Runene, a young native teacher dying of phthisis (pulmonary tuberculosis) "and whom we can ill spare". He meditates on a soul who knew his need of God. It is this need of God responded to:

> which brings the true ring, the true meaning and hope into
> every life under all circumstances. To ignore this, is what leaves
> a suspicion of unreality in the background of so many lives.
> How can a man care much about the means, when he has not
> yet settled what the end is which he is to live for? The desire of

---

pdf/58912907.pdf>, accessed 14 June 2021. Weeder also refers to further work and a film on Williams (pp. 24–5).

54   James, *Cowley Fathers*, p. 121.

55   Rousby, *Under Table Mountain*, pp. 9–14 (Julia), pp. 30–2 (Mercy Ndilele).

God points always true to the true end of every man created in
God's image for God.[56]

Congreve's attitudes to the people of all races whom he met were complex
and not easily characterized. He understood the contrasts of tribes and
nations: "The Zulu is a gentleman of his own kind, and a Xosa in his—as
different as a typical Yorkshireman finds a typical Oxfordshire man."[57]
He spoke of "lower races",[58] but while he did not believe all people to be
equal, it was Christianity, not inherent superiority of any kind, which
raises one man above another, and the response of the Christian must
be to offer Christ. If to be a missionary is wrong, then Congreve would
readily plead guilty; but he did not subscribe to Social Darwinism or to
a biological theory of race. He thought the removal of African men from
"the healthy natural conditions of their traditional life in the Kraal"[59]
to the cities was "uncivilizing". Fundamentally, for Congreve there was
no innate superiority of white people or their way of living. Speaking
of the Bantu he said, "[S]etting their points of inferiority against ours,
to me they remain our equals."[60] The "higher races" were made so by
their adherence to Christianity, and he remarked, "[W]hat unpleasant
and unpromising people our ancestors must have been before grace and
truth came to them a thousand years ago."[61] He was comfortable with
speaking of "different sorts of humanity", and wrote that it is "interesting
to compare the character and intelligence" of peoples. His conclusion was
always that what civilizes and raises is faithfulness:

> I remember how the bright intelligence of a pure native Xosa girl,
> and her faithful memory, used to cheer me despite the dullness
> or inattention of our dear English and Dutch children. And now

---

[56]   Congreve, "The Need of God", pp. 55–60.

[57]   Congreve, letter to Miss Kebbel, 19 December 1900, SSJE/6/5/2/4/10, f. 20.

[58]   Rousby, *Under Table Mountain*, p. 7.

[59]   Ibid.

[60]   Congreve, letter to Miss Kebbel, 15 February 1902, SSJE/6/5/2/4/11, f. 31.

[61]   Congreve, Copies of letters to friends and associates, 23 December 1903,
SSJE/6/5/2/7.

the child to whom I turn quite sure of a good answer, when the higher races fail me, is a small coloured Cape boy, who has the gentle humanity of the African native and the intellectual light of Christianity in his brown face.[62]

If Christianity rather than biology makes the difference, a society permeated with the faith will be superior to one which is "heathen", and if the faith is lost then it will slip back to barbarism. Preaching to the white community in Cape Town Cathedral, Congreve sounded a note of hope for both black and white society through the life of Christ:

[A]part from the directly missionary duty of the church, there is our part to take in creating a Christian public opinion, in awakening among ourselves a sense of our social and political duties to the native races. Here is a sphere of hope for us to do our part in raising the native races out of savagery, and what is worse—savagery with the added vices of a corrupt civilisation.[63]

For Congreve there were great signs of hope in the changes achieved in the lives of the girls in the home at Lillebloem, who were "of all colours— wild creatures out of a wicked life, but with human nature hidden under the hard skin of vice and selfishness . . . some of them become as frankly good as they were frankly bad."[64] Speaking to the black congregation in St Philip's, Congreve made the same point:

The Saints are not all English people, all sons of the British Empire, but of *all* nations and tongues. They are of all races and colours and make up *one* people, God's People, One Empire, Christ's Empire: and whatever their language, Dutch, English, Kafir, they belong to us, if we belong to Christ. *And every one of them is noble*, every one has Christ's righteousness *and we belong to them* and they care for us and watch our battle with sin and

---

[62]   Report on St Philip's Mission, p. 10.

[63]   Congreve, South African Sermons, SSJE/6/5/3/16, f. 27.

[64]   Congreve, letter to Miss Kebbel, 15 February 1902, SSJE/6/5/2/4/11, f. 16.

pray for us, and call us to be of good cheer and to fight manfully
to follow Christ as they did—*we are never alone*: if any of you has
no home in this world, you have what is better, you have your
home in the heart of Christ and have the companionship and
love of all the saints.[65]

The impetus for mission was that all people need the civilizing power of
Christ. Before that power came to them, black Africans were "heathen"
at best and at worst morally undermined by their contact with the vices
of corrupt white Africa; the Malays were similarly in need, though harder
to reach for "the vices of slaves are dignified and protected by the laws
of Islam".[66]

Cape Town at the turn of the twentieth century was a melting pot of
peoples of different languages and cultures. Insofar as he had politics,
Congreve shared the assumptions of the imperial elite of which he was
a member. Nevertheless, it was not from the lexicons of political theory
but from Scripture and his understanding of God that he reflected upon
society. Preaching on the text of "those that are undefiled in the way",[67] he
quoted St Paul, "[T]here is no difference between the Jew and the Greek
. . . Whoever shall call upon the name of the Lord shall be saved,"[68] and
went on:

> [W]e do not ignore necessary social distinctions, nor even
> their prejudices, but we can treat them as belonging only to the
> discipline of 'the way'. From the point of view of the necessities
> of our earthly life here today, we submit to them; but in Jesus
> Christ we have gained a new point of view; 'for our citizenship
> is in heaven;' and from that point of view 'there is no difference.'

---

[65]   Congreve, South African Sermons, SSJE/6/5/3/16, f. 42. Emphasis in the
        original.

[66]   Report on St Philip's Mission, p. 19.

[67]   Psalm 119:1.

[68]   Romans 10:12.

Knowing God, rather than any improvement in social or economic wellbeing, is the key to contentment:

> Happiness, which is spiritual life, need not really be hindered by unavoidable temporary social barriers, for spiritual life has its source in Christ, where "here is no difference between Jew and Greek." The newborn man, no matter what his social position, seeks his happiness in God; and finding it in Christ, walks in glory and in joy whether on the pavement or in the street below with the cattle, because he walks with Christ the King, who was born among the cattle in the cave of Bethlehem.[69]

As one who sought to live mortified to the things of this world under vows of poverty, chastity and obedience, Congreve could not consistently teach that happiness could lie in the achievement of better wealth or position in this world. This was not, however, a justification for neglect of the plight of the poor and the marginalized. Congreve's instinctive trust in the establishment gave him what may have been a rosy view, but he understood it to promote social mobility. His understanding of what he called the "English idea of government" was that "its duty is to ensure every human being under its rule, without distinction, a fair chance of doing the best he can for himself and rising as high in the social scale as God has given him the faculties to rise".[70] In the context of the Boer War, he spoke against what he saw as the Dutch refusal to offer "Christian civilization" to Africans and deprecated the fact that "the Dutch believe God has created Brown races for slavery or low-wage labour". Congreve was not merely a British imperialist denigrating the enemy. If the Dutch were misguided by warped theology, there was selfishness also among the English "which would deliberately thrust back the native races, and keep them locked in ignorance and degradation, to be used for cheap labour supply only at the white man's convenience". He thought the government needed support to ensure "whatever advantage for native races has been gained by the present conflict has been secured and made permanent

---

[69]   Congreve, *Spiritual Order*, pp. 120–1.

[70]   Report on St Philip's Mission, pp. 19–20.

by the charity of the church bringing them to Christ that they may be 'free indeed'".[71] Because the Church brings Christ, who is the source of civilization, while "the law says the Native can rise, *if he can*, the Mission shows *that* he can".[72]

Congreve had a high understanding of monarchy but did not simply subscribe to a theory of divine right. The death of Queen Victoria in 1901 moved him deeply ("the greatest calamity we have ever had to face as a people") and clearly many others as well:[73]

> The day the news of the death of Queen Victoria reached us at Cape Town we met a poor coloured Dutch speaking peasant woman on the mountain slope; we understood one another at once, there was little need of words, she pointed to her crêpe badge of mourning, and passed with her sorrow. We met other coloured people of the poorest class all in tears at the news.[74]

Following the Queen's death, he preached a sermon in which he set out his thoughts on the ordering of human society. Taking as his text 1 Timothy 2:1–2,[75] he adumbrated the Christian duty to pray for earthly rulers. "Loyalty to the Head of State is not personal nor dependent on benefits received." God makes the King "most religious" in the sense "not

---

[71]   Ibid., p. 22.

[72]   Ibid., p. 23. Emphasis in the original.

[73]   Congreve, letter to Miss Kebbel, St Agnes Day 1901, SSJE/6/5/2/4/10, f. 13. "We thank God for the Queen's noble life, and will rejoice in her rest. Since I lost my mother I have never had a loss that was so keen perhaps and personal to me as this—the dear Lady came to visit us boys when I was at school in some state, with the Prince Consort, and the Royal Children, and got a week's holiday for us."

[74]   George Congreve SSJE, "The King", in *The Cowley Evangelist*, July 1911, p. 147.

[75]   "I exhort therefore, that, first of all, supplications, prayers, intercessions, and giving of thanks, be made for all men; For kings, and for all that are in authority; that we may lead a quiet and peaceable life in all godliness and honesty."

of personal devotion but of having a duty and privilege". For Congreve, a duty was always a means of self-sacrifice and an opportunity to turn away from what one would have chosen for oneself to what God has asked. In contrast with most political theory that the first duty of Government is to keep the citizens secure, Congreve says that the King's "first duty in being first in his Empire is the defence of religion". In this context, "loyalty to the sovereign springs up when that sovereign is loyal to God. To obey the King in all things lawful is to acknowledge God's authority over us." Congreve did not believe in divine right, nor was he simply a royalist, for "God does not determine a single form of government." In Scripture, there are examples of God's people living under Judges, in a Republic and in a Kingdom. "But always God kept for Himself supreme authority." Human society requires order, which raises the question of obedience:

> Whom to obey? The state? We cannot rejoice to obey a statute book—the law of the land is a disagreeable necessity to obey. God helps us by giving us a person to obey—a Chief of State . . . I can give with joy to my King what I give grudgingly to the state. Because the king reigns by God's grace I can offer my obedience joyfully to God . . . What I do not feel inclined to do for the personal merit of the tax collector I do loyally for the love of my King and what I do or suffer for my King I do or suffer joyfully for Christ.[76]

There remained limits to authority, whether political, social, or economic. He wrote home presciently to Assheton:

> [T]he "Colour Question" begins to loom. It seems to me quite insoluble and to contain future terrible things. Education; mixed marriage; university; political rights; such vast questions we learn gradually to face, and touch the little springs of movements that are going to be great rivers of the progress of mankind two generations hence.[77]

---

[76]   Congreve, letter to Miss Kebbel, January 1901, SSJE/6/5/2/4/10, ff. 16–20.

[77]   Congreve, letters to Assheton, 8 October 1901, SSJE/6/5/5/9, f. 919.

Congreve understood Christian fellowship to be the antithesis of worldly division and the basis of a better ordering of society. Better fellowship would bring better conditions for workers. He might have been mistaken in looking back to a golden age when mutual flourishing rather than profit gave the motive to trade and in which there were "old Christian business methods in which workmen were associated in trade-guilds under Christian rules", but he recognized and publicly deprecated exploitation when he saw it. "The Board of Directors cannot be expected to entertain sentiments of individual and personal interest in the hands employed. They are paid to have regard to dividends, and personal regard to the workers naturally drops out of consideration." The African gold mines were a doleful example:

> [N]otice the remarkable indifference to the workers that appears in the excessive percentage of deaths among the Kafir boys who work for them underground. Is there not there a flat contradiction given by the world's business methods at the present time to the Christian "fellowship with one another," that was a vital characteristic of society in the church of St John's day?[78]

Far from being cultural imperialism, Congreve viewed the spread of Christianity as a good for all since it brings fellowship and is the root of culture for all races. He advanced the example of Indian Christians, whose population increased because their religion taught them to care for the sick and the poor and not to expose their infants. Society and culture rest on fellowship, and the primary fellowship is the Fellowship of man with God which is:

> the very foundation of the Being of the Son of God Incarnate. His Fellowship with the Father is from everlasting, is consubstantial, a divine unity. And His manhood taken into God is the type of our fellowship with God, and the means of it. He communicates

---

[78] Congreve, *Interior Life*, pp. 240–1.

Himself to the members of His Body, shares with them His Death, His Resurrection, His Ascension, His states and glories.[79]

The church itself needed also to be challenged and Congreve wrote with frustration:

It is surprising to see how easily fashionable Christianity at the present time drops the idea of Fellowship. The Kafir sexton of the South African Cathedral is at work there all Sunday morning preparing it for the white congregation who will arrive presently for their Communion. This makes it impossible for him to go for his own Communion to the church some distance off, where the people of colour worship. The refinement of the white Christians forbids him to communicate at the cathedral at all, since no coloured person is allowed to kneel at the same altar with them.[80]

As Congreve's time in South Africa extended beyond the initial plan that he would stay only for a year or so, he became more and more clear that the plight of all peoples—African and European—can only be helped by the opening of hearts to God. The Boer War progressed, leaving destruction in its wake. Characteristically it was the sight of a bird settling on a large cactus rather than a thorn bush that gave him the simile with which to express his thought:

Do I want to help South Africa? There lies my next duty, and there is the blue sky spread over me and my duty, and the cactus,—to look up there is to pray: let me do my day's work in the spirit of prayer, and I have begun to build up the ruins. A fine canary-throated bird has just alighted on the cactus[,] canary coloured and black and grey beak, a link for the cactus to a higher life. But no such link for the Aloe, which gathers every nerve, every drop

---

[79]   Ibid., p. 242.

[80]   Ibid., pp. 241–2.

of sap in its heart to sharpen the point of the bayonet, and dares
the world to touch it.[81]

For all his love of the people and natural beauty of South Africa, Congreve
would have liked to have gone home. April as autumn seemed especially
strange, and he wrote to Assheton, "I live in the English April in my
thoughts, and listen to the cuckoo and want to see the daisies."[82] For
a time, at least, it was not to be. By the time he wrote this, bubonic
plague had broken out in the slums of Cape Town served by the Cowley
Fathers. The government forcibly cleared the slums and their people to
a "Location" outside the city, in the first act of segregation on racial lines
in South Africa, and Congreve's work was redoubled as he found himself
providing a church for the displaced peoples and preaching movingly of
hope in the face of warfare and disease.

---

[81]   Congreve, Copies of letters to friends and associates, letter to "N" (Selina
       Congreve), February 1902, SSJE/6/5/2/7.
[82]   Congreve, letter to Assheton, 7 March 1900, SSJE/6/5/5/9, f. 849.

CHAPTER 7

The Sorrow of Nature

In May 1900, Cape Town was a place of "continuous movement, continuing pressure towards the front—stores of all sorts being shoved up the lines day by day week by week to the bases. Traction engines groaning and puffing along the streets with wagon loads of provisions, blankets, materials for huts—towards the railway stations—the railway whistle works away every night . . . at the continual forcing along the main lines."[1] In the face of the early defeats, Congreve knew that "the Boers are tough and determined and it may be a long tussle",[2] but he never really expected the Empire to fail: "I think that we have nearly learned the Boers' kind of war—the strong and weak points—and I expect now that we shall soon convince them that their aggressive designs are impossible—but it has been at great cost . . . "[3] The war added to the work of the mission. The All Saints Sisters nursed Boer prisoners, and later Congreve took on the chaplaincy of a newly established mounted police training camp.[4] He did not enjoy the work, and his letters describe the indifference and disengagement of the men. "My police friends have souls too, but look up through a thicker veil than others of parade propriety, and a frozen mountain of lay reserve."[5] In another letter he wrote, "[I]t is a great step

[1] Congreve, letter to "N" (Selina Congreve), 28 May 1900, SSJE/6/5/2/5, f. 20.

[2] Congreve, letter to Miss Kebbel, 2 May 1900, SSJE/6/5/2/4/9, f. 9.

[3] Congreve, letter to "N" (Selina Congreve), 28 May 1900, SSJE/6/5/2/5, f. 20.

[4] Congreve, letter to Miss Kebbel, 2 May 1900, SSJE/6/5/2/4/9, f. 9.

[5] Congreve, letter to Miss Kebbel, Fourth Sunday in Lent 1903, SSJE/6/5/2/4/12, f. 12.

forward, as far as religious consolation goes, to pass from the mounted police service to the Kafir worship."[6]

Congreve was personally involved. His nephew Walter, now a Captain in the Rifle Brigade, was serving on the staff of Lord Roberts. At the Battle of Colenso in December 1899 he was severely wounded, and was awarded the Victoria Cross for going out to seize some guns which had become exposed and for bringing back from the action the mortally wounded Freddy Roberts, son of the Field Marshal.[7] Walter was sent back to Cape Town to recover, where "Uncle George" read poetry to him in hospital and "introduced him to everyone who was anybody in the clerical world at the Cape at the time from the Archbishop down".[8] The two also visited the house (and private zoo) of Cecil Rhodes, whose philanthropy had supported the Sisters.[9] Walter joined his uncle in church activities, on one occasion attending the baptism by immersion of seventeen African men.[10]

On the day that Walter started back to the front in February 1900, he made his communion at the hands of his uncle.[11] In June and July 1902, Cape Town was *en fête* for the victory parade following the Boer surrender. Congreve wrote to Brother John: "I shall feel how much

[6]   Congreve, Copies of letters to friends and associates, letter to "N" (Selina Congreve), 30 December 1902, SSJE/6/5/2/7.

[7]   Thomas Pakenham quotes Walter Congreve's descriptions of the action in *The Boer War* (London: Weidenfeld & Nicolson, 1979), pp. 235, 237, 315. He was less forthcoming to his uncle: "WNC is only reserved as to his own achievements of which one can extract only monosyllables or chaff." Congreve, Copies of letters to friends and associates, letter to Mrs Torr, 15 January 1900, SSJE/6/5/2/7.

[8]   Leslie H. Thornton and Pamela Fraser, *The Congreves, Father and Son* (London: John Murray, 1930), pp. 34–41.

[9]   Congreve, in "Reminiscences", SSJE/6/5/5/2, p. 38, remarks that in Holy Week 1902, "Mr Rhodes is dying and we are all sad." The funeral train was to use SSJE's altar cross and two candles "Gladly lent in his honour".

[10]   Copies of letters to friends and associates, letter to Mrs Torr, 15 January 1900, SSJE/6/5/2/7.

[11]   Thornton and Fraser, *The Congreves*, p. 41.

nicer and more suitable it is for age to rejoice in his cell, with the loyal multitude, than to be hustled about, and have his pocket picked in the street."[12] Congreve reported to John that on 25 June, rather than go to the public lunch with speeches to celebrate the Boer surrender with Lord Kitchener, General French and "other great people" Walter had "slipped away" to lunch at the Mission House.[13]

Walter was not the only one of Congreve's nephews fighting. Another, Francis, was also at the front.[14] In June 1902 a letter arrived from him (actually after the Boer surrender), telling of "treks and drives". Congreve heard that he was covering the rear-guard of a convoy and fighting all day. It was with "huge relief" that news of peace came.[15]

The war had been fought in two distinct phases. Despite the success of Roberts' army, the victories of 1899–1900 did not bring peace.[16] Congreve felt that the guerrilla war which followed was "savagery, senseless and cruel—making the land derelict".[17] He also felt it to be counter-productive: "[I]t is discrediting the whole Boer cause and making it to stink in the noses of the Boer sympathisers in the colony,—it is simple robbery and murder, it has produced a great demonstration of loyalty here in

---

12   Congreve, letter to Br John, 21 July 1902, SSJE/6/5/2/2/3, f. 16.

13   Congreve, letter to Br John, 25 June 1902, SSJE/6/5/2/2/3, f. 4.

14   Son of George's younger brother, another Walter, he was commissioned Second Lt 18 December 1900; Congreve, letter to Miss Kebbel, 16 July 1901, SSJE/6/5/2/4/10, f. 33.

15   Congreve, letter to Br John, 21 June 1902, SSJE/6/5/2/2/3, f. 2.

16   Pakenham notes, in *Boer War*, pp. xvii, 457, that the successes of General Buller's forces in 1899–1900 are often overlooked. In many ways Buller worked out tactics that, had he not been discredited, could have made a significant difference in 1914–18. The generals who commanded Corps and Armies in the later conflict were the cavalry officers formed by their experience of leading mobile columns across the Veldt. Walter Congreve—a Rifleman—was also a Corps Commander in the Great War. The Congreves were pro-Buller: "We all feel very sorry about Gen Buller"—Copies of letters to friends and associates, letter to Jervoise [?], 13 November 1901, SSJE/6/5/2/7.

17   Congreve, letter to Br John, 6 July 1902, SSJE/6/5/2/2/3, f. 16.

Figure 13: Walter Congreve. George's godson and
favourite nephew, Walter won a VC in the Boer War
and commanded a Corps in the Great War.

Cape Town."[18] He made no mention of the British policy of establishing concentration camps for the Boer population. There was, however, a camp in Cape Town in which Congreve was himself ministering. Bubonic plague had broken out in the city in February 1901. It was not understood that it had been carried by flea-ridden rats, imported from Argentina with the fodder for horses, and the disease was blamed on the poor living conditions of the black population. The response was to segregate them in a camp known as "The Location", at Ndabeni.[19] The only exceptions were those who were housed at the Society's St Columba's Home, for whom the well-connected Congreve achieved an exemption.[20]

Congreve described conditions at the Location: "8000 natives, mostly heathen, enclosed within a barbed wire fence five miles off on Maitland flats."[21] The salt marshes were "a lovely flat in summer, but I do not know how the natives will stand it in winter. I am afraid it will be exposed windy and damp".[22] Corrugated iron huts were laid out in streets, and Congreve described the "boiling pots of porridge" on the camp fires and "all the disturbing elements of civilisation being forgotten and left behind". In addition to the Segregation Camp at the Location, there was a Plague Camp where victims of all races were treated. A nurse wrote to Congreve to say that "most of the plague patients belong to the church", and to describe how "our 'boys' night and morning, six of them, sing the hymns together; and one, who cannot sing, whistles the tune." Congreve described this as "Christ's feast in the wilderness, the joy of grace keeping life fresh, and awaking songs in the silence and strangeness of the plague camp".[23]

---

[18] Congreve, letter to Miss Kebbel, 15 January 1901, SSJE/6/5/2/4/10, f. 1.

[19] This was the first compulsory segregation of people on the basis of race in South Africa.

[20] Copies of letters to friends and associates, letter to Miss Sharman, 25 April 1901, SSJE/6/5/2/7; Report on St Philip's Mission, p. 30.

[21] Copies of letters to friends and associates, letter to Miss Sharman, 25 April 1901, SSJE/6/5/2/7.

[22] Copies of letters to friends and associates, letter to "N" (Selina Congreve), Easter Eve 1901, SSJE/6/5/2/7.

[23] Congreve, *Spiritual Order*, pp. 281–2.

In this, Congreve was beginning to articulate a concept of "spiritual refreshment" with which he was able to help the Fathers, and others who were part of the mission, to remain focussed on God in all the "busy life of duty". The description of the singing in the plague camp was part of a Lent address on "Work and Worry" given (on Refreshment Sunday 1901) to the Nurses' Guild of St Barnabas Cape Town. He said, "[T]he Lord's remedy for the over-strain of our life is not 'arrange your work better,' or 'work harder,' or 'give up your holiday.' No, but 'come unto me, and I will give you rest.'" Congreve did not teach repose, but refreshment: "Christ could not be the companion of an idle desultory life; the idler must live under the perpetual curse of depression and bad conscience." In the heart of Jesus whose yoke is easy and burden light,[24] we find "the only sphere of perfect relief from care and fretting". The fundamental problem is "isolation from God. The soul was created for God, to work in God, to bear its sorrows to God."

The alternative is what Congreve called "worry", which he defined as "working with an uneasy conscience, dragging along a chain of responsibilities not fully faced, duties neglected, and a feeling of despair of ever getting one's work and oneself right". The medicine for this is not simply a break. "It was very likely *not* change of air I wanted, or relaxation from work, when the doctor said I needed rest; it was another need which mere cessation of work does not supply."[25] Refreshment comes from sharing work with Christ, to be working with and for him. To be released from "unshared responsibilities" is to work "at home" in the fellowship of Jesus Christ where work does not exhaust, "but invigorates and refreshes us".[26]

To serve the population of the Ndabeni Location, the Fathers immediately sought to build an "iron church" dedicated to the

---

[24] Matthew 11:30.

[25] Congreve, *Spiritual Order*, p. 282.

[26] *Ibid.*, pp. 277–87.

third-century African bishop and martyr, St Cyprian.[27] The £500 needed[28] was not immediately available and worship began in a tent. Congreve preached the first sermon there, taking as his text, "Beloved, let us love one another: for love is of God; and every one that loveth is born of God, and knoweth God."[29] Congreve reminded his hearers that the Children of Israel had worshipped in a tent in the wilderness, a sign that we are not at home in this world, but our true home is God himself. Even among the displaced, Congreve was not concerned directly for worldly comfort. "We worship in a tent because we are poor, but not as poor as Christ who had nowhere to lay his head." The tent in the wilderness was "a glorious and happy place because God came there, and He will come to this tent in the Holy Eucharist". The congregation must love one another "because if we do not love one another we have no fellowship with God and have no kind of good in us". The sting came in his call to radical love of enemies: "Do not say I cannot love my enemy because I cannot feel glad to see him. Never mind that: try to do him some good—pray to God for him, love him and that may change him, turn an enemy of God into a friend of God." Love is thus missional. Congreve cited again the example of Bernard Mizeki who "asked the Bishop, if you could send anyone to make my tribe Christians. The Bishop said, no you can go yourself." The reward of missional love is immediate, but spiritual: "God gives love not to cheer a little few sad years in this dying world, but to give you now at once in the world the love that never dies."[30]

Throughout his time in South Africa, faced with the suffering caused by war, sickness and prejudice, Congreve preached hope. He saw God shining through the world around him, and especially the natural world that so delighted him despite the grimness of the city and the plight of its population. He was no escapist but looked squarely at the suffering and squalor, and nonetheless saw God. Robben Island, off Cape Town,

---

[27] Bishop and theologian, born c. 200; Bishop of Carthage in North Africa 249–58.

[28] Copies of letters to friends and associates, letter to Miss Sharman, 25 April 1901, SSJE/6/5/2/7: "We hope to run up a building at once but we need £500."

[29] 1 John 4:7.

[30] Congreve, Sermons at St Columba's and St Cyprian's, SSJE/6/5/3/15, ff. 18–23.

where the Fathers often kept retreat and helped with the chaplaincy, was for Congreve a microcosm of Africa and her needs, and a sign of hope out of suffering for her peoples.[31] He found it beautiful: "[I]t is a sandbank 3 miles long, covered with a gold flower that smells like chamomile, but must be a Tansey. Rough gold and fine green leaves everywhere."[32] But it was also:

> a sanctuary of the sorrows of Christ. Here are detained until they die, apart from their families and friends on the mainland, more than five hundred lepers; here are, besides, three or four hundred lunatics, and some seventy coloured convicts working out their penance. The island is a prison, but the Prisoner is Christ, the stricken and afflicted Man Who has no form or outward beauty, rejected of men, the Man of Sorrows, acquainted with grief.[33] One morning I was allowed to kneel with the lepers to receive the Holy Sacrament in their church. Here was Mount Calvary, and Christ suffering upon the cross in the person of His stricken members.[34]

Hope came because through the very suffering there was joy in Christ. At the lepers' Eucharist the people were "so happy and devout", and Congreve looked on "all this glory and joy with the contrast of the bodily ruin and decay of fallen man, who comes there to praise God and give thanks for redemption and eternal life with lips that are already marked for death".[35] On another occasion, preaching to leper women about to be baptized, he pointed across the water to the homes "they would never again visit and their people they would never again see" and spoke of passing through the water of baptism which would open for them fellowship in God with

---

[31] Robben Island later became infamous as the prison which held Nelson Mandela.

[32] Congreve, "Reminiscences", SSJE/6/5/5/2, f. 33.

[33] Isaiah 53:3.

[34] Congreve, *Spiritual Order*, pp. 51–8. This meditation, "The Sorrow of Nature", was originally sent as a letter to Walter Congreve.

[35] Congreve, letter to Miss Kebbel, 31 July 1903, SSJE/6/5/2/4/12, f. 29.

all whom they loved.[36] There was no romanticization or false joy on which a false hope might have been built, but a clear-eyed acknowledgement of the suffering over which Christ triumphs. He recorded an occasion on which a Lay Brother[37] went to spend a day with the lepers on Robben Island:

> [I]t was a dismal, wet day, and the young man and boy patients were feeling thrice discouraged. Our Brother had not one word to say, he could only listen in silence to their bitter complaining, separated forever from their homes, to die in prison as it were, merely because they were sufferers. The distress was sharp, what balm had he for such sorrow?[38]

The answer was a reading of the last chapters of the Bible, containing the proclamation of the New Jerusalem:[39]

> The leper boy read all that to his dispirited fellows, and afterwards our Brother found them no longer bitter or complaining, but patient and willing to be comforted. It was that mystery which S Paul calls the "comfort of Love"[40] that made the difference. And the good of Love is not merely that it can make miserable people a little more comfortable for the moment, but, because it comes from God, it brings the miserable to God,—and makes their very misery a vessel to hold all the more of the joy of God's love. "Your sorrow shall be turned into joy,"[41]—become the occasion, the very material of new joy.[42]

---

[36] Congreve, letter to "N" (Selina Congreve), 3 November 1902, SSJE/6/5/2/5, f. 55.

[37] Possibly Br John.

[38] George Congreve SSJE, "Love Never Faileth", in *The Cowley Evangelist*, February 1913, p. 27.

[39] Revelation 21 and 22.

[40] Philippians 2:1.

[41] John 16:20, cf. Jeremiah 31:13.

[42] Congreve, "Love Never Faileth", p. 27.

Robben Island was a source of hope for Congreve even from afar. On a stormy night on the mainland:

> on my way home looking out—seaward into the utter darkness, I caught sight of the calm steady spark of the Robben Island Lighthouse, an hour's sail away to the north which is always my symbol of hope—and so transcends all the other little frightened twinkles from the ships . . . The ascension of our Lord to prepare a place for us is like that calm light far out at sea in the darkness and storm.[43]

Hope for Congreve is not a passive virtue, but requires the active cooperation of the will:

> The cactus has only to sit on its wall for 100 years and express dimly the splendour of God's thought by its strange vitality and slow development of a splendid flower. But I have to fit myself by discipline to listen for the Divine Word, to hear, rejoice in, live by, and respond to it.[44]

In an Advent Address, he wrote that hope:

> is no vague natural poetry in us, like our blind longing for the first signs of spring coming after winter. It is an energy of conscience, reason, and will, set upon things above, seeking the highest and the loveliest; yes, an energy of our highest faculties, and *all* of them, even of our earthly body, because we know that we are not created only to *think* of what is highest, but to suffer and strive for it, attain, and possess it.[45]

---

[43] Congreve, letter to "N" (Selina Congreve), The Sunday after Ascension 1904 (?), SSJE/6/5/2/5, f. 37.

[44] Congreve, letter to Assheton, 19 February 1902, SSJE/6/5/5/9, f. 962.

[45] Congreve, *Spiritual Order*, p. 61–2. Emphasis in the original.

For Congreve, the "Sorrow of Nature", the yearning of the natural world for the Creator, is a cause and source of hope for all creation. Late one evening, standing on the summit of Robben Island:

> a flight of curlews passed me with their wild cry, out of the dark into the dark. The sea made its perpetual moan, uttering the burden of the endless sorrow of a world that cannot rest until man is restored to God. I was conscious of this sorrow of the world everywhere—in the lingering traces of glory departed in the West, in the presence of the unmoving cloud masses, in the cry of the wild birds, and in the voices of the sea far and near. But I knew that sorrow can never be the whole meaning of nature. With all the solemnities of the close of day out at sea, there falls a majestic sadness everywhere; but why do I submit to its influence, and seek the fellowship of its pain? Why do I listen so hungrily to catch the burden of the breaking waves? To drink the sorrow of the fading light, and the passion of the evening star? Who ever turned to sorrow for sorrow's sake? I find that there is always woven into the sorrow of nature a joyful mystery, which, if it is ever named by men, is called beauty, or love, or praise. If I strain my ear to listen to the sorrow of the sea, it calls me far away from myself, and all that is base, on into this sphere of the infinite, to hear the music of eternity.[46]

A writer who more usually spoke of the dawn and of the spring than of winter and sunset, Congreve understood sympathy with nature as an active means of grace, not merely a static sign or a cause of feelings: "I am sure that whatever power nature may have, it has not only from God originally, but in God also, from moment to moment." Because "nature in all its forms is an utterance of the Word of God, not merely as He dwelt from all eternity in the unity of the Blessed Trinity, but of the Word made Flesh," those who share Christ's humanity have a sympathy with the whole of creation, and can come to him through it:

---

[46] Congreve, *Spiritual Order*, p. 53.

> When "the gentleness of heaven is on the sea,"[47] I know why it is
> so lovely, and whence gentleness comes to us in nature. Nature's
> secret, the character of mystery which haunts it, is a reflection of
> the infinite Person from Whom it has its being and destiny. In
> the vast silence and gloom of nightfall at sea I find the fellowship
> in sorrow of a world fallen from God, and its yearning to return
> to the lost fellowship of His kingdom.[48]

Nature can be a means of hope for those who suffer because it is not
merely a sign of God's past or even continuing action of creation, but
because it is united with humanity by Christ's act of redemption:

> When I hear all the waves of the sea mourn for man, this is
> no feigned conceit of affected phrase for me. If I am in Christ,
> nature really shares my sorrows and mourns with me, because
> God in Christ girt creation to Himself, and bore the sins and
> pains of the whole world in His breaking heart upon the cross.
> The sympathy which I find in nature is the pulse of the heart of
> the true Mourner for the world's sin—the heart of Him Who
> carried all our sorrows.[49]

Nature can be a means of hope, because it too is somehow caught up by
God in his redemptive work and thus helps to lead human beings to him.

A comparison with Father Benson's reply to a correspondent on the
"future of the beasts" is instructive. Benson wrote, "[T]here is a future
for beasts probably, but probably not in any sense a personal future."
A personal future is reserved for humanity because participation in
the personal life of God is opened by the Incarnation. "How beasts
and Angels (fallen and unfallen) relate to this we cannot tell, but our
predestination is to something altogether surpassing theirs." For Benson,
creation thus becomes indifferent and he concludes characteristically, "for
now we have to train ourselves under the discipline of God to be worthy

---

47 From Wordsworth's poem, "By the Sea".

48 Congreve, *Spiritual Order*, p. 56.

49 Ibid., pp. 56–7. The reference at the end is to Isaiah 53:4.

of that Kingdom".[50] Congreve took a slightly different view, remarking in answer to a similar question that animals do not touch merely the surface of our soul:

> . . . but the best and deepest parts of it . . . Our interest in every creature is a spiritual one, not created to stop in the creature which awakens it but meant to go further on into God . . . Our love for creatures teaches us of God, it helps us to tie our wills up to God and His perfect purpose for every creature.[51]

For Congreve, the salvation of human beings and nature are woven together. Drawing on St Paul's words, "The whole creation groaneth and travaileth together,"[52] he wrote:

> [T]here is a real unity in creation, animate and inanimate, of man, his dog, and his horse, the wild beasts, the sea with its sorrow and its glory. We who both in body and soul are built up of lower created forms, share the humiliation of the created universe; but if we suffer together, we are associated also in a common hope, for as members of Christ we lift up and restore to God our fellow creatures by our thanksgiving for the use of them.[53]

Nature is not to be left behind as we move into God but remains a means to him, though Congreve is always clear it is not an end in itself:

> When after storms you open your window on a perfectly still and lovely spring morning and breathe freely the sweet air, the peace and the beauty, that manifestly is not meant merely to end in a

---

[50] Benson, Correspondence from Cowley, Letter to Lady [?] 22 December 1899, SSJE/6/1/2/9/2.

[51] Congreve, letter to Miss Kebbel, 1894, SSJE/6/5/2/4/3, f. 6.

[52] Romans 8:22.

[53] Congreve, *Christian Progress*, p. 265. This address, "The Fellowship of Man with All Created Things in Sorrow and in Hope" (pp. 257–69), was given in 1908 on Iona.

bodily sensation, such as the feeling of refreshment and a good appetite for breakfast: it must be meant to carry our spirit on to God and eternity.[54]

It is in this light that Congreve was able to say that "God has given us all things richly to enjoy."[55]

The key scriptural text for Congreve's consideration of nature and beauty was the description of the Son of God in Hebrews 1:3 as the brightness—Congreve used the words "effulgence" and, more usually, "outshining"—of the Father's glory:

> Christ, the Word of God, is the Perfection . . . of human nature and of human life . . . He has come not to hide the glory, but to make it shine forth according to their capacity in every body and soul into which He comes . . . If God really is in the world reconciling it to Himself in Christ, then . . . dullness, sin, and sadness . . . [cannot be] the real basis and substance of human life.[56]

Natural beauty is the sense:

> . . . into which God flashes revelations every day, by which He makes you aware of a mystery,—of something you call beauty, which passes from some external object you look upon into your intelligence, by which you become assured that love, and not mechanical necessity, governs the world.[57]

Because beauty has its source in God Incarnate, it cannot be looked upon directly: "[E]ye has not seen, nor ear heard," by nature, the divine glory;

---

[54] Congreve, Copies of letters to friends and associates, letter to Annie C. Lane, 18 December 1900, SSJE/6/5/2/7.

[55] Congreve, letter to Miss Kebbel, 1894, SSJE/6/5/2/4, f. 12, quoting 1 Timothy 6:17.

[56] Congreve, *Christian Life*, pp. 264–5.

[57] Ibid., p. 267.

but to the regenerate, "God has revealed them by his Spirit."[58] Nor can beauty satisfy, since it always points beyond itself:

> I thank God that we can never be satisfied with any created beauty or interest, that we can never get more than a passing glimpse of external perfection, that while we look at it it fades; And yet I thank God that we do get these glimpses of the beauty that as it fades suggests to us every moment the need of the eternal beauty; they set on fire our delight in loveliness, and awaken both the longing and the hope of perfection.[59]

In the very "*transitoriness* of beauty we are constantly reminded of its true significance".[60]

Since beauty is a revelation of God, for Congreve the true artist is the man or woman of prayer, who sees the fact that "God touches things as He passes through creation, and makes them burn for an instant with the beauty of His secret passing."[61] Without this, "the passion for and pursuit of beauty are often regarded as a mere fashionable form of folly, because so few realise its true nature, and how wonderfully it tends to ennoble human life."[62] Congreve continues with an acute observation on secular culture: "Merely sensual delight in beauty stops in the pleasure of the created form, and having exhausted it, turns wearily to look for another equally disappointing satisfaction."

When beauty does not lead on to God it brings a person "no permanent solace . . . Rather it tends to weary him of his commonplace companions, and to lead him into the same solitary world of dreams, to rest in a vague sympathy with the suffering and waiting universe."[63] It was the weary sterility of the Clayton & Bell windows in Frankby church which Congreve had criticized. God could make up what was lacking

---

[58] Congreve, *Spiritual Order*, p. 323, quoting 1 Corinthians 2:9 and 10.

[59] Congreve, *Christian Life*, p. 309.

[60] Congreve, *Spiritual Order*, p. 321. Emphasis in the original.

[61] *Ibid.*, p. 319.

[62] *Ibid.*

[63] Congreve, *Christian Progress*, p. 272.

in an artist. Of the windows he had written, "Daylight makes colours passionate with or without the artist's assistance, so I hope well for our windows."[64]

Congreve's view that art without God is wearisome is echoed clearly in Ninian Comper's famous remark, that "The purpose of the church . . . is to move to worship, to bring a man to his knees, to refresh your soul in a weary land." Comper went on, "For mankind in the mass the neglect of beauty spells the hardness and narrowness either of a puritan or of a materialist."[65] In this again, Comper was effectively quoting Congreve who wrote, "[I]n contrast with the contemptuous view of the Puritan and of the sensualist, it is startling to discover how Theology speaks of beauty only with bated breath".[66] For Congreve, the Puritan rejection of beauty in favour of "a morally pretentious and insignificant plainness" is as wrong as the sensualist's "glorious self-complacency" in using beautiful things only for "comfort and convenience". The godly person will find that beauty reveals God:

> For want of better teaching beauty will often mean nothing more to a man than the pattern of a silk or of a wallpaper. But there will be another whose eyes are open, who finds beauty everywhere: it carries a message from God to him, and he rises with reverence to hear what the Lord God will say to him by it.[67]

Congreve's thought throws light on the reasons why ultimately Comper was interested in more than merely the functional aspect of a church. Though Comper is seen, not without reason, to have developed into an early Modernist, a church could not simply be a "housing for an altar"

---

[64] Congreve, letter to Assheton, 2 February 1863, SSJE/6/5/5/9, f. 153, and see above p. XXX.

[65] J. Ninian Comper, *Of the Atmosphere of a Church* (London: Sheldon Press, 1947; reprinted in Symondson and Bucknall, *Sir Ninian Comper*, pp. 231–46) pp. 9–10.

[66] Congreve, *Spiritual Order*, p. 316.

[67] Ibid., p. 319.

without also considering the need for it to be beautiful, and echoing Congreve he wrote:

> This would seem to be the Creator's purpose towards Man in giving him the beauty of nature, and it should be the purpose of all art. In art Man partakes in this purpose of his Maker and objectively he brings the best of all that He has given him to create of beauty (in liturgy, poetry, music, ceremonial, architecture, sculpture and painting) to be the expression of his worship.

While Comper thought "mankind in the mass" needed beauty, he concluded that "the saint and the mystic may pass directly, without the aid of external beauty of art, and even of nature, to God himself."[68]

For Congreve, however, the experience of beauty is equally for "mankind in the mass" and the mystic. He quoted Anselm: "God is absolute beauty" and "His Only Begotten Son is the revelation of the invisible uncreated beauty of God." Thus "the beauty of the creature is that subtle indescribable quality in it which you cannot arrest or analyse, which is at once the true artist's inspiration and despair, because it is a Divine mystery, 'the brightness of the Eternal Father's Glory.'"[69] Congreve wrote:

> Once we have seen this, and understand it, we no longer need to see beautiful forms and lights in nature; their beauty is not in them; they change and pass away, but that mystery of fairness[70] which came through them and touched our Soul, was the Eternal Light which abides. We can seek and contemplate that splendour

---

[68] Comper, *Atmosphere of a Church*, pp. 9–10. On Comper as a Modernist, see Symondson and Bucknall, *Sir Ninian Comper*, pp. 208–9.

[69] Congreve, *Spiritual Order*, p. 317. The reference is to Anselm, *Cur Deus Homo*, 1.1. The quotation is from a hymn by Bishop James Woodford (1820–85), "Brightness of the Father's glory".

[70] Congreve uses "fairness" here to mean "loveliness", not "even-handedness".

in our daily private prayer, under the dullest circumstances, and all the pressure of common life.[71]

It was characteristic of Congreve to assert that mystic experience comes in and through daily life and is neither a special grace nor dependent on a particular way of living. Elsewhere he came back to the mystic experience we can have in the contemplation of God beyond nature:

> The man of faith and prayer is the man whose eyes are open, who never rests on the symbol of created beauty, but passes straightway through to the contemplation of the Eternal Substance, the uncreated beauty of God, by prayer and thanksgiving. It follows that the man of prayer is the true seer, the lover and priest of natural beauty; he alone knows its deepest and highest significance; he does not rest his joy in it; he raises it to God in his thanksgiving, when he has it, and transcends it; he is independent of it; it passes and he lets it go joyfully, but leaves him with the unchanging Beauty. He will not be excited by the enthusiasm of art, not because he is insensible to beauty, but because in his communion with God he possesses it always; God is always "revealing it to him by His Spirit."[72]

Congreve explored the means of this revelation through nature in a sermon on St Columba, preached on Iona after his return from South Africa:

> We were sitting just now on the rocks watching the tide running up the Sound,—the waters a sea of glass,[73] blending unspeakable blue and purple and green with the silver and gold of the sunshine; and we were asking ourselves what such glory of colour could mean for us ordinary people who behold it . . . Presently the Chapel bell called us home to Evensong, and as we

---

[71]   Congreve, *Christian Life*, p. 269.

[72]   Congreve, *Spiritual Order*, pp. 323–4; cf. 1 Corinthians 2:10.

[73]   A reference to Revelation 15:2.

sang "Magnificat" and the Creed, the mystery of the splendour
of the colours of the sea and the sunshine, and the white crested
waves, kindled in our praise; the words were old, but the meaning
was new to us. The splendour which we had seen just now with
perplexity, found its expression in the psalm; colours melted, as
it were, into the words, and brought an infinite significance into
the song. The splendour meant the beauty of God Himself,—the
kindness and love of God to man appearing in our Lord Jesus
Christ; but it was waiting for the psalm to utter the mystery of
the Divine Name, of which all created glories are but echoes. You
have passionate tone and colour suggested in nature everywhere,
but no one can tell us what the unexpressed joy or the sorrow
is, until God's praise gathers them into their true unity, and they
become spiritual music in our psalm. Strange colours and the
sea awake the heart to hunger for higher things than sufficed
us before; but the praise of God brings us by the power of the
Holy Spirit an inward unveiling of the mystery, which the colours
made us desire, and wistfully suspect the hidden presence of. The
psalm interprets nature to us, and us to ourselves, by waking in us
the need of God, which we share with the suffering and waiting
creation, and by uttering our thanksgiving, by which we bring
every creature into the blessing of the divine purpose.[74]

Scripture is the means by which the inarticulate sense of beauty can be
brought to become praise of God. A spirit of poverty is also required:

But it was not the daily conventional recitation of the psalter by
itself that revealed to Columba the significance of nature. It was
primarily the mystery of the cross accepted inwardly as the new
ground of a converted life ... By dying with [Christ] to every
shred of pride, ambition and anger of his youth, he rose to live
with Him Who is the Life of all creatures. In proportion as we
are dead to all selfish use of things, the creatures of God begin
to reveal to us the glory and virtue that they have of Him ... It

---

[74] Congreve, *Christian Progress*, pp. 280–1.

is only the man who is dying to himself, the pure of heart, who learns to hear and to see mysteries in nature.[75]

In February 1900, Congreve wrote to Father Page from a retreat the Fathers were making by the sea in Cape Town. It was typical of Congreve's leadership that he drew the community away from the busyness of their life to the contemplation of God. Because for him to come to God through nature was to come to the reality at the heart of things, the retreat was the opposite of escapism. The letter sets the beauty of nature in the foreground and offers through it a profound revelation of God. There is also a darker note of the trouble and difficulties of the world. Taken together, it sums up Congreve's work in Cape Town in another example of the marvellous writing that Africa inspired in him, and the letter is worthy of lengthy quotation:

> I have climbed up into a sort of eagle's nest, where several masses of granite meet and support each other, shelter me from the sun, and give me a seat. I look out across the bay, landlocked, like many a highland sea-lough, shut in by mountains; sometimes a copje,[76] a thousand feet of red or yellow sandstone, battered and seamed, but proof against the siege of the ages, splendidly built up upon, perhaps a thousand feet of primeval granite:—mountains each as like Table Mountain in its stratification and form, as the children in one family are like one another.
>
> From my granite chair I look across the bay, which is blue, because it takes in and gives back all the cloudless blue overhead, much deeper in tone than the blue above, because it has its own depths of blue water below, besides the blue which it receives from above. But the blue of the water is shot with many other mysteries of colour: the green sun-suffused veldt-bush weaves reflected gold and green into the blue water; a shadow from some (to me) unseen cloud, sends a purple stain through the blue and gold and green; the sea-tangle gives a darker purple still to the

---

[75] Ibid., pp. 281–2.

[76] A mountain outcrop.

shallows which hide it. Looking down from this height into the sea below, I see places where the white sand at the bottom is clear of the dark sea-tangle, and those places are of the palest sea green, transparent as a jewel. The large rounded loose stones that border the bay, among which the clear water runs up and carries a fringe of white foam,—these stones are of a deep red gold colour.

Across this scene sea-gulls flap leisurely, and some black divers, like cormorants, fly swiftly only just above the water.

Then there is a sound of the sea breaking close at my feet, and miles away, with many tones, nearer and further off, and now the clang of a sea-gull's cry. Sometimes looking seaward we can just make out on the horizon a speck, and a faint train of distant smoke, which is some big ship carrying a regiment and guns to Natal. We do not know what is happening there these days; we seem to live in "a world where nothing can go wrong",[77] a world where sleep could never be disturbed by any fear; but even the profound peace of this place turns out to be only a passing away of storms, a resolution of discords. For just below is the ruin of an old Dutch fort, with two old guns, engraved 1711, rusty and half buried in the sand, and on the opposite side of the bay, there are traces of Dutch empire in ruins. And there are dykes and chasms in the stratification of the mountain opposite, torn by wild forces of nature in ancient times. But the Dutch forts are grass-grown mounds, and the distorted rocks are tapestried with wild sweet-geranium and mezembryanthemum. Storms and disorder visit this quiet place still, no doubt, but they are not eternal; they pass and make way for the kingdom which cannot be shaken, for our Eucharist and retreat,—the kingdom of peace.

[The same evening, later.] This is the Vigil of the Feast of the Purification;[78] it is after Compline, and the Community and all the mountain creatures are asleep, lizards, the meer-cats, the conies, the sea-birds: the mountain opposite that lately in the sunshine was all gold and green, is a pall of blackness now,

---

[77]   From Wordsworth's poem, "The Cuckoo-Clock".

[78]   Candlemas (2 February).

outlined against a sky of dark blue that sparkles with stars. The bay is blue that is almost black, and the mountain is blackness itself; a murmur of the sea comes as gently as the breathing of one who sleeps; but the silent stars are all awake, and tingle with life and splendour.

Here we have had two peaceful days hidden in the heart of wild Africa: it is the loneliest place you can imagine; the moment you leave the cottage you are lost in the tangle of wild bush, where there is no path. Everything is beautiful and everything is conscious of an eternal unrest. The gentle undertones of the sea and its dreams express this to me while I am writing; Retreat does not discover rest for us in nature, but reveals to us our fellowship with all creation in the noble pain of unrest, and in the desire of God. To-morrow morning (if the world gets safely through another night), we shall be celebrating the holy mysteries in honour of the Presentation of Christ in the Temple, and shall find the rest which the Blessed Mary found, but which nature is still waiting for. May all our Brethren at home welcome today in their Festival the Salvation which nature cannot find, and which even prophets and Kings desired, but did not see,[79] Christ, a Light to lighten the Gentiles, and the Glory of His People Israel.[80]

The work continued, and each year Congreve thought it would be time to go home. It is not clear when he stepped down as Superior. As early as January 1901 he wrote to Miss Kebbel, "just two more mails and I slip out of office into retirement and the joy of a back seat and the happiness of helping a really able and good Father in any way I can."[81] In any event, Congreve was the doyen of the Community in South Africa, and whether or not Superior, he offered spiritual leadership among the brethren. At last, after Easter 1904, he had the call to return to Cowley. Even then

---

[79]   Cf. Luke 10:24.

[80]   Congreve, *Christian Progress*, pp. 320–3. The meditation is entitled "The Shore"; the final phrases of the quotation are from Luke 2:32, part of the canticle *Nunc dimittis* traditionally sung at Candlemas.

[81]   Congreve, letter to Miss Kebbel, 15 January 1901, SSJE/6/5/2/4/9, f. 2.

there was a hiccough: with farewells all made, a telegraph came in April saying simply, "Congreve stay".[82] He finally sailed in late August. He left, as always, under obedience and mortified to his own will in the matter, but he allowed himself to write, "I am sorry to be leaving this ancient land of buried histories, wild hearts, and gentle savages and to leave so many kind friends and brethren behind . . . but it will be a happiness to see the green fields again and the daisies and the dear people at home."[83]

---

[82] Congreve, letter to Miss Kebbel, 9 April 1904, SSJE/6/5/2/4/13, f. 17.

[83] General correspondence, Transfiguration [6 August] 1904, SSJE/6/5/2/3, f. 35.

C H A P T E R   8

The Security of Duty

On returning from South Africa in September 1904, Congreve had just
turned sixty-nine. While he was not as fit as he had been, and already in
the last year had found difficulty climbing up to Lillebloem, he was still
hale.[1] He cherished happy memories but was pleased to be back. He had
written of holidays in the past:

> [O]ne of the nicest parts of going abroad I think is (it is an
> Irishman who writes) the coming home. What treasures you
> will have of stories and remembrances and photographs to share
> with your people.[2]

At first there was no definite plan for him, and he made a visit to Assheton
in Rugby.[3] After a few months at Cowley he went to London, where the
Society was in the process of establishing a permanent presence, though
what would become St Edward's House was not yet built.[4] His book
Christian Life, a Response continued to sell well, and in the years after
coming home, he published more collections of sermons and papers.[5] He

---

[1] Congreve, Copies of letters to friends and associates, letter to "N" (Selina
     Congreve), February 1903, SSJE/6/5/2/7.
[2] Longridge (ed.), *Spiritual Letters of Fr Congreve*, letter of 16 May 1888, p. 20.
[3] Congreve, letter to Miss Kebbel, 26 September 1904, SSJE/6/5/2/4/13, f. 41.
[4] James, *Cowley Fathers*, pp. 167–72 gives a full account of the foundation of
     St Edward's House.
[5] Congreve, *Christian Life, a Response, with other Retreat Addresses and
     Sermons* (London: Longmans, Green & Co., 1899). *The Parable of the Ten
     Virgins: Addresses Given in Retreat* (London: Mowbray, 1904) was followed

was in demand to give retreats and as a spiritual director, and he wrote prefaces for others' books.

The Society of Saint John the Evangelist was becoming well known, and Congreve was becoming one of the better-known Fathers, a "figure" in some church circles.[6] During this period of active retirement his teaching adumbrated ideas he had been speaking and writing about for years, now developed and mature. He continued to support Ninian Comper, who was also becoming more widely appreciated. In 1909 Congreve was recalled to Oxford, to spend the last years of his life there.

When the Great War broke out in 1914, he was personally involved—as in the Boer War—through his family, with seven nephews or great-nephews on active service, and it was Congreve who was asked to speak for the Community.[7] His forthright support of the war from a Christian perspective challenges today, though it was welcomed by his contemporaries both in the Society and more widely. Congreve's concepts of Christian Patriotism and the "safety of duty" are more nuanced than might at first be thought. He was personally touched by the bereavement of war, meaning that he taught from painful experience, not from comfortable theory. His teaching is arresting and helpful, neither a simplistic retreat into grief or despair—which he believed to be sinfully negligent of God's providence and care—nor a jingoistic acceptance of militarism, which he believed to be evil. Rather, he offered a way of facing and approaching the violence which blights every age, and coming to it as a Christian. Congreve articulates a teaching which was felt to be helpful at the time and still has much to offer, even though his was a voice largely drowned out by the war poets whose influence has been so great on subsequent assessments of the sacrifices of the conflagration of 1914–18.

When encouraging Benson that he should resign as Superior General, Congreve had suggested that the two of them might go to London to

---

by *The Spiritual Order, with Papers and Addresses written for the most part in South Africa* (London: Longmans, Green & Co., 1905).

6   James, *Cowley Fathers*, p. xvii.

7   Congreve, Copies of letters to friends and associates, letter to Sr Isolda (Congreve's niece, a member of the All Saints Sisters of the Poor), 22 March [no year], SSJE/6/5/2/7.

fulfil an ambition of Benson's to establish the work of the Society there.[8] Now, fifteen years later, Congreve was sent to a house which SSJE had rented in Westminster as the first stage of realizing the plan.[9] Congreve liked it in London, characteristically enjoying the natural beauty of the parks.[10] Money was being raised, with building works undertaken, at what was to become St Edward's House in the shadow of Westminster Abbey, and Congreve attended the laying of the foundation stone of the Chapel there in July 1905. The House itself was ready in November.[11] Congreve would go into the Abbey, often for Evensong, and at the end of 1908 was delighted when Ninian Comper was commissioned to make a window to commemorate John Bunyan. Congreve noted that the commission arose after the Dean of Westminster saw and liked the All Saints Hospital Chapel in Cowley St John. It is probable that Congreve was instrumental in winning Comper the Oxford commission, and possible that he had spoken of Comper to the Dean. The Bunyan window was a success—Congreve's own verdict was that it was "a fine window, nobly done, almost totally hidden by a monstrous architectural structure raised by the Nation to the memory of Mr Pitt".[12] When there was controversy the following year about the first of Comper's windows in the north aisle of the Abbey, depicting abbots and kings, support came from the Provost of Eton, another of Congreve's contacts.[13] It was also around this time that Father Waggett introduced Comper to the Earl of Shaftesbury, from whom Comper received an important commission for

8 Congreve, Correspondence with Fr Benson, 21 January 1890, SSJE/6/5/2/1, f. 112. James, *Cowley Fathers*, p. 168 narrates Benson's initial opposition.

9 13 Dartmouth Street.

10 Congreve, letter to Miss Kebbel, 25 June 1905, SSJE/6/5/2/4/14, f. 20.

11 Congreve, letter to Br John, 17 November 1905, SSJE/6/5/2/2/6, f. 18.

12 Congreve, letter to Br John, 20 October 1911, SSJE/6/5/2/2/12, f. 25. Comper visited Congreve at Cowley in 1913 and told him that he was designing his Henry V window; Congreve, letter to Br John, 14 February 1913, SSJE/6/5/2/2/14, f. 4.

13 Symondson and Bucknall, *Sir Ninian Comper*, p. 159.

the chapel at Wimborne St Giles. It is inconceivable, given how close he remained to Waggett, that Congreve had no hand in this as well.[14]

Congreve remained full of enthusiasm for Comper and his work, which he felt much more interesting than Bodley's: "[A]ny work by NC is like good music; there is never anything faded, or negligent or commonplace in his work, but every line has distinction, strength, beauty".[15] For all his influence on Comper's theology and concept of beauty, perhaps Congreve was not as aware of the artistic development of his protégé, whom he understood as working straightforwardly in the tradition and inspiration of the art of the Middle Ages.[16] Whether the artist would have agreed, drawing as he did on a much wider and less mediaeval inspiration, it was certainly true that—as Congreve hoped—Comper became more widely appreciated.

Congreve himself was in demand as a spiritual director, and wrote spiritual letters to a wide range of correspondents.[17] He moved in the upper circles of society and the church as easily as among the poor in the parishes where he preached and led retreats. The saintly Bishop King of Lincoln asked Congreve to visit him in his last illness.[18] Adeline, Dowager Duchess of Bedford, a penal reformer and great supporter of the Society of Saint John the Evangelist, was a friend, and Congreve, who more than

---

[14]   The circumstances of the Shaftesbury commission at Wimborne St Giles are given in Symondson and Bucknall, *Sir Ninian Comper*, p. 112. For Congreve and Waggett see Woodgate, *Father Congreve*, p. 89. Their correspondence has not survived. See also Congreve, *Christian Progress*, p. 324 (the last page), a letter of Waggett's entitled "In the Mission House Garden". For Waggett on Congreve, see Waggett, "Father Congreve", in *The Cowley Evangelist*, May 1918, pp. 127–32.

[15]   Copies of letters to friends and associates, letter to Miss Sharman, Third Sunday of Advent 1909, SSJE/6/5/2/7.

[16]   Congreve, letter to Br John, 18 December 1908, SSJE/6/5/2/2/9, f. 35.

[17]   Longridge (ed.), *Spiritual Letters of Fr Congreve*, 15 August 1898. A further collection was typed (by Frances, Ninian Comper's sister) and sent to Longman's but rejected, and Mowbray rejected a collection of the Assheton correspondence in 1930. See SSJE/6/5/5/6 and SSJE/6/5/5/8.

[18]   Congreve, letter to Br John, 4 March 1910, SSJE/6/5/2/2/11, f. 9.

Figure 14: Fr Congreve. A mature religious, author and spiritual director, Congreve was, humanly speaking, perhaps his most productive in his 70s.

once visited her and celebrated in her private chapel at Chenies, wrote a preface for a book of hers.[19] Eton welcomed him back when in the spring of 1911 the Head Master, Lyttelton, asked to consult him, possibly about the "spiritual crisis" he was undergoing at the time.[20] It was on this occasion that Congreve saw his first aeroplane: "a biplane navigating the upper regions very high up, but not so far off we could not see the little man driving his machine, which was sailing as smoothly as possible across the sky".[21]

It was not surprising, given this higher profile and the success of *Christian Life, a Response* (which had seven impressions by 1907), that he should be asked for more, and his next book—a series of retreat talks, *The Parable of the Ten Virgins*—was published in 1904. The success of this volume encouraged Father Page to "order" Congreve to publish more of his papers. He drew on material he had written in the years in South Africa, and *The Spiritual Order*,[22] containing some of his best writing and dedicated to Walter, now Colonel Congreve, came out in 1905.[23] In 1908, Congreve was called upon to give a paper at the Pan-Anglican Congress

---

[19] Rod Garner, "Gilding the Cages of Others: the life and work of a philanthropic duchess compelled by her faith", *Church Times*, 20 August 2020. Congreve wrote a preface for Adeline Marie Russell [Duchess of Bedford], *An Autumn Easter* (London: Mowbray, 1911). He went to Chenies in 1906 after Easter when he celebrated in the House Chapel for a congregation of sixteen, "the first time there has been a celebration there". (Congreve, letter to Miss Kebbel, 14 April 1906, SSJE/6/5/2/4/21, f. 37.) Congreve was there again "to celebrate in the house chapel" in 1912, and surely at other times too. Congreve, letter to Miss Kebbel, 3 August 1912, SSJE/6/5/2/4/21, f. 15.

[20] Congreve, letter to "N" (Selina Congreve), 26 May 1908, SSJE/6/5/2/5, f. 16; cf. Congreve, letter to Br John, 17 November 1905, SSJE/6/5/2/2/6, f. 18. On Lyttelton's "Spiritual Crisis", see Cyril Alington, *Edward Lyttelton, An Appreciation* (London: John Murray, 1943), pp. 22–6.

[21] Congreve, letter to Br John, 18 May 1911, SSJE/6/5/2/2/12, f. 6.

[22] Congreve, *The Spiritual Order, with Papers and Addresses written for the most part in South Africa* (London: Longmans, Green & Co., 1905).

[23] Congreve, letters to Br John, 28 April 1905, SSJE/6/5/2/2/6, f. 4; 19 June 1905, SSJE/6/5/2/2/6, f. 6.

on "Sisters, their Vocation and Special Work", returning to a subject on which he was now seen as the leading expert. It is noteworthy that he was the only male among those who presented to the Congress on the ministry of women.[24] In 1909 the publishers asked for more, and the result was *Christian Progress*, largely papers reprinted from the Society's journal, *The Cowley Evangelist*.[25] In 1913, he published a further collection, *The Interior Life*, which he described as "odds and ends".[26] When he received yet another request for a book in 1914 he wrote, "I laugh when I get a request like that from Mr Longman. I feel like a kitchen knave invited to sup upstairs with the king."[27] During 1916, he collaborated with Father Longridge to produce an edition of Benson's letters,[28] and wrote a preface for the reissue of Benson's *Divine Rule of Prayer*. This was the fifteenth preface he wrote for others, mostly produced in the period after he returned from South Africa.[29] An invitation to be the Select Preacher before the University of Oxford in 1917 was declined on grounds of ill health, but in the last two years of his life he worked on a final collection

[24] Congreve, "Sisters, their Vocation and Special Work", in *Pan-Anglican Papers, being problems for consideration at the Pan-Anglican Congress 1908*; SC Group 5, *The Church and its Ministry: The Ministry of Women, Section 2, Organised Associations* (London: SPCK, 1908).

[25] Congreve, *Christian Progress, with other Papers and Addresses* (London: Longmans, Green & Co., 1910). Congreve notes the request from Longmans in Letters to Br John, f. 36, letter of 10 December 1909.

[26] Congreve, *The Interior Life, and Other Addresses* (London: Mowbray, 1913). "Odds and ends" was a remark to Br John: Congreve, letter to Br John, 14 June 1912, SSJE/6/5/2/2/13, f. 16.

[27] Congreve, Copies of letters to friends and associates, letter to Mrs Torr, 8 May 1914, SSJE/6/5/2/7.

[28] Congreve and Longridge (eds), *Letters of R. M. Benson* (London: Mowbray, 1916).

[29] Richard Meux Benson SSJE, *The Divine Rule of Prayer* (Second Edition, London: Mowbray, 1916). For other prefaces, see the Bibliography.

of papers, published posthumously, *Treasures of Hope for the Evening of Life*.[30]

Congreve was not a controversialist, but he did write about contemporary issues and had a hidden influence on others, such as Adeline Russell who used her position as Dowager Duchess of Bedford to intervene in the treatment of prisoners in Portugal, forcing the UK government to put pressure on the Portuguese; she became chair of the European War Fund supporting military hospitals.[31]

At the end of his Pan-Anglican Congress paper, Congreve touched on an issue which was becoming more important for Religious, when he stated that bishops do not have an inherent right to be the Visitors of Orders.[32] It was a rare foray into ecclesiastical debates on an issue on which SSJE would later support other communities.[33] Congreve was not immune to the worries of church politics, but he turned to God in the face of them. In 1913, two Anglican bishops in East Africa attended an ecumenical conference at Kikuyu in Kenya at which they celebrated Holy Communion and communicated some of the non-Anglicans present. Bishop Frank Weston of Zanzibar delated the Bishops, William Peel of Mombasa and John Willis of Uganda, to the Archbishop of Canterbury, asserting heresy. The scandal caused great trouble to many Anglo-Catholics concerned about the doctrine of the Eucharist and the necessity of episcopacy, which they feared was under threat from those who sought in the mission field to abjure the divisions of the old world.[34] Congreve told a priest that for a few days he had fretted over it, but that

---

[30]   Woodgate, *Father Congreve*, p. 81; Bull, "George Congreve", p. 99. Congreve, *Treasures of Hope for the Evening of Life* (London: Longmans, Green & Co., 1918).

[31]   Garner, "Gilding the Cages".

[32]   Congreve, "Sisters, their Vocation and Special Work", pp. 7–8.

[33]   Benson's authority had rested on his position as parish priest; James, *Cowley Fathers*, pp. 50–70. For this issue in a later generation, see Dunstan, *Labour of Obedience*, p. 125.

[34]   On Kikuyu, see H. Maynard Smith, *Frank, Bishop of Zanzibar* (London: SPCK, 1926), pp. 145–70; Roger Lloyd, *The Church of England in the Twentieth Century*, Vol. 1 (London: Longmans, Green & Co., 1946), pp. 97–100; Luke Miller, "The Winds of Change: 1914–45", in William Davage (ed.), *In This*

"things soon get into their proportions by getting into their relation to other things".[35] In the end, Congreve was convinced that the Church of England, being inherently catholic, would not turn away from her fundamental nature.

He had always been unwavering in his rejection of Roman Catholicism. There was never any doubt in Congreve's mind that he was a catholic Christian where he was. He wrote, "I had many such impressions and attractions [to the Roman Catholic Church], but I have always felt convinced they were temptations offering me easy ways out of spiritual difficulties."[36] When Frances Comper, Ninian's sister, was troubled about her place in the Church of England, Congreve wrote to her, "The only reason to be a Roman Catholic is not, does it help me or is it satisfying, but is Rome the only true church? . . . I feel that loyalty to the Church is like loyalty to the King, a virtue in each sphere." Though he was well aware of the arguments and rested his rejection of Roman Catholicism on his rejection of the doctrine of infallibility and the "modern Papal claim to universal authority",[37] his focus was always on God, rather than upon points of doctrine. "We do not get hold of truth and beauty by asking questions, the defective policeman's instrument, but by love of the loveliest."[38] It might have been Congreve whom Maturin described when he spoke of the convert who looks back at:

> men who are far better than themselves, who feel as keenly as they
> do the difficulties of which they complain, but who bravely set
> them aside, and remain where they are, and do the work God has
> given them to do, and treat all these questions as temptations.[39]

Sign Conquer: A History of the Society of the Holy Cross 1855–2005 (London: Continuum, 2006), pp. 124–5.

[35] Congreve, Copies of letters to friends and associates, letter to the Revd P. H. Leary, Vicar of St Augustine's Kilburn, [undated], SSJE/6/5/2/7.

[36] Congreve, letter to Miss Kebbel, 18 March 1897, SSJE/6/5/2/4/6, f. 12.

[37] Longridge (ed.), Spiritual Letters of Fr Congreve, p. 198.

[38] Congreve, Copies of letters to friends and associates, letter to Frances Comper, 15 August 1914, SSJE/6/5/2/7.

[39] Maturin, Price of Unity, p. 279.

Catholic he certainly believed himself to be, but for all his love of Comper's churches, Congreve was not a ritualist. His background was of an austere Irish Protestantism, and he remained true to it. He felt that processions and ritual "fuss" were not helpful to the cultivation of a Christian interior spirit, and would have limited great rituals to Easter Day and "perhaps" Pentecost in order to emphasize the "religious quietness" of other times:

> How delightfully silent and still God's triumphs and processions—the ritual of nature—is—the gardens of wild flowers along the railway banks—the cloud capped towers of the sky—the pageantry much grander than we can make, and the angels arrange it all and take it away so quickly afterwards so that no one saw the scene shifting.[40]

In Westminster Abbey he would pass by the grave of his ancestor William Congreve in Poets' Corner, but "somehow he never has anything to say to me".[41] Whatever he thought of his ancestors, he was close to the living members of his family. Congreve's brother (Walter's father) had died while Congreve was in South Africa, and a younger generation was coming forward.[42] When Congreve was living in London, Billy (Walter's son) was at Eton and growing fast, as the last Edwardian summers passed by and the clouds of renewed war gathered on the international horizon.

Despite their radical poverty and rejection of the world, the Cowley Fathers were by no means unpatriotic. Late at night on Coronation Day 1911, Congreve heard Benson in his cell singing "God save the King", and he was personally delighted when Walter was appointed CB in the Coronation Honours.[43] Congreve was proud of the careers of his nephews, and especially that of Walter, chronicling his promotions in

---

[40] Congreve, letter to "N" (Selina Congreve), St John the Baptist 1899, SSJE/6/5/2/5, f. 1.

[41] Congreve, letter to Br John, 14 August 1905, SSJE/6/5/2/2/6, f. 14.

[42] Benson, Correspondence from Cowley, 1899–1908, SSJE/6/1/2/9/4.

[43] Congreve, letters to Br John, 23 June 1911 (Benson singing), 30 June 1911 (Walter's CB: Companion of the Order of the Bath), SSJE/6/5/2/2/12, ff. 14, 15.

his correspondence.[44] Walter had not been the only Congreve to serve in South Africa against the Boers—as well as Francis Congreve, John Shea (married to a niece, one of Walter's sisters) had won the DSO (and would later receive the surrender of Jerusalem as a Divisional Commander under General Edmund Allenby in 1917).[45] In 1901, Congreve had sympathized with a sister-in-law that all three of her sons were now serving, two in South Africa and the third in India.[46] Billy Congreve was commissioned into the Rifle Brigade in 1911, and his brother Geoffrey was a Cadet at the Royal Naval College, Osborne in the same year.[47] Walter was promoted to the rank of General in 1912.

Congreve's personal links in the military, as well as his own direct experience in Cape Town during the Boer War, made him well aware of the reality behind military pomp and circumstance, and he had been touched in his life by the human cost of war. He knew that soldiering "is not about living at home and showing off in uniform in fine weather".[48] He had helped nurse Walter from the wounds he sustained at Colenso, and in 1902 had shared the frustration of the family who had come out to Johannesburg to see Walter but who were unable to do so because the expected peace with the Boers did not materialize.[49] As chaplain to the Cape Mounted Police in the same year, Congreve reported how his men had "come on a laager of 14 Boers: rushed them, killed one, taking the rest prisoners", and he knew the rough violence and dehumanizing tendency

---

[44] Congreve, letters to Br John, 27 October 1906, SSJE/6/5/2/2/7, f. 10 ("WNC may get a Brigade."), and 29 December 1911, SSJE/6/5/2/2/12, f. 31 ("WNC is in command of 3,000 officers and men.").

[45] Francis became a Lt Col; see Thornton and Fraser, *The Congreves*, pp. 106, 145, 225 (Francis), 140, 146, 271 (Shea). For Shea, see also Archibald Wavell, *Allenby: A Study in Greatness* (London: Harrap, 1940), pp. 186–7, 229–31. Shea was later General C-in-C Eastern Command India.

[46] Congreve, letter to Miss Kebbel, 13 July 1901, SSJE/6/5/2/4/10, f. 33.

[47] Congreve, letter to Br John, 31 March 1911, SSJE/6/5/2/2/12, f. 1. Geoffrey served as a Midshipman at Jutland in 1916 and was killed on active service at sea in the Second World War.

[48] Longridge (ed.), *Spiritual Letters of Fr Congreve*, p. 54.

[49] Congreve, letter to Miss Kebbel, 15 February 1902, SSJE/6/5/2/4/11, ff. 5–6.

of war, describing in one letter the boasting of a militiaman who told him that he had killed a native in cold blood.[50]

Congreve's first-hand experience meant that in 1914, now back in Oxford, he was well placed to help his Community—and a society at large whose experience was the Victorian *Pax Britannica*—to understand and reflect on the outbreak of the Great War. As a respected teacher with military connexions, his views were sought. Father Benson was noted for his conviction that the end of the world was very near. For him, modern conflicts were the birth pangs of the new age. During a crisis with Russia in 1878 he wrote:

> We learn of the drawing near to war. I hope it will call the English nation out of this miserable life of self-indulgence. We must pray God garners to give us some fresh recruits for our own military movements.[51]

Congreve was less apocalyptic in his approach, but he "felt" the War. It was said of him:

> Father Congreve was *in* it utterly. He was on fire for justice, the justice menaced by the enemy. He had no tolerance for pacifism, which is, I suppose, not the temper that loves Peace, but the temper that prefers Peace to Duty.[52]

While he was not "blind to the evils war occasions or brings to light, or to the faults and sins of soldiers" he was touched by stories of chivalry and care for friend and foe through which he discerned the presence of

---

[50]   Congreve, letter to Miss Kebbel, undated 1902, SSJE/6/5/2/4/11, f. 41 (the attack on the laager); Congreve, "Reminiscences", SSJE/6/5/5/2, f. 25 (the man shot was "a native servant of the Boers" killed for having British horses).

[51]   Richard Meux Benson SSJE, Correspondence with Br Beale, 10 April 1878, SSJE/6/1/2/4, f. 15. The Disraeli Government mobilized on 27 March in anticipation of war with Russia.

[52]   Waggett, "Father Congreve", pp. 129–30.

Christ.[53] Despite this "feeling" for the War and the terrible casualties and upheavals it brought, Congreve placed it in a wider context, as a war like others rather than making the war itself the context for all else.

The scale of death is what marks out the Great War, and Congreve was alert both to the numbers and to the sting of personal bereavement.[54] This was to him a fact of war, not of the World War specifically. On a visit to Eton to see Billy in 1905, he had noted the new memorial in the chapel to 300 boys killed in the Boer War, and the bronze images of Victory specifically donated by two mothers of only sons.[55] More directly, in 1903 he had supported an acquaintance who came to South Africa to search for her son's memorial; she was referred to Congreve as one who knew the people who cared for the soldiers' graves and, importantly at a time when the dead were buried where they fell, the locations.[56] He was aware, even from the beginning, that the World War was characterized by a new scale. He wrote to Brother John, "I excuse myself omitting the year in the date of my note—it seems as if this was the last year of all, the end of all things, the beginning of the endless age." News from France had come of "the great fatigue of war, the heavy work for the men, the endless business for the commanders". It took Billy Congreve five days at sea to get to the front, followed by long marches ("one day of 26 miles and sleep out in the field in the rain").[57]

Once again, the family were considerably committed. Within weeks of the outbreak, Congreve had "eight nephews in harness in this war and [I] am glad". They included the two Generals, Walter Congreve

---

[53] Bull, "George Congreve", pp. 99–100.

[54] George Congreve SSJE, "The Peace of Jerusalem", in *The Cowley Evangelist*, October 1914, p. 218.

[55] Congreve, letter to Br John, 17 November 1905, SSJE/6/5/2/2/6, f. 18; Congreve described this visit and the memorial again to Sister Selina: letter to "N" (Selina Congreve), 16 May 1905, SSJE/6/5/2/5, f. 16. About 22,000 British soldiers were killed or wounded in the Boer War, in the First World War about 703,000.

[56] Congreve, letter to "N" (Selina Congreve), 6 September 1903, SSJE/6/5/2/5, f. 29.

[57] Congreve, letter to Br John, 2 October 1914, SSJE/6/5/2/2/15, f. 7.

and John Shea, a Major and more junior officers, all quickly engaged. Francis Congreve—now a Captain in the Field Artillery—and John Shea were mentioned in dispatches by October 1914.[58] A godson went to the trenches direct from school.[59] They were united by letters and by prayer; Walter noted in his diary:

> [S]tayed in a clergy house exactly like Cowley in all ways and felt much at home. Its cells, plain cleanliness and silence in corridors, garden, chapel, refectory, all like the Mission House. Its priest is a gentleman and good to look at. Church in the village commencing at 10 so attended. Could not understand a word, but its chants are those of Cowley and I felt very full of our three "Religious" and wrote to them after. Slept in a cell and enjoyed being in one again.[60]

Death came close. Within a few days of Billy's appointment as ADC to General Hubert Hamilton, the General was killed.[61] Major Arthur King, married to one of Congreve's nieces, was killed in action on 15 March 1915. Billy risked his life in a failed attempt to bring King's body back.[62] Unsurprisingly, Congreve had more sympathy for the leaders than historians have shown until recently, noting that "it is very hard work for the generals. W gets about four hours sleep out of 48."[63] Despite all this,

---

58 Congreve, letter to Br John, 23 October 1914, SSJE/6/5/2/2/15, f. 9, 11. He looked forward to more decorations: "I believe Charles Congreve will get some notice in November." Later in the war, Shea commanded the 30th Division in Walter's XIII Corps.

59 Congreve, Copies of letters to friends and associates, letter to Miss Gore Browne, 22 March 1915(?), SSJE/6/5/2/7.

60 Thornton and Fraser, *The Congreves*, p. 119. The "three religious" were Congreve, Sr Selina and Sr Isolda.

61 Presumably Billy's appointment was not unconnected with the fact that Hamilton had served with Walter on Kitchener's staff in 1900–2.

62 William (Billy) Congreve, *Armageddon Road: a VC's Diary 1914–1916*, ed. Terry Norman (revised edn, Barnsley: Pen & Sword, 2014), p. 6.

63 Congreve, letter to Br John, 13 November 1914, SSJE/6/5/2/2/15, f. 11.

Congreve set the World War in proportion; notwithstanding the scale of suffering and death, he was able to approach it using frameworks and ideas that were familiar.

That war is an evil in itself was clear to Congreve, but he placed that evil in a wider context. War is "probably no worse than other evil processes of civilization, corruption, oppression, mortality, godlessness, competition".[64] In a series of letters which he and Father Hodge wrote in 1916 to a pacifist correspondent, T. V. Morley, Congreve gave a classic exposition of Christian just war theory, drawing on Augustine and Tertullian, whose views Morley had quoted in writing to Hodge (who seems to have asked Congreve for help in replying). While rejecting "'jingo' utterances of any bishop or priest", Congreve was clear about the rightness of the causes for which his family and his nation fought, and that it is licit for a Christian to fight.[65] These were views he had long held in the face of past conflicts. In 1899 he had said that the struggle against the Boers was ultimately to the benefit of the African peoples, because British rule would not tolerate slavery and would impose justice, whereas the Dutch would impose the one and withdraw the other. In this he expressed views held by contemporary politicians.[66] He did not, however, always assume that "England" was the necessary champion of virtue.[67] In 1895 he wrote sharply about gunboat diplomacy:

> I suppose these horrible big guns and rams and torpedoes are to express roughly [i.e. forcibly] great principles. They send a few thousands of us into the air, into eternity—but a great principle has been maintained. Brute sin has to be awed by brute force. The only thing I can see would be if our captains on land and sea could come to recognise that Queen Victoria's service means

---

[64] Copy of correspondence between Fr Congreve and Fr Hodge on war, SSJE/6/5/2/9, f. 4.

[65] Ibid., f. 5.

[66] For instance, Lord Rosebery: see Warren, "Church Militant", p. 66.

[67] Congreve used "England" to mean all the nations of Britain, and the Empire.

Christ's service, and that the country they have to defend is our
City Jerusalem.[68]

In a sermon on the "Peace of Jerusalem" in October 1914, Congreve
developed the idea that a true patriotism leads to a love of God who in
Jesus Christ was himself a patriot for his own land. "Mary's son took the
natural virtue of the patriot, and rooted it in God. Our love of England
is to be rooted in Christ's love of His country, and . . . is to grow up to
new heights, and unknown endeavours . . . capable of strange degrees
of self-sacrifice." In the crisis of the nation, people whose faith has been
lukewarm turn back to him and to love of the Heavenly Jerusalem, which
is the homeland of all nations and peoples. Real patriotism thus implies
love of neighbour:

> It is true we cannot love other Countries just as we love England,
> because our state is still incomplete and imperfect . . . But when
> our love of England, such as it is, grows out of . . . our union with
> God in the heart of Christ, it gradually enables us to feel for other
> countries besides our own. The Catholic Church becomes our
> new country; we have lost nothing of our old love of England, but
> it no longer stops there,—it will always be reaching further, loving
> more . . . Because we are united to Christ we may learn to love
> England with the same generous self-sacrificing love with which
> He loves Jerusalem; Patriotism with us is to grow to something
> greater than it ever reached in pagan ages.[69]

Once again, the principle is that civilization in all respects is enhanced
by Christianity.

This greater patriotism is served by the faithful warrior: "[A] man of
battles and business should have gentle Christian thoughts in his mind

---

[68]   Congreve, Copies of letters to friends and associates, letter to Miss Gore
       Browne, 7 November 1895, SSJE/6/5/2/7. Her brother was a Naval
       Commander.

[69]   Congreve, "The Peace of Jerusalem", p. 220.

all the time."[70] Since war is an evil, properly to profess arms is to combat evil: "A good man does not become a soldier to create war but will seek to give war the best results possible and to conduct war as well as possible: chivalry, thoroughness, consideration, care for men."[71] Congreve saw unselfishness in those who go to serve, which is the beginning of holiness, and the opening of the path to self-sacrifice. Duty thus becomes a path to holiness. Billy Congreve's fiancée, Pamela Maude, thanked "Uncle George" for helping her to understand "the eternal security of duty known, and the love of God" as Billy went back to the Front in November 1915. Billy and Pamela married in April 1916.[72]

Billy became for Congreve what his father Walter had already been, an example of the Christian warrior who "suffers whatever there is to suffer in Christ's service".[73] They lived up to this ideal, Billy writing letters from the front reflecting on his faith, which show Uncle George's teaching took root:

> I could not ever have a swelled head because I know it is not me who does well. I remember in that little book [Brother Lawrence's *The Practice of the Presence of God*] Uncle George gave me, and which I always carry, came the words "I cannot do this unless thou enablest me" and often and often have I said those words to God, knowing their truth, and knowing too that this help *would* come, and it ALWAYS has. So one could never feel *proud* of what one did could one? And there is only the feeling in one of greater and greater joy as each time one feels more secure in God's love.[74]

---

[70] Congreve, letter to Miss Kebbel, 25 August 1910, SSJE/6/5/2/4/19, f. 11.

[71] Copy of correspondence between Fr Congreve and Fr Hodge on war, SSJE/6/5/2/9, f. 5. Note the implied viewpoint is that of an officer.

[72] Congreve, Letters to friends and associates, letter from Pamela Maude, 6 November 1915, SSJE/6/5/2/6, f. 5.

[73] Congreve, Copies of letters to friends and associates, letter to Sr Bertha Mary, 17 January 1900, SSJE/6/5/2/7.

[74] Thornton and Fraser, *The Congreves*, pp. 330–2.

Figure 15: Billy Congreve. Pamela's letters to "Dear Uncle George" show his influence on her even before her marriage to "My dear boy", as Congreve called Billy, who was killed seven weeks after their wedding. Walter and Billy remain one of only three fathers and sons both to be awarded VCs.

Nevertheless, if reward came for duty done, it would be a reward for something essentially unselfish, and so Congreve was able to feel pride in the promotions and awards conferred on his nephews, which included one of the first ever Military Crosses, awarded to Francis in January 1915.[75]

Since duty is a path to holiness, those killed in the course of duty have had the opportunity to "offer their lives to God for duty".[76] During the battles at the beginning of the Boer War, Congreve had commented on the "solid happiness" of the wounded and fallen "because they have the grace to do their duty to God and to their country at great cost, which is worth more than to die on a feather bed".[77] In 1917, he returned to the idea of duty, which:

> brings to the serviceman the call of God. This call of God named duty comes from Calvary: "greater love hath no man than to lay down his life for his friends."[78] The call is not to *mere* loss of life or limb but to SACRIFICE, to CONSECRATION. Willingly to offer all to God is not to be a loser. Nothing is lost that love asks for and is willingly sacrificed to love. Thus the call of duty carries with it to the soldier, as to others, the inspiration of immortal hope.[79]

Since for the Christian, warrior or otherwise, death is not the end, death is not the worst thing that can happen. For Congreve, the fact of the resurrection removed from the World War, unique in the scale of the killing though it was, its particularity. His message to those grieving the

---

[75] *London Gazette*, 1 January 1915—"for distinguished services in time of war". He later won a DSO (Distinguished Service Order).

[76] George Congreve SSJE, "Repentance and Hope: The Third Year of the War and the National Mission", in *The Cowley Evangelist*, September 1916, pp. 193–9.

[77] Congreve, letter to Miss Kebbel, 22 December 1899, SSJE/6/5/2/4/8, f. 34.

[78] John 15:13.

[79] George Congreve SSJE, *The Fourth Year of the War, Hope Through Suffering: A sermon preached in Oxford, on August 5th 1917* (Oxford: Mowbray, 1917), pp. 11–12. Author's emphasis.

casualties of war was what he had taught the lepers on Robben Island. In the face of death, whatever the cause, the Holy Spirit is the Comforter, coming into the world of death to lift souls to God.[80]

The key thing, therefore, is a personal relationship with God; and so Congreve taught that the soldier and the civilian have the same spiritual needs, since both are engaged in spiritual warfare which is more important than the battles of the world.[81] Thus in 1900, as he prepared to see Walter back to the front following his recovery from his wounds "to be shot at again by the Boers", Congreve wrote to a member of the All Saints Community who was mourning the death of a Sister in terms that equate the soldier and the nun:

> It seems to matter less for the moment whether we win or lose in the war, whether our dear people who are fighting ever come back, or are left buried in a trench on the border—the Sister's rest shows the real, the Eternal Issue of things. She has fallen in war: that is an honourable way to slip out of the probation of life—the Religious Life used to be called—"the warfare" —*militia*.[82]

For Congreve, the perspective is so clearly on the soul's relationship with Christ that the distinctions of the places in which that relationship grows are of no consequence. This was illustrated when he received the news of the death of Basil Maturin, who was drowned when the *Lusitania* was torpedoed by a German submarine in the Atlantic in 1915. Like Congreve he was terrified of the sea, but he was seen on the deck helping others into the lifeboats and hearing confessions. His last recorded action was to throw a child into a lifeboat. Congreve was deeply moved, but clear that in the face of death, "Christian character ennobles what is merely horrible."[83]

---

[80]   John 14:16.

[81]   George Congreve SSJE, "The God of All Comfort: a Sermon in the Society's Church on Whitsunday, a day of national sorrow for the loss of Lord Kitchener and his Staff at sea", in *The Cowley Evangelist*, July 1916, pp. 145–52.

[82]   Congreve, Copies of letters to friends and associates, letter to Sr Bertha Mary, 17 January 1900, SSJE/6/5/2/7.

[83]   Congreve, Preface to F. M. M. Comper, *Book of the Craft of Dying*, p. xxix.

While Congreve was too old to fight himself, other members of the Community went to war.[84] Father Waggett was the first to leave, in September 1914, and in France became an unofficial chaplain in General Walter Congreve's camp. Later in the year he joined the Royal Army Chaplains' Department and was three times mentioned in despatches. In March 1917 he was invalided home because of the strain. Lay Brothers enlisted in the ranks, and Brother Walter Frederick was killed on 23 April 1917.[85] Father Conran was also mentioned in despatches and awarded a Military Cross. He had developed a method of evangelization among the soldiers based on a rosary, and like Waggett was discharged by 1917.[86] By then, there was a desperate shortage of chaplains, and following a call from Archbishop Davidson, Father Strong, Father Wigram[87] and three novices were released for active service. Wigram was also awarded a Military Cross, and Brother Michael became very well known for distributing crosses among the soldiers, estimating that he gave away over six thousand, all of which he made himself. Even with all this first-hand experience of the war, it was Congreve who was asked by the community to speak for them. At least four times, he preached major sermons for the Society on the theme, two of which were published in *The Cowley Evangelist* and two as pamphlets.[88]

---

[84]   The information in this paragraph is drawn from Brian Taylor, "The Cowley Fathers and the First World War", in W. J. Sheils (ed.), *Ecclesiastical History Society, Studies in Church History, Vol. 20: The Church and War* (Oxford: Blackwell, for the Ecclesiastical History Society, 1983), pp. 383–9; SSJE/10/6; and Congreve, General correspondence, 13 March 1917. See also James, *Cowley Fathers*, pp. 220–38.

[85]   On the death of Walter Frederick, see James, *Cowley Fathers*, pp. 251–2. The Second Station of the Cross in the Church at Cowley St John is dedicated in his memory.

[86]   On Waggett's hospitalization on returning home and Conran's chaplets, see Congreve, Letters to friends and associates, 13 March 1917, SSJE/6/5/2/6, f. 61.

[87]   On Father Wigram, see <http://www.thepeerage.com/p60922.htm#i609214>.

[88]   Congreve, "The Peace of Jerusalem" (October 1914), "The God of all Comfort" (July 1916), "The Third Year of the War" (September 1916), *The Fourth Year of*

The most powerful of these sermons was preached in August 1916 at
the opening of the third year of the War. The terrible losses of the first
day of the Somme had just been endured, and Congreve's family had lost
Major King in 1915. Then in the fighting around Hooge, on 20 July 1916,
Billy was shot and killed by a sniper:

> My dear boy killed at the front! Everything is happy about him.
> He was—and remains, not only a very gallant gentleman, but
> he possesses the best of all qualities that go to make "the happy
> warrior" the love of God—a habit of prayer.[89]

At the time of Billy's death, he and Pamela had been married seven weeks.
Their honeymoon together had been just ten days.[90] Their daughter was
born in March 1917.

It was thus in raw and deep personal bereavement that Congreve
preached on "The Third Year of the War and the National Mission".[91] In
the pressure of the war, Congreve began, the Christian should "seek rest
in God who made both us and our enemies for Himself". As always when
approaching God, a spirit of repentance is required, "but we do not repent
of the war. We may be beaten, but we will never be traitors to God and to
all honest men by repudiating engagements of honour and friendship to
save our skin." Congreve was clear: conscience "demanded" that Germany

---

the War (August 1917). In addition, "Seek Peace and Ensue It", in *The Cowley
  Evangelist*, August 1914, pp. 169–75.

[89] Congreve, Copies of letters to friends and associates, letter to Frances Comper,
  17 August 1916, SSJE/6/5/2/7. The reference is to Wordsworth's poem, "The
  Character of the Happy Warrior". See also *ibid.*, letter to Frank Thorne, 2
  August 1916.

[90] Pamela had written to "Uncle George" on 30 April to ask him to come to their
  wedding. Congreve, General correspondence, letter from Pamela Maude,
  30 April 1916, SSJE/6/5/2/3, f. 89. On Billy, see Thornton and Fraser, *The
  Congreves*, Pamela's memoir of her first husband and father-in-law. (She
  married Billy's best man after the War.) Also William (Billy) Congreve,
  Armageddon Road.

[91] Congreve, "The Third Year of the War".

be stopped from "devouring Belgium, France, Servia, and a few other countries". Because the pursuit of the war was morally right, it was therefore Godly, and "the light of grace shines on the decision". Although at the beginning the duty had simply been to oppose aggression, as time had gone on a wider significance had been revealed: "we are fighting a philosophy in Germany which says that the only virtue is strength. Thus the Christian ideal of self-control, loyalty to Christ, mercy, justice, truth is dismissed forever. This is the religion of pure selfishness glorified." As a result, "we know now without any possible doubt that this is a holy war . . . Not let merely for our lives, but to save all that remains of Christian civilisation and goodness in the world from perishing."

The greatness of the sermon lies in the fact that Congreve then turns to apply these concerns also to England. The very same selfishness is evident also among his own people. England:

> needs repentance to be worthy to serve Christ and make the sacrifice needed. Repentance from national social sins: slums; criminal classes; social isolation of the rich and the poor; the mass of the neglected; open and secret moral corruption; exclusion of religion from school; feebleness of mission; divisions of Christendom.

The only way to deal with the sins, and therefore to rise to the self-sacrifice needed to pursue the war properly, is "national repentance served by private contrition". Congreve went on, "except by that link with God that restores our spiritual life and energy—our own conversion—we cannot reach to help any other souls."

Congreve saw that if the war is against an anti-Christian evil, then repentance is required at home: "our repentance will show which side we have chosen". He therefore called his hearers to pray, reminding them that prayer is always an exercise of hope. Congreve concluded movingly by quoting from a letter that a young Billy had sent him when he was in South Africa. It thanked him for a little prayer he had sent for the boy to say for his father. "It is difficult to link such a man to the child writing that letter of long ago, but the link is his prayer." Just a few days before his death Billy had written from the front to say that "prayer is our only help:

we feel always that we are close to God, and that He will help us to keep close to Him, and not be lonely". Congreve concluded: "The child's prayer of 16 years before had grown by now into the good soldier's prayer, and the Christian husband's prayer with power now to keep them together and all the time 'close to God.'"[92]

Congreve had written perceptively at the conclusion of the Boer War about the need to secure the victory over the "the Dutchman's principle of ruling the native races by closing to them the door of Christian civilisation".[93] He was afraid that his own people would close that door. As the World War wore on, he was concerned in similar ways. He was so clear in his support for the War and so firm in his view that German aggression needed to be countered that the passages in his sermons which rejected wholesale condemnation of the German people did not attract the anger directed, for instance, at Lyttelton following a sermon at St Margaret's Westminster in 1916.[94] In that year Congreve discussed with the Principal of Pusey House, Darwell Stone, an article from an American newspaper reprinted in the *Morning Post*, which traced the growth in England of hatred for the Germans. Congreve agreed with Stone that there was "enough of a real spirit of hate to be alarming".[95] He prayed that the outcome of the War should indeed lead to a better world, and looked forward presciently to the social changes which would accompany peace.

On 5 August 1917 Congreve preached on the "Fourth Year of the War: Hope Through Suffering": "The evils fought against in international relations touch also most deeply the very roots of our own personal and social life at home, and that we can never go back to tolerate evils amongst ourselves that we scarcely noticed before."[96] Congreve recognized that

---

[92]   Congreve, "The Third Year of the War", pp. 12–13.

[93]   Report on St Philip's Mission, p. 20.

[94]   "In 1914 how else but armed resistance to hold back the flood of German invasion? . . . Am I to look on if a man is murdering children or ill treating women before my eyes?" Copy of correspondence between Fr Congreve and Fr Hodge on war, SSJE/6/5/2/9, f. 4.

[95]   Letters to friends and associates, letter to Darwell Stone, 23 September 1916, SSJE/6/5/2/6, f. 7. The newspaper clipping is *ibid.*, f. 40.

[96]   Congreve, *Fourth Year of the War*, p. 10.

there was great work to come for the Church once the war was over: "The upheaval of the world war will leave great questions for the English Church and our society will have to show some lead to the many who look to us for some direction to guide them among various movements that unsettled times give rise to."[97] But he knew it would be for others to take up that work; for Congreve was now old, and his own sacrifice was soon to be complete.

---

[97]   Congreve, General correspondence, letter to Fr Bull, 5 April 1916, SSJE/6/5/2/3, f. 51.

Figure 16: Nofamile Noholoza, the old African
communicant, "radiant within" despite "a life as low
in its circumstances as you might well find".

CHAPTER 9

Growing Old by Leaps and Bounds

Nofamile Noholoza was an impoverished, "entirely uneducated", elderly African Christian who lived in a hut outside Cape Town. Nofamile's vigorous faith and tenacious commitment to Christ was—to the Cowley Fathers who met him—a powerful example of the difference made by Christ. George Congreve found in him an example of how to live in old age so as to die well. Congreve taught that Christian old age and its special circumstances are part of the joyful gift of life. Life is sanctified because, in Christ's incarnation, divinity has been united with our humanity so that all aspects of human life are transformed and become a gift by which we may come to God. Of the destitute, sick and dying Nofamile he wrote:

> Here is a life as low in its circumstances as you could well find, and here is the mystery which changes all things, the Christ by the Word and Sacraments coming to the man as he goes through his vale of tears, and leaving him radiant within, while the external gloom and sorrow remain. Here is joy in the Lord in a life emptied of every other element of joy—joy associated with humblest penitence, with liberality abounding out of deep poverty, with a habit of frequent communion with God alone on the mountain and in the Sacrament, and with manners cheerful, gracious and simple: joy in such companionship attests the mystery of the Incarnation—Christ coming into the individual soul that welcomes Him, and changing it into His own likeness. The old Kafir communicant singing in his solitude through wintry weather the song of the Child without sin born to save, may well awaken us to welcome Him better who once came to His own and His own received Him not. But the welcome of a

great joy in the Lord comes only from hearts established in great
love and great penitence.[1]

Congreve wrote about age itself, not how to fend off or mitigate ageing
such that middle age is simply extended and the period of decline is
minimized. He felt old from a young age, having been born into a world
of shorter life expectancy than the one in which he aged; but that did
not mean that he felt decrepit. In 1903 he wrote to Miss Kebbel, "an old
friend—we were curates together—writes 'one grows old—at least an
Irishman does—by leaps and bounds.'"[2]

From the time of his return to Oxford in 1909, when he was himself in
his late seventies, Congreve was given the duty of helping with the care of
the aged Father Benson and saw at first-hand how what he described as
the "solitude of age" can open paths to a deeper communion with God.
In Benson, Congreve saw an example of ageing he formulated in terms
of a renewal of childhood. Himself full of many memories, Congreve
offered ways in which memory may become the means of joyful
thanksgiving rather than a cause of sorrowful nostalgia. He taught that
age gives a person both opportunity and training to develop graciousness
and hopefulness as tools to combat the depression and fear which can
overtake those facing the end of life. Congreve did not neglect death
itself, both the process of dying and its meaning. His own death when it
came, exemplified his teaching.

Nofamile was the example of one whose utter destitution was turned to
riches by the living presence of Christ in his life. In beginning to think
about old age and death, Congreve began with the joy of earthly life.
Life is joyful because of the incarnation. Because Christ has shared it,
human life is "no longer that pathetic drama of infancy, growth, and

---

[1]   Congreve, *Treasures of Hope*, pp. 94–7, and Congreve, letters to Miss Kebbel,
5 January 1904, SSJE/6/5/2/4/13, f. 6 (a photograph of Nofamile) and 8 March
1904, SSJE/6/5/2/4/13, f. 10, in which Congreve reports that he has told the
story of Nofamile's "radiant love" to "the white people here who are always
asking if any good can come out of Native Africa".

[2]   Congreve, letter to Miss Kebbel, 8 July 1903, SSJE/6/5/2/4/12, f. 26.

decrepitude, the contemplation of which weaned Gautama [Buddha] for ever from all love of it", but is "the merciful opportunity of ever-deepening penitence and renewal, the splendid opportunity of a growing fellowship with Christ in doing the works of Christ".[3] The extension of life, even in suffering, is a blessing because it increases the opportunity:

> Growing old is not decay—mere failure of life. It is life prolonged for the highest purpose; the object of growing old is to grow in love—to learn at last to exercise that gift of God's love shed abroad in the hearts[4] of members of Christ by the Holy Ghost—a gift which in our youth perhaps we had hardly discovered. Our interest in one another, young or old, is that gift of God that is in each of us, that new life that does not grow old.[5]

Suffering in old age was for Congreve part of the gift, be it the physical suffering of sickness and frailty, loneliness as a result both of the death of contemporaries and inability to communicate, or mental anguish from fear or depression at the loss of previous strength and authority.

At the end of her life he talked with Mother Harriet, the foundress of the Clewer Community, who told him that old age had stripped from her the authority she had had in her community, the activity which she had relished and sought all her life, and everything which had made "her long life exceptionally successful". It was not that these things were not painful for her, but that the emptiness and sense of forsaking that, Congreve said, "others would have regarded as a final catastrophe, the failure of a whole life's anticipations", she had accepted, "I do not say with edifying resignation, but with a face radiant with joy". She said, "I think when you have lost everything you have in the world as I have, such a wonderful new life comes into you."[6] "Edifying resignation" would be a pagan response, that of the Stoic. By contrast, for the Christian Christ has

---

[3] Congreve, *Treasures of Hope*, p. 93.

[4] Romans 5:5.

[5] Congreve, *Treasures of Hope*, p. 102.

[6] Congreve, *Treasures of Hope*, pp. 149–50; see also Congreve, *Interior Life*, p. ix.

brought an assurance of a position in God where "isolation, loneliness, uselessness, powerlessness disappear", therefore:

> It is no longer the question how to endure a lonely, withered, and useless life without cowardly complaining; in Christ [the Christian] has come already to the City of the living God, the heavenly Jerusalem, to innumerable hosts of angels, to the festive assembly of the first-born enrolled in heaven.
>
> In Christ he has reached that centre, which holds the whole truth about everything, and the truth sets him free.[7]

Mother Harriet and Father Benson had in common that they had given up the Rule of their communities. Their characters were different. In 1904 Benson, now eighty-one and himself newly called back to Cowley from America, had welcomed Congreve's return from Cape Town as "a delight to many, but especially to me. I had looked forward to our next meeting in another world. However there are so many changes in invalid life that it seems as if even Cowley is another world."[8] Although describing himself as an invalid, it seemed at first as if the Father Founder would remain as vigorous as ever. Well into his eighties he would slip out and go to London to serve at St Peter's London Docks, in what was then one of the roughest areas of the capital.[9] He approached the onset of frailty with his wonted toughness. At eighty-five, he fell and dislocated his shoulder, but nevertheless went to church and Compline in the chapel, saying nothing until others noticed his pain. It was only when he understood he could not remove his surplice (no one knew how he had managed to get it on) that he allowed Congreve, now back in Oxford and "in charge" of looking after him, to help him and summon a doctor.[10]

---

[7]   Congreve, *Treasures of Hope*, pp. 135–6; cf. Hebrews 12:22–23, John 8:32.

[8]   Benson, Correspondence with Fr Congreve, September 1903, SSJE/6/1/2/21, f. 14.

[9]   Congreve, letter to Br John, 14 August 1908, SSJE/6/5/2/2/9, f. 15.

[10] Congreve, letter to Br John, 15 January 1909, SSJE/6/5/2/2/10, f. 3; Woodgate, *Father Benson*, pp. 174–5.

Benson's hearing began to fail, as did his sight, despite two successful cataract operations.[11] Congreve noted, "[I]t is very serious to think what a life that implies for him in our regime which has so much silence, and in which the social and conversible element is limited."[12] One of Benson's last outings, in 1913, was to vote in the Oxford University Convocation against what he considered the dangerous innovation of opening theology degrees to men of all religions and no religion. By then he was more a link with the past of Pusey and Newman than a living power: "Yesterday Convocation was a notable gathering. Father Benson in his curule chair made the historical highlight in the scene."[13] He was now struggling to get to the church,[14] and largely confined to his chair, the library, and his cell where Congreve would say Compline with him each evening. In the afternoons, Congreve went to the library to read to Benson and say Evensong with him. This could be an uncomfortable duty as the Father Founder would sit very close to the fire even in the hottest weather.[15] As infirmity constrained Benson more and more, Congreve discerned in him an inner growth and expansion. Congreve found in this a model for those who age:

---

[11]   Congreve, letter to Br John, 28 January 1910, SSJE/6/5/2/2/11, f. 3. The operation was at the end of 1909.

[12]   Congreve, letter to Br John, Palm Sunday 1909, SSJE/6/5/2/2/10, f. 14.

[13]   Congreve, letter to Br John, 9 May 1913, SSJE/6/5/2/2/14, f. 8; Congreve was away from Oxford at a "Poona Meeting" in London. A curule chair has an 'X' shaped frame forming the legs and arms, and if the brace which forms the back is removed, it can fold. Pictures of Fr Benson in old age show him in an upright arm chair or a Glastonbury Chair; since the curule was originally specifically the throne of the Roman magistrate, Congreve's remark might have referred more to Benson's continuing authority than the design of his seat. Later Benson's chair became Congreve's—see below p. XXX.

[14]   Congreve, letter to Br John, Palm Sunday 1909, SSJE/6/5/2/2/10, f. 14.

[15]   Congreve, letter to Br John, 12 July 1912, SSJE/6/5/2/2/13, f. 19. See also Woodgate, *Father Benson*, p. 171; "Fr Benson sits by the fire while we are all stewing in a heatwave."

> One has heard of old people dying because they came to feel
> their work was done; they had nothing left to live for. There was
> nothing like that for the old Father. Deaf, blind, unable to move,
> left alone,—he was as much *alive* as ever, that as God no longer
> wanted him to be governing and managing and working, his life
> [was] set more freely than ever, and more joyfully towards God.[16]

It was not that Benson's interest in the world did not remain keen. Despite
Congreve's preference for poetry,[17] Benson wanted news of the latest
scientific discoveries and current affairs,[18] although, said Congreve:

> [H]e never now expresses the strong uncompromising views that
> he used to settle affairs with—he listens with interest and good
> humour but does not comment; as if his part of life was written
> on a page that is turned over, and the affairs of today been a fresh
> page of which he has no part.[19]

Benson, whose sermons and meditations were always long, had taught
silence, and now—in old age—lived it. Benson had said that "Silence
is the complement of praise; the silence of Religious is never mere
repression of sound. It is like the pause in music, out of which the music
springs new-born."[20] In a meditation on St John, Congreve might have
been describing Benson:

---

[16]   Congreve, letter to "N" (Selina Congreve), 1 August 1915, SSJE/6/5/2/5, f.
49. Emphasis in the original.

[17]   Woodgate, *Father Congreve*, p. 70.

[18]   "The Father is very much interested in the mystery of the rays that see through
the wall of flesh and exhibit the secrets of bones." Congreve, letter to Br John,
15 January 1909, SSJE/6/5/2/2/10, f. 4. Again, "He is keenly interested in the
elections, and in the new comet and in the sad floods in Paris." Congreve,
letter to Br John, 28 January 1910, SSJE/6/5/2/2/11, f. 4.

[19]   Congreve, letter to Br John, 14 February 1913, SSJE/6/5/2/2/14, f. 4.

[20]   Congreve, *Treasures of Hope*, p. 194.

> Many words seemed necessary in youth in order to bear witness
> to the truth; now in old age life seems to express better without
> words. The old Christian is doing the truth of which he could
> in youth talk eagerly, which now lies appropriated and secure,
> affirmed by the faithful tenor of a life of few words.[21]

Silence is a gift: We should not, taught Congreve, resent the silence of
old age. Busy Christians have "felt sometimes that our salvation almost
depended on our getting away now and then in Retreat from the strife
of tongues . . . [a]nd now God is rewarding faithful activity by calling the
soul on to Himself in quietness."[22] Moreover, the silence of old age brings
the opportunity for a change in the quality of conversation, imposed as
the old person is ignored, or—not hearing—is unable to join in with easy
conversation which can be a mask for a failure of relationships:

> The talk of the world is generally the mutual exchange of ideas,
> the mind's market-wares, often trivial things, between persons
> separated in heart. The speaker brings forth in words whatever
> subject happens to turn up on the surface of life, and contrives
> to pass the time, but leaves the treasure of the heart absolutely
> hidden. The hearer takes what is offered with courtesy, and pays
> back in words of no greater consequence, and so time is passed,
> but neither gets a glimpse into the heart of the other. They talk
> in order to hide the habitual and infinite separation that divides
> them. Silence for them means an awkward confession of mutual
> incapacity of being interested in each other.[23]

In age, the difficulty of conversation allows for an increased quality both
of words and silence.

While the silence imposed by age can expand true conversation,
Congreve noted that pain drives people in on themselves. The aged
sufferer:

---

[21]   Ibid., p. 198.

[22]   Ibid., p. 187.

[23]   Ibid., p. 192.

The late Rev. Father Congreve, S.S.J.E., Cowley

Figure 17: Congreve in extreme old age. Sending a picture of himself
to his sister, Congreve remarked that a photograph is "a shade of
a shade"; but it conveys something of his childlikeness in old age.

stretches out desperate hands to clutch some support, and finds its absolute isolation. The people and circumstances of our ordinary social and family fellowship are present as usual, or within reach, but the soul finds to its despair that its consciousness of suffering is incommunicable. It shuts the soul up within itself, out of reach of the cheer of our ordinary social surroundings; there is the soul alone with its enemy, the pain.[24]

The only release from the intolerable burden of solitary pain is in "the Fellowship of the sufferings of Christ".[25] With Christ who suffered for us, and who is united with the Father, the Christian may pray "Thy will be done" and the soul finds itself no longer alone with its pain. "Love, the deliverer, has appeared, and has opened a door for [the soul] into the secret place of the Most High."[26] Pain thus becomes not a route into the self and solitude, but a way of sharing Christ's selflessness in his Passion:

> The suffering was the fire perfectly annealing the Lord's Humanity in the fellowship of Divine love, through the supreme experience of difficulty in the sacrifice of self-forsaking. His human Soul, which had the natural capacity of growth by experience, found its complete union with the will of the Father in its last act of abandonment, in which He took into His own heart, besides the horror of all our sins, all the suffering of all battle-fields, all broken hearts, all spiritual despairs and desolations.[27]
>
> And so my pain was the key that opened for me the door of my prison—my solitude, and admitted me into the immensity of a new world—the sympathy of Christ, Who in His Passion chose

---

[24]   Ibid., p. 126.

[25]   Cf. Philippians 3:10; 1 Peter 4:13.

[26]   Congreve, *Treasures of Hope*, p. 127. Cf. Psalm 91:1.

[27]   Here Congreve echoes John Henry Newman, *Discourses Addressed to Mixed Congregations* (Birmingham: Birmingham Oratory, 1849), Discourse XVI, "The Mental Sufferings of our Lord in His Passion".

to suffer the pain of every human soul, because on the Cross He
took that soul and all its sin and suffering into His heart.[28]

Pain thus becomes a means of union with Christ, and in Him with the
Father,[29]and the aged Christian may "[r]ejoice in as much as ye are
partakers of Christ's sufferings".[30]

This means that the small "pinpricks" of life can become precious as
opportunities to suffer some little with Christ.[31] Moreover, the direction
of life itself towards death is a cause not of fear but of joy:

> Life becomes more serious and mysterious and sorrowful every
> year . . . We take steps nearer the edge of time . . . But as we get
> by experience closer to the sorrowful mysteries, we are also to be
> getting close to the joyful mysteries . . . sorrow is always turning
> to joy because of His triumph over evil . . . Here might be an open
> road for us as we grow old, leading us unto the many unknown
> countries of blessing.[32]

Writing to Brother John, Congreve expanded on the theme.
Fundamentally, the source of joy in old age is participation in Christ, for
what participates in eternity is assimilated to the incorruptible, and old
age is a renewed—or rather re-experienced—childhood. The Christian
experiences a "lifelong springtime because the truth that is in us cannot
be touched by old age". Congreve went on:

> I do not know of any living illustration of this victory over age and
> infirmity so exhilarating as Father Benson who still shuffles into
> Chapel and back. This is no exterior conquest of pain or holding

---

28   Congreve, *Treasures of Hope,* pp. 127–8.

29   Congreve quotes John 14:23; 17:21.

30   Congreve, *Treasures of Hope,* p. 128; 1 Peter 4:13.

31   Congreve, letter to Br John, 19 February 1909, SSJE/6/5/2/2/10, f. 10. For a
     comparison of Congreve with St Thérèse of Lisieux in this line of thought,
     see Miller, *Sorrow of Nature,* pp. 1–9.

32   Congreve, letter to Miss Kebbel, 11 March 1903, SSJE/6/5/2/4/12, f. 7.

off of age, but a reassertion in the midst of the trials of age of the
joy of knowing God and growing in him.[33]

Congreve, who was often described as being himself "boyish" in old age,
even saw this renewal of childhood as applying to society, and it was
for him an antidote to the despair about the direction of the world felt
by so many in old age: "The decay of reverence is in every age a great
anxiety—but with the eternal decay I suspect there is in Christendom
an eternal rejuvenescence, renewing of what had been lost."[34] When
Congreve himself was ill in Holy Week 1909, Benson came to visit him,
and Congreve remarked to Brother John that he was "a shadow as far as
bodily presence goes—but in spirit, in will, affection and minds—still
strong and younger than any of us".[35]

In the same letter, Congreve told John that his life-long friend Richard
Assheton was "dying at his sister's house in Folkestone, and I am not
well enough to go to him". Congreve was outliving many who had been
close to him and knew the aspect of solitude in old age which is repeated
bereavement. In 1890, he had suffered a major break with his past with
the death of Mrs Barton, who had given such a refuge at Caldy in his years
at Frankby, and where he had often stayed during his religious life.[36] There
was perhaps a hint that Benson was mellowing. In 1910, when *Christian
Progress* was printed, Congreve included his sermon on the occasion of
the dedication of two lamps in memory of Mrs Barton for the Cowley
Mission House Chapel. He read this "Memory of Caldy Manor" to Father
Benson, and wrote afterwards to Brother John that he was "surprised
to find it was a real pleasure to him—we were so wholesomely trained

---

33   Congreve, letter to Br John, 14 August 1890, SSJE/6/5/2/2/9, f. 15.

34   Congreve, letter to "N" (Selina Congreve), 9 September 1902, SSJE/6/5/2/5,
      f. 15.

35   Congreve, letter to Br John, Palm Sunday 1909, SSJE/6/5/2/2/10, f. 12;
      Congreve, letter to Miss Kebbel, 18 May 1909, SSJE/6/5/2/4/18, f. 18,
      enclosing a copy of Assheton's funeral service paper.

36   "The phrase 'Mrs Barton's Death', while it brings tears to my eyes, makes me
      laugh, it is so manifestly untrue." Copies of letters to friends and associates:
      letter to Miss Sharman, 28 January 1890, SSJE/6/5/2/7.

to have our heads snapped off perpetually that it is an astonishment to find that the dear old Founder can be pleased with any little thing his ignoramuses can do—he could be tender and generous at need, but tenderness and gentleness have grown in him".[37]

There were other forms of bereavement. While he was still in South Africa the last of his brothers died, and Burton Hall—his family's main home in England—was sold. He was honest enough to note in himself "the oddest feeling . . . It leaves a vacancy in one's feeling of one's place in the world, and illustrates splendidly . . . the difference between real and unreal things." Benson wrote to him "all the associations of Earth pass away for those some who are left longer." [38] When just home from South Africa Congreve's attention had been arrested, while visiting the chapel at Eton, by the sight of a new memorial to the headmaster of his time.[39] Sister Selina died before he did,[40] and the death of Father Page on 25 October 1912 prompted a reflection on mortality, when he wrote to Brother John:

> [W]e all have our warnings that our opportunities are passing—
> my beautiful razor which I think you found for me at Cape
> Town its handle is broken and the blade is wearing out—and I
> am myself so dilapidated that I do not think I am worth keeping
> in repair.[41]

---

[37] Congreve, *Christian Progress*, pp. 14–23. Congreve, letter to Br John, undated, early 1908, SSJE/6/5/2/2/10, f. 4.

[38] Benson, Correspondence from Cowley, 9 January 1902, SSJE/6/1/2/9/4; Congreve, Copies of letters to friends and associates, letter to "N" (Selina Congreve), February 1903, SSJE/6/5/2/7. See also Congreve, letter to Miss Kebbel, 8 January 1902, SSJE/6/5/2/4/11, f. 1.

[39] Congreve, letter to Br John, 17 November 1905, SSJE/6/5/2/2/6, f. 18. (The journey from Westminster in a motorcar took an hour and a half because of traffic.)

[40] Woodgate, *Father Congreve*, p. 89.

[41] Congreve, letter to Br John, 25 October 1912, SSJE/6/5/2/2/13, f. 25.

Benson died in January 1915, and Maturin went down with the *Lusitania* just a few weeks later. Congreve was entering a stage in life in which old friends were "now nearly all gone".[42]

In common with many old people, his mind turned to the past, but not to nostalgia—rather a positive use of memory as a recollection of the "delight" which God has given, which rejuvenates and is an aspect of the gift of childhood in age:

> We can still recall for our delight . . . something of the mystery of the world as we looked upon it on first arriving here. To do so sets us back where we were when we first found ourselves in this world, the youngest in a Christian family, and that is very near to God . . . There is always the heart of the boy in the old man, if he will only remember; for there is in him always recoverable the heart of the child of God, and [the] inheritor of the Kingdom of Heaven.[43]

In 1912 he was sent a packet of his correspondence with Richard Assheton, and a lifetime of memories was awakened: "I described the racket in my quiet vicarage, with two delightful children staying with me—little Walter and little Geoffrey his youngest brother who died—playing coach horses in my drawing room."[44] Far from being a cause for morbid sadness, these messages from the past stirred thanksgiving and remembrance of the gifts of God given over many years. In one of his South African sermons, he had noted "the contrast of Rousseau who sees a plant not noted for 30 years and is struck by a pang of regret for lost time"; and a soldier "sorrowing at Cape Town for the people left behind who sees on the mountain a glade of green and flame coloured flowers that speaks to him of the love of God".[45] The mistake of nostalgia is to separate a sad

---

[42]   Congreve, letter to "N" (Selina Congreve), 20 May 1913, SSJE/6/5/2/5, f. 17.

[43]   Congreve, *Treasures of Hope*, p. 155; cf. Romans 8:17.

[44]   Congreve, letter to Br John, 13 December 1912, SSJE/6/5/2/2/13, f. 28.

[45]   Three Addresses on the Spiritual Life, St Faith's Chapel, Lent 1905, SSJE/6/5/3/11; Address 3, "Progress by Conflict".

present from happiness in the past. Whether it be a soul before or after conversion or the memories of an old Christian:

> Christ when He calls us does not break our life in two, and leave
> the earlier part behind, thrown away—but calls us on up to better
> things, bringing on with us all our past memories, and all we tried
> to do right—raising it to what is better—His call is like the call of
> spring to a tree that is leafless and dead in winter, it puts life into
> all there is in the tree—awakes it all—rouses the old root and stem
> and branch—new energies—fruitfulness—joy.[46]

Memory of the past had the capacity to rejuvenate in the present:

> [T]he joy of one's childhood has its sparkle still down at the
> bottom of one's heart quite out of sight of men. And the spring
> (it seems a wonderful personal favour that one may see it once
> more) touches me almost more tenderly and joyfully than ever.[47]

Congreve himself had felt old almost from his entrance to Cowley.[48] He had been brought up in a world in which sixty was a good age, and wrote even at the beginning of the twentieth century about an "average lifetime" of thirty-five years.[49] His were the usual experiences of ageing, ("It is a curious experience to find that one does not pick up as easily at 50 as at 30"),[50] but his asthma and general physical weakness dogged him. He was often unable to sleep[51] and suffered from "bad heads" and gout. In 1899 he told Sister Isolda, his niece in the All Saints Community, that he had been knocked over in the street, "not, as you heard, by a Hansom Cab, but

---

46   Congreve, South African Sermons, SSJE/6/5/3/16, f. 23.

47   Congreve, Letters to friends and associates, 19 March 1912, SSJE/6/5/2/6, f. 50.

48   Woodgate, *Father Congreve*, p. 23.

49   Congreve, *Treasures of Hope*, p. 188.

50   Congreve, Correspondence with Fr Benson, April 1886, SSJE/6/5/2/1.

51   A fact he mentions in passing in many letters written in the night when sleep would not come.

by a vulgar grocer's van". Congreve broke his leg: it mended well enough, and "after a fortnight limping with a stick I am walking better than ever before".[52] He was ill in Lent 1908, again in 1909, and in 1911 had bad rheumatism; in 1915 he had a "big operation" followed by eight weeks in hospital, some shorter stays and two further "smaller operations". He contracted shingles in 1917.[53]

All his life Congreve faced a mental struggle with low moods. "It is not *years* that make souls grow old, but the having nothing to love, nothing to hope."[54] Whether or not he was in fact what would now be recognized as depressed, he did not recognize his moods to be in any sense an illness, responding entirely in terms of looking away from the mortal and the decaying to God.[55] So he wrote in a private letter, "I often feel the depression and sometimes the irritation that the burden of years suggests, and which one's loyalty rejects quickly."[56] More publicly, he taught in his published writing that:

> ... morbidness, despondency, given way to, means, "I believe in nothing but my deadness, and decay,—myself, and the things around me that are seen, that are temporal,—that is all I have

---

[52] Congreve, Copies of letters to friends and associates, letter to Sr Isolda, 26 January 1899, SSJE/6/5/2/7. See also Waggett, Correspondence with Fr Page, 2 January 1899, SSJE/6/16/1/1, f. 61. "I am delighted to hear Fr Congreve's accident was not more serious."

[53] Congreve, Copies of letters to friends and associates, letters to Frances Comper, August 1914 and 15 August 1916, SSJE/6/5/2/7. Congreve, General correspondence, 12 October 1911, SSJE/6/5/2/3, f. 65 (rheumatism); 13 July 1915, SSJE/6/5/2/3, f. 59 (operations); 12 October 1917, SSJE/6/5/2/3, f. 63 (shingles).

[54] Congreve, *Christian Life*, p. 164. Emphasis in the original.

[55] Woodgate believes Congreve to have been depressed (*Father Congreve*, p. 23). His letters and papers show him grappling with feelings of sadness and being "low". His response was to call himself to acts of will, which would be appropriate as a response to general moods but not to clinical depression. It is, of course, impossible to know.

[56] Congreve, General correspondence, 12 October 1911, SSJE/6/5/2/3, f. 67.

to live for or be interested in, and I see death through all these things." But we will remember that Jesus Christ is the death of despondency and weariness; He brings immortality to light, because he is the Life.[57]

Part of the cause of depression of mood in old age was the sense of "youth unfulfilled".[58] Congreve's answer to this was to note that "it does not matter very much whether [our fortunes and destinies on this planet] be high or low. They will never be high enough to content the smallest mind among us, for the smallest mind is made in the image of the Infinite. And if they be very poor and low, they can hardly be poorer or lower than the cave of Bethlehem . . . "[59] Congreve had not been the only postulant to Cowley who could not go to the missions, and Benson's own hopes had been dashed by the request of Bishop Samuel Wilberforce for him to stay in Oxford. The Founder taught that sickness is one of:

> God's greatest gifts, and those who are kept back by some bodily infirmity have a very special mission of grace committed to them by Almighty God . . . it is better to be professed by God in a weakness that we cannot shake off, than to be professed by our own lips in a life that is always liable to be damaged by the vacillation of human will. How great is the blessing of being in a state of life which we have not chosen.[60]

Now, after nearly half a century of a life he had not chosen, but through which great blessings had come, Congreve prepared to "give an account of his stewardship"[61] and reflected on what use an old person can be. The fulfilment of any soul, young or old, is ultimately the same:

---

[57]   Congreve, *Christian Life*, pp. 165–6; cf. 2 Timothy 1:10.

[58]   Woodgate, *Father Congreve*, p. 23.

[59]   Congreve, *Christian Life*, p. 167.

[60]   Richard Meux Benson SSJE, Unpublished correspondence, letter to Br Gardner, 17 February 1877, SSJE/6/1/2/7/9.

[61]   Congreve, letter to Br John, 20 September 1912, SSJE/6/5/2/2/13, f. 22. "This is the 39th anniversary of being received at Cowley—and I shall have been

The real value of [a Christian's] active service in the day of his strength was the love with which it was done and lifted up to God in sacrifice. And now that God bids him put all his work aside, He tests His disciple to prove whether in his activity he sought himself, or God only. If he has worked hard purely for the love of God, he will welcome God's will in his helplessness, as joyfully as before he welcomed it in his power to work. Love kept him joyfully and vigorously at work then, and now love, that grows always more brave, sends him joyful and contented into silence and vacancy, if that is the discipline by which God wills that love is to ripen and be perfected.[62]

More than acceptance in love, the aged bring a new and special blessing: "They can no longer work for us, but in their infirmity they give themselves more simply than ever to God, and we find that in consequence their power to help and bless us has advanced through that which threatened to end it."[63] This is seldom understood:

There is hardly anyone who understands old age. People are very kind and deferential, and one finds oneself put, so to speak, on the chimneypiece as a bit of an old china to be treated with respect, dusted occasionally with care and replaced, and left there—a china ornament on the chimneypiece has some relation to life that goes on in the house, but only a symbolic and distant one . . .

To be treated this way is depressing, but only:

if one gives way to thinking of oneself. But grace keeps old age alive and fresh with thoughts of others, with affection for the young, with tender and humorous remembrances of dear people who are with Christ, and with the eternal youth of love to God

---

over 52 years in the priesthood. And soon it will be time to give an account of my stewardship."

[62]   Congreve, *Treasures of Hope*, p. 12.

[63]   Ibid., pp. 12–13.

and man for God's sake. Not an old chimneypiece ornament but
a tree planted by the river of water, that brings forth his fruit in
due season; his heart also shall not wither[64]... Nature tends away
from other people so no one understands, but new nature comes
out into the open, and takes interest in other people's lives and has
not time to dwell on self... and in increasing solitude is always
finding ways open to God and passing on through the gates of
the City—Jerusalem which is above.[65]

There are practical challenges to growing old, and Congreve faced them
on various levels. "The telephone is musical again, and I am learning
to take courage and converse with it."[66] His attitude was a mixture of
firmness and practicality. As Miss Kebbel became less able to get about,
he exhorted her to continue to try to get to church. "Submit to every
physical disability with the greatest goodwill, but cheerfully decline to
submit to limitations created by mere indisposition of mind or will."[67]
Congreve was clear that God has given us medicine, and had no time for
wallowing in sickness, encouraging his readers to use what remedies are
within reach, but to deal with infirmities "as master, not as their miserable
drudge".[68] Like many old people he would often doze off (though he had
always thought that meditation is better made in the morning than in
the evening), and reassured one correspondent who was worried about
snoozing through her prayer time, "I am sure the Eternal Love is not on
the watch to set down in the Book of Doom our failures and dullness
through infirmity."[69] His hearing and sight began to fail. "I no longer hear
the canticle of the creatures... And now in the stillness I become aware

[64] Cf. Psalm 1:3; Jeremiah 17:8.
[65] Congreve, letter to Miss Kebbel, 18 July 1904, SSJE/6/5/2/4/13, f. 44. This
is, in fact, a letter to "Nina and Auntie" and probably should be archived at
SSJE/6/5/2/5.
[66] Congreve, letter to Br John, 19 April 1904, SSJE/6/5/2/2/5, f. 2.
[67] Congreve, letter to Miss Kebbel, 14 April 1906, SSJE/6/5/2/4/12, f. 33.
[68] Congreve, *Treasures of Hope*, pp. 135–6.
[69] Longridge (ed.), *Spiritual Letters of Fr Congreve*, p. 69.

of One Who lures me into the wilderness in order that He Himself may speak to my heart."[70]

Congreve took all this as a further stage in the call of God to life, rather than as frustration to be avoided or mitigated. He described the process as "our last spiritual Retreat":[71]

> Insensibly the years are leading us out of the conflicting interests, claims, appeals, eagernesses of life, the strife of tongues, into a quiet world of solitude and silence. Being no longer able to take our part in the general struggle of life in the world, the world leaves us alone. Too infirm perhaps to share in the exercises of a spiritual Retreat, God calls us aside that we may attend to Him in a Retreat in which He Himself is the Conductor.[72]

Not merely imposed silence, but other aspects of ageing offer opportunity to advance in the things of God:

> The quietness and retirement of age offers us the occasion to reach a higher kind of prayer than we could learn in the days of our activity, the prayer of absolute and affectionate self-surrender to God. The mortifications of bodily infirmity cordially accepted set the soul free to die to earthly attachments, to find wings, to aspire and to advance in contemplation.[73]

With this attitude the body itself—for all its infirmity and pain—ceases to be in any sense an enemy or prison for the soul. Not for Congreve any sense of Platonic dualism, seeing the mind or soul as a prisoner of the body, even in the face of significant disability. Mortification of the body is a stage in the process which leads to its glorification. "I am glad we are not obliged to speak of 'our vile bodies', but our 'bodies of humiliation' which

---

[70] Congreve, *Treasures of Hope*, p. 190.

[71] Ibid., p. 168. "The Last Spiritual Retreat—Silence" is also the title of Chapter XXIV, pp. 187–199.

[72] Ibid., p. 189.

[73] Ibid., p. 168.

is kinder and truer."[74] Humiliation for Congreve is a positive beginning in a path that leads to exaltation.[75]

Benson had written to Congreve on this subject, and again there are instructive differences in their approach. Speaking of the distinction of body and soul Benson wrote of "the one with its category of locality, the other with its freedom from all categories. To the one with its passivity, all the ills of [*sic*] the flesh is heir to in this present world, or the other with its participation in the activity of God." Benson is saved from a strightforward dualism by his view that spiritual things have a greater reality than material things:

> One does feel that existence is not of earth, but only in God who calls us out of the world. God is the source of all reality and the "struggle of grace" is as real as the place where we have to struggle.[76]

This echoes Congreve's teaching of the emptiness to be filled, both of the soul and of the material world, but Congreve goes further than Benson and is more balanced:

> When you look down into that empty cup of your own nature, you never find what you want in it; it was created empty in order to be filled. Bring it empty as it is to the fountain; leave off contemplating your own emptiness and contemplate the eternal love as He is in Himself.[77]

Material suffering for Congreve is a positive tool. Commenting on the crowds who "floated after Jesus on the easy current of popular enthusiasm", he wrote:

---

[74] Congreve, letter to Br John, 23 October 1914, SSJE/6/5/2/2/15, f. 9.

[75] Cf. Philippians 2.

[76] Benson, Correspondence with Fr Congreve, undated, SSJE/6/1/2/21, f. 5.

[77] Woodgate, *Father Congreve*, p. 30.

The Lord turns round with a certain scorn to repel the ovation of this great multitude. He opposes the severity of the truth to their torrent of emotion, and scatters it into spray. He welcomes no love but that which will suffer the loss of all things for his sake, and will die to the gratification of the most innocent natural feelings, even to the natural instinct of self-preservation, for the supreme love of the infinite loveliness."

Congreve goes on, "why does our Lord confront enthusiasm with sacrifice? Because in a fallen world pain is the necessary test and the purification of love." The Christian must therefore live by the mystery of the cross, and "in a prayerful life each soul is taught of God by degrees the secret of Sacrifice – learns 'how good it is to suffer'".

These last words, Congreve notes, were Fr O'Neill's on his death bed, his first friend at Cowley whose mortified life seemed to Congreve to shine with God's splendour.[78] Congreve's great example of this was always his first friend among the Fathers, Simeon Wilberforce O'Neill, whose mortified life in Cowley and Indore seemed to Congreve to shine with God's splendour.

For Congreve, the material world is not ultimately lost in death, because there is ultimately no distinction between matter and spirit: "[M]atter has no existence apart from the Divine Energy of which it is the *forma-formata*." The distinction between the spirit world and the material world is therefore ultimately false: "[W]e being of this world think matter as real and spirit its vague concomitant, but 'we shall see differently'." He believed that:

the doctrine of material permanence is dualistic. When a man no longer uses the "vegetable life of grass" then it has nothing more to do with the man and is not his flesh at all. If the vegetable bit *has* real life then there are two independent real existences, matter and spirit; which seems to be contrary to scientific investigations,

---

[78]   Congreve, *Parable of the Ten Virgins*, pp. 78–9.

and (what is far more important) the simplicity of the creature
ceases to testify to the Unity of the Creator.[79]

Thus if any part of life is eternal, then it all is, and the material, natural
world has its place in eternity as much as the spiritual. Here is a
concomitant to Congreve's view that the natural world partakes both in
the fall and in the redemption of humanity.

There is a last fear of the dying Christian, which is the loss of confidence
in faith at the end. Congreve had seen this at first hand in the death of
his mother, a devout evangelical, to whom he was close and whom he
nursed as she died. He recalled her confiding in him the darkness that
engulfed her soul, and how he had written to an uncle asking for help.
No letter back came in time, but when it did arrive it called Congreve to
the understanding that faith is not a matter of feeling, but of will, and that
the darkness of doubt can be a time in which love is refined—as offered
but receiving no palpable reward—and therefore shorn of selfishness.
He recalled:

> [B]efore her death when we were alone together she said a few
> words to me which made me know how all the pain was fulfilled
> and paid by the happiness she had in the Lord's love and His
> goodness to her.[80]

For Congreve himself, there was no hint of such a trauma, though he
would probably not have expressed it had he suffered it. His last letter
was full of confidence. Though confined to "my arm chair—Fr Benson's
old chair which he lived in in his last few years", and remaining in his
cell "without any prospect of getting about again", he wrote that "the sun
shines in my room all day just now, my brethren are wonderfully kind."
His correspondent was a penitent who may also have been dying, for
Congreve wrote:

---

[79] Letter to Assheton, [No specific day] May 1884, SSJE/6/5/5/9, f. 503.

[80] Congreve, letter to Br John, 12 July 1902, SSJE/6/5/2/2/4, f. 12.

I have taken your confession with my own in my prayer, and asked for grace that we may be released from the weight of our burden and in the joy of forgiveness bring to our Father in Heaven joyful service. I cannot give you any idea how long life here is likely to hold out; I do not believe the doctor expects any recovery—I think it is some heart failure, and might end any time—and probably before long. I am not up to writing much—God bless you always, dear friend, you and your flock.[81]

One of Congreve's most powerful examples of hope in the face of despair is, typically, drawn from nature:

I once stood in a place, one might suppose the saddest in the world. Behind the Prisoners' Chapel, within a high walled County Jail, there was a small and dark plot of ground, shut in by high palings, and locked,—a prison within a prison; it was a plot where were buried those who from time to time had been executed in that prison for murder. Here it seemed that I stood on the very verge of the place where love is not, and rest cannot be for man. But here, I could not fail to remember the grace of the King of Love upon the Cross, His prayer for the murderers, His promise to the dying thief, His welcome to the penitent first after His resurrection. I saw, also, that there was at least a short time in the day when one ray of sunshine might reach this place of shame; and that there was on one and another of the nameless mounds a rose tree planted. Who cared to plant the rose on the unhonoured grave? There must been at least one person here who believed that the felon's execution was not the conclusion of the whole matter for him. Was it his wife or his child who got leave to plant the sign of love and hope there? How clearly the Rose tree, growing in such a place, sang to me the creed of the Catholic Church: " . . . and the third day He rose again from the dead . . . I believe

---

[81]   Congreve, Letters to friends and associates, 19 February 1918, SSJE/6/5/2/6, f. 55.

in the Forgiveness of sins, the Resurrection of the body, and the life everlasting. Amen."[82]

In the end:

> . . . the noblest guesses leave the secret of death undisclosed. We leave it without anxiety, for we leave it with God, Who is not merely the Arbiter, but the Father and lover of souls; sure at least of this that the revelation when the cloud lifts, will be lovelier than our loveliest thoughts about it; for we are convinced that it is not merely some benevolent purpose of God that death has to reveal to the loyal soul that goes forward into the dark to seek Him, but God Himself.[83]

---

[82]   Congreve, *Christian Progress*, pp. 42–3.

[83]   Congreve, Preface to F. M. M. Comper, *Book of the Craft of Dying*, p. xxxvi.

CHAPTER 10

His Gift of Himself

George Congreve died on 18 April 1918. His last book, *Treasures of Hope for the Evening of Life*, was almost ready and was published later in the year.[1] In his last years, and especially after Benson's death, he was—as it were—the Fathers' Father, to whom all the Brethren had specific permission from the Superior to turn for help and advice.[2] In 1915 he had collaborated with Fr Longridge to edit and publish a volume of Fr Benson's letters, and now Longridge prepared some of Congreve's for publication. Congreve had commented that, while Benson's letters were fascinating to him, they were "wonderfully outside the interests of most church people today".[3] By the same token, it was not long before Congreve's own books began to go out of print. An attempt in the 1920s to publish a selection of his letters to Richard Assheton and other correspondents was rejected by publishers who, ten years before, had solicited books from him.[4] A small biography by Mildred Woodgate was published in 1956, but her work on Congreve was thin by comparison with her book on Benson, and Father Dalby (a Superior who had not known Congreve) commended her in his Foreword for finding so much to write about one "whose life

---

[1] *Treasures of Hope for the Evening of Life* (London: Longmans, Green & Co., 1918).

[2] General Chapter Minute Book, Superior's Address to Provincial Chapter, 29 December 1916, SSJE/2/5/1.

[3] Congreve, Letters to friends and associates, 13 July 1915, SSJE/6/5/2/6, f. 59.

[4] Congreve, letter to Br John, 14 June 1912, SSJE/6/5/2/2/13, f. 13; "Mowbray proposes to publish a volume of odds and ends which I am to give him towards the end of the year."

Figure 18: The Cloister at Cowley St John. The Cherry Tree in full blossom as it was on the day of Congreve's funeral. In some ways the tree was a symbol of the life of the community, and Congreve a great part of its springtime.

was so essentially hidden and seemingly uneventful".[5] Except for those who treasured up copies of old books of devotion, Congreve was then almost entirely forgotten except for a brief mention of his writing about Saint Columba by A. M. Allchin in lectures given in 1979.[6] Recently a revival of interest in Ninian Comper has at last seen Congreve's name mentioned other than in footnotes.[7]

Congreve's relevance to the concerns of the modern church in his teaching on mission, community and prayer is clear. He speaks also to issues of beauty, ageing and death, which are of interest to many who do not share his faith. Assessment is most needed of the relevance of Congreve's reflections on nature, race and warfare. He was not a "Green" writer in the modern sense; his response to war, and especially the First World War, is shocking to modern sensibilities moulded by a twentieth-century consensus; his view on race and empire challenges twenty-first-century stereotypes of Victorian thought. Yet a century after his death, a world facing religious violence and imperial legacies—good as well as bad—has much to take from Father Congreve's teaching.

Modern "Green" concern begins with fear for the environment at the hands of humanity and seeks preservation of that which is under threat. The concept of stewardship is central to much Christian reflection on this. Congreve begins with the sheer loveliness of creation. He described (in the third person) how as a boy in Italy he first came to understand natural beauty when he saw a shrine:

> for the cheer of devout wayfarers, giving him, where he might
> have expected the image of a saint, a text from the Vulgate instead.
> He read there: "*Pulchritudo agri mecum est*" ["The beauty of the
> land is mine"] . . . [H]ere was a clear message from the Word of

---

5   Woodgate, *Father Congreve*, Foreword by Father Dalby, p. vi.

6   A. M. Allchin, *The Dynamic of Tradition* (London: Darton, Longman & Todd, 1981), pp. 140–1.

7   Symondson, "'An Ass or a Devil'?"; Symondson and Bucknall, *Sir Ninian Comper*.

God, suggesting to the lad a higher source of his joy in nature
than he had ever suspected; it set him wondering.[8]

Congreve taught that Nature "shares the burden and no less mysteriously
reflects the destiny of mankind".[9] Nature is under no more nor less
threat than the human soul with which it shares the Fall, and in whose
redemption it will come to partake. "Christ is risen and ascended, not for
us alone, but for all creation, and it is through that door opened in heaven
that we begin to recognize the true significance and delight of nature."[10]
Nature for Congreve is a sacrament which points beyond itself to God;
he describes an unforgettable experience one evening on Robben Island
when he came out of the chapel alone. Eagerly he pressed on:

> up the white road that led to the lighthouse on the highest point
> of the island. I made haste in hope to catch a glimpse of the
> sunset, for though the western horizon was hidden from me by
> the rising ground, there was a reflected glow that told of it high up
> in the sky as clear as crystal crossed by a few bars of violet cloud
> at rest . . . [O]ld age awoke in me a hunger to reach beyond the
> solitary darkness through which I walked, and inspired me with a
> conviction that there lie mysteries of love and beauty to discover,
> just beyond the verge of our senses, for a soul that desires them—
> mysteries of which such scenes in nature are a sacrament.[11]

Congreve was interested not so much in the preservation of the natural
world as in its redemption. His writing invites a different way of thinking
about nature, one which is not focussed on the world itself, but on the
Creator. He points a way to a Christian environmentalism which is alert
to nature, loves the beauty of creation, but looks always beyond it to
God and is not trapped in a sterile attempt to preserve what is inherently
mortal.

---

[8]   Congreve, *Treasures of Hope*, p. 108; Psalm 50:11 (49:11 in the Vulgate).
[9]   Russell, *Autumn Easter*, Preface by Congreve, p. x.
[10] Congreve, *Treasures of Hope*, pp. 109–10.
[11] Ibid., p. 173.

Such an environmentalism avoids the temptation to grasp at nature as a sort of possession, even in order to preserve it from harm, and contributes to the growth of the human soul in love and contemplation of God. It is possible to be mortified to the things of this world, to embrace poverty, but still to love them and rejoice in them:

> We do not reject the pleasure that belongs to healthy humanity—pleasure in society, and friendship, in art or in nature, in food. It is worldliness in lawful pleasure, pleasure we rest in selfishly [that we reject]. Pleasure [is wrong if] we fail to consecrate it by making it a means of union with God by our thanksgiving.[12]

In his sermon at Congreve's funeral the Vicar of All Saints Margaret Street, Fr MacKay, said of Congreve, "like all truly mortified people he could take pleasure in simple comforts when affection put them his way".[13] His speculation that any distinction of matter and spirit is ultimately dualist is striking and would repay more thought.[14] In the end, nature demands our attention because it reveals God who is calling to us who are part of it, and for Congreve the revelation is clearer precisely because it eludes direct observation:

> This lofty and mysterious power which nature has to compel our reverent attention is the point at which the things we contemplate transcend themselves, and touch the infinite. The beauty of the creature begins just where it eludes your observation and pursuit. You are conscious that it calls you to rise and follow further out of yourself than you ever dared, on towards the infinite, invisible Perfection. I have seen, I have heard, something which has left me more dissatisfied with myself than ever—which has left me all longing for the loveliness that alone satisfies, and that is, I am more sure than ever, within my reach, and close to me;

---

[12] Congreve, Sermon notes, SSJE/6/5/3/1–18. Second notebook, "The World".

[13] H. F. B. MacKay, "Funeral Sermon for Fr Congreve", published as "Fr Congreve" in *The Oxford Journal*, May 1918.

[14] See above, p. xxx.

something, too, which I fear, for it bids me forsake myself, and
follow the Uncreated Beauty to its home in the heart of God. Thus
the contemplation of God in nature leads to the contemplation
and desire of God in Himself.[15]

It is perhaps in the face of the First World War that Congreve seems at
first sight to be most hopelessly out of touch and irrelevant, uselessly
preaching the pieties of a lost Victorian world in the face of the suffering
of modern warfare. This seeming irrelevance stems from the fact that
what subsequent generations have seen as a unique experience and a
point of disjunction, Congreve insisted on setting in a context, moreover
the context of self-sacrifice. This is, however, what makes him important
to hear now, and gives him a new relevance.

Self-sacrifice was the basis of Congreve's whole approach to the
Christian life. Because he believed Christianity to be the principle of
civilization, self-sacrifice is the basis of the civilized life. In a sermon on
Romans 6:5, preached in 1916 and published in *The Cowley Evangelist*,
he said, "If we have been planted together in the likeness of His death
we shall also be in the likeness of His resurrection." Partaking in Christ's
resurrection is not something for the future, but "begins with our Baptism
and is to go on every day of our life in the world now." He went on:

> Christ's death and His heavenly risen and ascended life together
> constitute His sacrifice; and that, all of it, belongs by covenant
> to the Christian when he accepts Him as his Saviour in Holy
> Baptism . . . Our Lord is offering his eternal sacrifice, His death
> and His heavenly life, for us forever in heaven. And that sacrifice
> offered there continually is the ground of our acceptance as
> members of Christ, and of our right to draw near to God in any
> way . . . the whole life of a good Christian is meant to be a life of
> continual approach to the Father through the mediation of our
> ascended Jesus who is our heavenly sacrifice.

Congreve continued that it is clear that Christ's sacrifice:

---

[15]   Congreve, *Treasures of Hope*, pp. 173–4.

will develop its own essential virtue in his members, but in many
different forms of self-surrender . . . every Christian has his call
of God however ordinary his lot may be; and that call is in every
case a call to sacrifice, to a complete self-surrender.[16]

Self-surrender does not lead to emptiness and gloomy renunciation of
good things, but on the contrary the mortified person is filled with joy
which comes from fulfilling the purpose for which we are made, a joy
which is more than any passing happiness in the things of this world.
This "emptying to be filled" characterized Congreve's whole teaching on
the religious life, was exemplified in his own life, and was his message to
both religious and secular people.

Congreve believed a nation can be mortified when it acts in a way that
is selfless and requires self-sacrifice. He believed the Empire had acted in
such a way in 1899 in resisting the Boers.[17] Though he felt that "English"
government was fundamentally moving in the right direction, he was
not naïve and was aware that both individuals and nations have warped
motives. After describing a mission service amongst African labourers
on Table Mountain "and the sense of brotherhood among us, black and
white as Christians; and the new ideal we had in common—the lovely
and dear Person of our Lord Jesus Christ", Congreve went on:

> and these most Christian of simple Christians—so they seem
> to me—are the creatures whom some upcountry farmers treat
> cruelly, regarding them as animals without a soul. It is true we
> English have often illtreated [sic] them by putting drink in their
> way and by much neglect; and it is little as yet perhaps that the
> Church of England has been able to do for them; but I am glad
> that wherever the English power reaches in South Africa it
> protects the native races.[18]

---

[16] Congreve, "Sacrifice", pp. 217–23.
[17] Report on St Philip's Mission.
[18] Congreve, *Spiritual Order*, pp. 336, 337–8.

After the Boer War and during the Great War he was concerned that any good that had been won might be lost in the peace, but nevertheless he believed that the principle was valid.

Nor was Congreve simply someone who thought that authority was always right. "Christ says to his soldiers, modern civilisation is full of sin, do not run and hide, but take your place in it and fight for righteousness, truth and charity. Renounce its evil *to the face*, by working against it for Christ."[19] This was counsel both for metaphorical soldiers of Christ, and for those who bear arms. Congreve cast Britain's response in 1914 in terms of self-sacrifice on behalf of invaded Belgium, and later in terms of the resistance to what Congreve understood to be an anti-Christian form of civilization based on selfishness and violence, propounded by Germany and her allies, of which the invasion of 1914 had been a symptom.

Historians' later focus on the proximate causes of the First World War, which seemed to some to be a series of unfortunate events in which one action triggered another, and the view which became ubiquitous, that the conflict was a pointless waste of life for what seemed little result, have perhaps blinded us to the clarity with which the issues were understood in Britain at the time, both strategically and morally. Congreve makes a moral case for national self-sacrifice to resist barbarism. At the individual level, soldiers were to find "security in duty", and Congreve maintained the view that those who fell made an ultimate act of self-sacrifice—even after the death of at least two of his close, and dear, relatives. He challenged the premise that "suffering is altogether evil and therefore anything causing suffering must be altogether evil and therefore war must be altogether evil"[20] and found evidence in the continuing stream of volunteers, even to the end of the war, that the spirit of self-sacrifice was growing in the nation, something which he saw as a good arising from the conflict.[21] Ultimately for Congreve death was not the worst thing that could happen, and therefore even large numbers of casualties, causing great sorrow, could be borne.

---

[19] Congreve, Sermon notes, SSJE/6/5/3/1–18. Second notebook, "The World".

[20] Correspondence between Fr Congreve and Fr Hodge on war (copy), SSJE/6/5/2/9, f. 5.

[21] Congreve, *Fourth Year of the War*, p. 5.

Setting the War in the frame of self-sacrifice allowed him to equate the self-sacrifice of an aged nun or of a secular Christian with that of a soldier at the front, and to draw the whole nation into the sacrifice. All are called to be the faithful warrior, whether or not bearing arms. It was a theology of universal self-sacrifice for an age of total war. Even less than nature, neither war nor peace are ends in themselves. Even the Great War should be set in the context of the love and grace of God. In all this, Congreve simply took seriously what his faith taught and applied it consistently. It is the theology of the official British memorials of the First World War. The Cross of Sacrifice which stands in British and Commonwealth War Graves Commission cemeteries was designed by Reginald Bloomfield, but Herbert Baker (architect of St Philip's in Cape Town) served on the committee and urged that a cross should be erected in all the cemeteries. Congreve's clear and unflinching justification of conflict in the moral context of self-sacrifice offers Christians embroiled in modern conflicts an opportunity for a clearer voice today when the churches often neither assert pacifism nor offer a positive justification for fighting, and are thus reduced at best to silent sympathy and at worst to hopeless irrelevance.

Since he believed Christianity brings civilization, Congreve was unembarrassed to speak of unevangelized peoples as "Child Races". Although he spoke out of a framework which uncritically assumed the differences of peoples (as of classes in society), he "treated all with the same courtesy", and it was noted of him that "he had respect for the image of God in [African people] and reverenced what he found in them of God and sought to understand it."[22] He wrote of a group of African labourers:

> [Y]ou never saw in England a gang of navvies so ragged, ill fed, and forlorn looking; but you never saw in English navvies the native courtesy, dignity, and gentleness of these sons of Africa. These men were our equals in manners. Were we equal to these

---

[22] Henry Power Bull, "In Memory of Father Congreve, A sermon preached in substance by the Father Superior General in the Society's church at Oxford on the 3rd Sunday after Easter April 21 1918", in *The Cowley Evangelist*, May 1918, refers to "[Congreve's] little Mirfield tract, *The Church and the Child Races*" (p. 106). I have been unable to find this tract.

unspoilt children of the wilderness, with their humble and cheerful courtesy?[23]

Congreve wrote powerfully of both the strength of Christ who "raised Christian slaves from the brutality of the slums of Rome to the spirit and fellowship of the saints and martyrs", and of the evils of western society, describing an African Chief who "sees his people—dockworkers— transformed by the vices of civilisation, and says 'this is hell.'"[24] Anything which undermines the influence of the civilizing power of Christianity threatens the regression of a people, and as much as he worked and prayed for what he considered the raising of the "heathen", he feared also the falling back of the civilized to "heathendom".

His fears after the Boer War that the South Africa of the future would not build on the sacrifice of the war were at first, sadly, justified. The Cape Colony which was so important to him soon passed, its dissolution beginning just a year after he came home.[25] Meditating on the sorrow of a bleak sunset on Robben Island, Congreve wrote, concluding what is the loveliest of his reflections:

> [A]nd tomorrow the sunrise and all happy things in the island will praise God with us for the victory of love through pain, and for the hope of the morning (it often comes to one or another prisoner here), which brings forever the end of sorrow and sin.[26]

The regime which grew out of the failures of the early twentieth century in South Africa maintained its prison on Robben Island. Surely Congreve would have rejoiced to see the release of the most famous of the island's prisoners, and South Africa begin a new trajectory.[27]

---

[23] Congreve, *Spiritual Order*, p. 332.

[24] Report on St Philip's Mission, p. 22.

[25] Pakenham, *Boer War*, pp. 575–6.

[26] Congreve, *Spiritual Order*, pp. 51–8; Miller, *Sorrow of Nature*, pp. 25–32.

[27] Nelson Mandela was held on Robben Island between 1964 and 1982.

That trajectory was, in part, prepared by Congreve and those like him. In 1912, one of the architects of British Africa wrote, not entirely approvingly:

> [T]he idea that there would be any serious demand on the part of the colonial peoples for a voice in their own taxation and government scarcely disturbed the forecast of any average imperialist . . . But, unfortunately for the ideals of the imperialist Britain of 20 years ago, education was permeating the British Empire in all directions . . . Missionary Societies were everywhere founding schools, colleges, and universities, attempting to make black, brown, and yellow people think and act like white Christians . . . impressing on them over and over again that once they were Christians and civilised, or even civilised without being Christians, they were the equal of any man, no matter of what colour or race.[28]

Congreve's contribution to stabilizing and expanding the work of the Cowley Fathers was considerable and, in this context, important for the future of many peoples. In the period in which the efforts of the Missionary Societies were rejected by the powers of the world, the work of men like Congreve was marginalized. Today, in a context in which missionaries come from Africa to help save Europeans from regression to "heathendom" for lack of Christianity, Congreve's teaching once again has relevance and importance.

Congreve, who noted that he "never attained the sixth form",[29] wrote in a way that was immediately accessible and attractive. Accessibility does not, however, mean that Congreve was lightweight. He has a way of coming at a subject that sets it in a new light, enabling it to be seen afresh. There is a directness which comes from the fact that his writings were either letters, retreat addresses or sermons. The prefaces he wrote for other people's books were perhaps less successful, though they showed

---

[28] Warren, "Church Militant", p. 68, quoting Sir Harry Johnstone, *Views and Reviews*, pp. 232–4.

[29] Congreve, letter to Br John, 18 May 1911, SSJE/6/5/2/2/12, f. 6.

the breadth of his reading and interest. He loved and read poetry as well as a wide literature, and drew on scripture, the writings of the Church Fathers and Christian classics. He could quote John of the Cross with confidence and knew the history of St Columba. A significant influence was Augustin Baker's *Sancta Sophia*.[30]

Congreve's handling of scripture was strikingly modern in that, when drawing spiritual conclusions, he avoided explicit engagement with biblical criticism. Benson, though he enjoined deep scriptural study was, following Pusey, careful of "the cleverness of critics"[31] and wrote, "controversy takes the place of Bible reading . . . [g]ood men fall unwittingly into such compromises with unbelievers, that the moral and spiritual value of the Bible is lost sight of in the attempt to rescue it from alleged difficulties."[32] Congreve was of the view that "criticism has done a great service to S Paul", since: "those who still doubt the genuineness of the history of the letters . . . are no longer [those who are] scientific but those who deliver brawling judgements, too idle, or unintelligent to examine the question".[33] In the years after the Great War this sort of view would be thought simplistic at best, and at worst would undermine confidence in the writer and may explain why to new generations Congreve seemed less worth reading than those who grappled more clearly with the "alleged difficulties."

Fundamentally, all Congreve's teaching was based on his own personal relationship with Christ. "We know (not nothing) but little of God." What helps us to understand is:

> [n]ot knowing creeds, but *personal* energies of trust, of hope.
> The real knowledge of God is not that which books of sermons

---

[30]   Augustin F. Baker OSB, *Sancta Sophia* (Doway: Patte and Fievet, 1657), ed. Norbert Sweeney OSB (London: Burnes & Oates, 1876).

[31]   Congreve and Longridge (eds), *Letters of R. M. Benson*, p. 310.

[32]   Ibid., p. 325. On Benson's approach to the Bible see Mark Gibbard SSJE, "Richard Benson: Man of the Bible", in Martin L. Smith SSJE (ed.), *Benson of Cowley* (Oxford: Oxford University Press, 1980), pp. 61–74.

[33]   Congreve, Sermon notes, undated sermon, SSJE/6/5/3/18.

give but the personal knowledge of spiritual affection based on likeness of character.[34]

He had learned this starting point of faith from his mother, and to the end she remained an influence on him. He was affected by her death, and in his last book he described beautifully and at length—in the third person—how as a boy, when on what he correctly feared would be a useless quest to bring her a doctor, he had been struck by a flower which led him to see the love and support of God even in suffering:

He started one day before sunrise alone on a walk of twenty miles along the Cornice road that overhangs the Mediterranean in North Italy. He saw the wrinkled sea in the early morning sunshine, without any comfort or delight in it, because he had left behind his dearest friend in the world—his mother—dying in much pain, in their villa among the olive trees by the sea. He was on his way to the city to seek surgical help, which he knew must be ineffectual. Dejected and without hope he trudged on refusing to look up at glories in sea and sky that seemed indifferent to his misery, till something arrested his steps, and the tenor of his bitter thoughts. He had noticed the withered bents, and weeds by the road-side, burnt up by yesterday's sun blaze, and thought of his own life withered with grief, and fear of a future emptied of the comfort of love; but here under the rock by the road-side one wild plant caught his eye, a small cranesbill, as fresh as if it were the first flower God ever made. Its one rose-coloured blossom had opened very early, and was filled with a drop of night-dew that sparkled in the light of morning by the dusty road-side. He stood for some moments gazing at this image of perfect beauty, freshness, and joy accidentally shown to him, till his eyes filled with tears, and his heart came to life again with trust in God . . . The little flower made him know at once and with absolute certainty that God would have in His holy keeping the saint he

---

[34] Congreve, General sermons, SSJE/6/5/3/17, f. 3. Emphasis in the original and punctuation altered for clarification.

left behind in mortal pain, not less lovingly than He cherished
His one wild plant by the road-side.[35]

In adulthood, he referred to Mrs Barton of Caldy as his second mother.
Other members of the family were important. Of them all, he was
perhaps closest to Walter, of whom he was proud not only because he
was a General and a winner of the VC—though he was proud of that—
but because he was godly and devout.[36] After the war Walter succeeded
Allenby as Commander, and effectively as military governor in Egypt
(where he and Lady Congreve attended the opening of Tutankhamun's
tomb in 1924). He became Governor of Malta where he died in 1927 at
the age of sixty-five. Francis, who was awarded a DSO, retired from the
army as a Lieutenant-Colonel in 1933 and served in the Home Guard in
the Second World War.[37] Geoffrey, Billy's younger brother, was made a
baronet in recognition of the service of his family. He too was awarded
a DSO, while serving in the navy in Norway in 1941, but was killed later
that year. There was one happy-ever-after: Billy's wife, Pamela, gave birth
to their daughter in 1917, and after the War married William Fraser, who
had been Billy's best man and had promised to look after Pam if anything
happened to Billy.[38]

---

[35]   Congreve, *Treasures of Hope*, pp. 108–9, from an article originally printed in
       The Cowley Evangelist, August 1916, p. 172.

[36]   Congreve, Copies of letters to friends and associates, letter to Mrs Torr,
       15 January 1900, SSJE/6/5/2/7. On Tutankhamun's tomb, Staffordshire
       County Record Office (D1057/M/U/18). A letter of Walter's containing his
       reservations about the Christmas Truce of 1914 was put on display at the
       Staffordshire Record Office in 2014: <http://www.dailymail.co.uk/news/
       article-2860468/WWI-General-Sir-Walter-Congreve-s-letter-reveals-
       reluctance-join-Christmas-truce-fearing-shot-fraternising-Germans.html>,
       accessed 30 August 2021.

[37]   DSO: *London Gazette*, 1 January 1919—"for distinguished service in
       connection with military operations in France and Flanders".

[38]   Robert Hamilton, *Victoria Cross Heroes of World War One* (Croxley Green:
       Authentic Publishing, 2015), p. 153. Sir Geoffrey declined to fund the
       publication of his Uncle George's letters to Assheton when Longman's rejected

Even more than his mother, Father Benson was undoubtedly the greatest influence on Congreve, who wrote about this difficult, austere saint, "He sometimes irritates and sometimes flattens me; but if I am saved at last it will be by God's mercy through Father Benson's teaching."[39] It was, however, Congreve's own engagement with that teaching—and in some respects his correction of it—that made Congreve so important for his own Community. After Congreve died, Father Bull, now the third Superior since Benson, wrote of him:

> His life was always so intimate with us here in this House that it seemed to each one part of his own, the constant factor, an influence always exerted, a standard of judgement, and of excellence, a reference on every occasion. Now he is gone we have to stand on our own feet, his children, please God, in spirit and in character, stronger, better, wiser, more persevering for our knowledge of him, and our love of him.[40]

In 1890 it was Congreve who took the lead in speaking to Benson about the government of the Society. It was Congreve who enabled the Fathers to work out how to live together in a functioning community, and he was significant in maintaining the religious character of the Society of Saint John the Evangelist when the suggestion was seriously put that it should reconfigure itself as a society of mission priests. If Congreve gave the Society a spiritual and theoretical basis to take forward from Benson's foundation, it was Father Page who, as second Superior General, gave it the practical and human leadership to embark on what have been described as its greatest years.[41] When Page died in 1912, Congreve remarked to Bull that:

---

them, as he had incurred considerable expense in the publication of Pamela's book about Billy and Walter, *The Congreves* (London: John Murray, 1930). Correspondence on the publication of Congreve's letters, SSJE/6/5/5/6, f. 1.

[39] Congreve, letter to Assheton, 5 November 1901, SSJE/6/5/5/9, f. 934.

[40] General Chapter Minute Book: Superior's Address to Provincial Chapter, August 1918, SSJE/2/5/1.

[41] James, *Cowley Fathers*, p. 172.

> time brings a certain test of faithfulness to a Religious Community
> . . . The old leaders have died: Hollings, Benson, Maxwell. I do not
> mean that we the individual members at any moment are worth
> anything, but the fellowship of our brotherhood grows richer and
> stronger with time—as the best of us are perfected one by one
> and belong to us more securely.[42]

That "secure belonging" was in no small part Congreve's own doing, though he would never have recognized nor accepted that fact. In England, the Society of Saint John the Evangelist has not flourished into the twenty-first century; without Congreve, it is hard to see how it would have flourished into the second quarter of the twentieth. In the last year of his own life, Walter Congreve wrote somewhat sadly to Father Puller from Malta. "I wish I could come and have luncheon once more as in the old days—you had some famous men. I hope there are others like them." That there were, at least for another generation, was in no small way due to his Uncle George.[43]

One of the men famous in the sight of God, though entirely hidden, was Brother John, with whom Congreve maintained a correspondence of nearly twenty years. After formative years together at Cowley, in which they became firm friends, John went to South Africa. By a twist of arrangements, John was in England when Congreve was in South Africa but returned to Cape Town as Congreve came back to London. Their letters are an example of Congreve's doctrine of ordinary friendships sanctified in the religious life, full of family detail and gossip as well as serious matters of faith, including strong support from Congreve in a period when John considered leaving the Society.[44] He died in 1930, mourned as "so much more than a serving Brother".[45]

---

[42] Congreve, General correspondence, letter to Fr Bull, 5 April 1915, SSJE/6/5/2/3, ff. 49–50.

[43] Frederick William Puller SSJE, Correspondence with friends and associates, 16 November 1925, SSJE/6/9/1/23, f. 2.

[44] Congreve, letters to Br John, 5 April, 7 May, 12 July 1902, SSJE/6/5/2/2/4, ff. 1–13.

[45] James, *Cowley Fathers*, p. 260.

For all his facility with words, there are points at which Congreve can verge on the sentimental, though he hated sentimentality. He signed off a letter to John, now in Cape Town, "Goodbye dear brother—tell me about the Honey Bird, the wagtails, as well as about the dear human creatures;" but he could use the power of description to evoke things of God and to offer encouragement. He reported to Brother John how he had visited his other great correspondent who preserved his letters, the by-now-bed-ridden Miss Kebbel, and read her "my little story of climbing Table Mountain. It revived her to have such a view of the ocean, the mountains and little Cape Town and S Philip's spread out far below our feet".[46] His descriptions of nature show him to be a master of prose. He was especially moved by spring, and two years before his death described what he must have thought would be the last time he saw what he would call the resurrection of the world from winter:

> I congratulate with all the new-born things in the garden—how they all trust instinctively in the sun, and disbelieve the winter, —the finery of the delicate catkins of the poplars and hazels— the merry and bold lilac buds almost in leaf and quite green already—the clear song of the blackbirds and thrushes—it is all as wonderful and delightful to me today as ever in my life—and Refreshment Sunday[47] is not less intelligible to me than when I was at Frankby. *Benedicat Terra Dominum* "O all green things that are in the Earth bless the Lord."[48]

It was typical of Congreve to remark that:

> Life seems to be like a garden more than anything—God gives us our nature, power of intelligence, affections, will—and then by sacraments he sows grace in the soil—plants trees of grace, and so seeds of grace which make little show today, but have heavenly life

---

[46] Congreve, letter to Br John, 27 October 1906, SSJE/6/5/2/2/7, f. 9.

[47] The Fourth Sunday in Lent, now often kept as Mothering Sunday.

[48] Congreve, Letters to friends and associates, 19 March 1912, SSJE/6/5/2/6, f. 50. An interesting use of the word "congratulate".

in them, and unless we neglect our garden, they are sure to grow up to wonderful beauty and grandeur and happiness in the end.[49]

His character was attractive and often described as "boyish"—even when old—and "joyful". Perhaps the best summary of Congreve, with the exception of the reference to "great bodily strength" is a description he himself wrote of the personality of Saint Columba:

> His unusual gifts of sympathy, enjoying life, society, friendship— as well as his rare intellectual powers and his great bodily strength and the magic of his wonderful voice, and courage, nothing was lost [in death]. His conversion was his sacrifice, his gift of himself with every faculty to God for ever.
>
> But the gift of his faculties to God who made them so noble did not mean their death and destruction—his love of nature he gave to God consecrated now. His delight in the colours of the sound where the sun shines—he did not *lose* his delight in it by giving it God—he consecrated it— and now he could not see it with the mere pain of a delight which cannot be expressed and ends in itself, but . . . with joy in the colour of the sea and in the waves, [his delight] given to God, [gaining] expression in consecration lifted up in His praise, given on to God, and [carrying] him in its joy to God—[becoming] music—[becoming] a habit. And now created beauty is always a sacred thing to him like the hymns of the sacred service . . . Now his old Irish love of his friends, love of his mother,—of young men and maidens—love of children—remains, but by the grace of the Holy Ghost Christ's love has come into all that capacity of love—and now that face of sympathy is not merely a face of enjoyment for him but a new face of sanctification for him and everyone he speaks to. [50]

---

[49]   Congreve, South African Sermons, SSJE/6/5/3/16, f. 23.

[50]   Congreve, General sermons, Sermon for St Columba's Day [no year], SSJE/6/5/3/18. Emphasis in the original. The punctuation and some words have been adjusted for clarity.

Figure 19: S Philip's Mission House Garden. For Congreve the beauty of the natural world is a means by which God calls us, and a garden is a sign of Grace at work.

Most Sundays during his years in South Africa, Congreve walked up the side of Table Mountain to Lilliebloem for the afternoon service in Lydia Williams's house, and would come home in the evening. There was a time for letter-writing before he set off. Once there was a storm, and darkness began to fall around the house where he was staying, the windows of which overlooked a storm-tossed Bay:

> I can trace the curve of the Bay in wrathful flame breakers. Further out what few ships there are, are tugging at their anchors and making themselves as small as they can. The clouds drive low, half melted with rain, or tower to enormous threatening height. Only our tall gum trees, tossing their heads in despair, are not swallowed up in storm and darkness. There is the steady sound of rain coming down in torrents. But now through the noise of the rain and wind comes the peal of Sunday evening bells in Woodstock town—the music all broken and scattered by the storm, only a note or two emerging every now and then from the welter of storm sounds, wild and sorrowful tones of a terrible music whose law is unknown to us. Darkness has fallen quickly and I shall have to beg a lantern by which to climb down to the road and to civilisation. The faithful bell has the victory. I can hear each gallant stroke calling the people to praise God, until now the whole peal bursts out in a lull of the storm, sounding so extraordinarily joyful just because of the world of sorrow on the sea and sorrow in the air which it conquers.[51]

Congreve's was a joy which conquered sorrow, a teaching which rewards study, a proclamation of the gospel which is more relevant and fresh now than perhaps at any time since his death. The day of his funeral was one of gentle weather, in the time of year which was his favourite:

> We laid his body to rest on the loveliest of spring days. There was a long procession of Religious, Priests and lay folk processing,

---

51 Congreve, letter to "N" (Selina Congreve), Sunday after the Ascension 1904(?), SSJE/6/5/2/5, f. 43. Woodgate, *Father Congreve*, p. 68.

preceding, and following the bier which his Brethren in Religion drew. All Cowley people uncovered and halted reverently; the boys in the day schools came along with us, cap in hand; the birds sang; the sun shone and the cherry tree in the Fathers' garden broke out into blossom.[52]

He was buried next to Father Benson in the Fathers' plot in the cemetery at St Mary and St John on the Cowley Road.[53] The international mission of SSJE was such that Benson was only the third member of the Society and the second of its priests to die at home.[54] Congreve was not buried next to Benson out of any honour: it was just that he was given the next plot in the row. It would have been as he would have expected and wished.

The place was marked, as was the Society's way, only by a simple wooden cross which, when in time it rotted away, was not renewed; but primroses flower there each spring.

---

[52] MacKay, "Fr Congreve". On the significance of the cherry tree, see James, *Cowley Fathers*, p. 373.

[53] Woodgate, *Father Congreve*, p. 89.

[54] James, *Cowley Fathers*, p. 228.

Figure 20: The Cowley Fathers' burial plot in the churchyard of SS Mary & John Oxford. The Fathers were buried with wooden grave markers which were not replaced when they rotted. Fr Congreve was buried to the right of the Celtic Cross, only the fourth of the Fathers to die in Oxford.

Bibliography

George Congreve—published works

Two Addresses given to the Associates of the Association of S John the Baptist at Zonnebloem, Cape Town in 1893 (Zonnebloem, Cape Town: The College Press, 1893).

Address on Preparation for General Communion (Oxford, 1895).

Increase in us True Religion: An Address by Father Congreve SSJE preached at the profession of the first novices to the Sisterhood of the Holy Childhood, St Margaret's Day, July 20th 1896 (Oxford: Mowbray, 1896).

Christian Life, a Response, with other Retreat Addresses and Sermons (London: Longmans, Green & Co., 1899).

Of Advance in Lent, Churchman's Penny Library No. 17 (London: Mowbray, 1899).

The Christian Mystics: a Paper for the Cape Town Clerical Society (Zonnebloem, Cape Town: The College Press, 1900).

Annual Report of St Philip's Mission Cape Town (Oxford: Society of Saint John the Evangelist, 1902). SSJE/9/2/4/5.

The Parable of the Ten Virgins: Addresses Given in Retreat (London: Mowbray, 1904).

The Sacrifice of Christ (Oxford: Society of Saint John the Evangelist, 1904).

The Spiritual Order, with Papers and Addresses written for the most part in South Africa (London: Longmans, Green & Co., 1905).

"Sisters, their Vocation and Special Work", in *Pan-Anglican Papers, being problems for consideration at the Pan-Anglican Congress 1908;* SC Group 5, *The Church and its Ministry: The Ministry of Women, Section 2: Organised Associations* (London: SPCK, 1908).

Christian Progress, with other Papers and Addresses (London: Longmans, Green & Co., 1910).

The Interior Life, and Other Addresses (London: Mowbray, 1913).

"On Devotional Reading", in Cary, Lucius, *Notes of a Retreat* (London: Mowbray, 1915).

The Third Year of the War and the National Mission: A sermon preached in the church of S John the Evangelist Oxford, August 6th 1916 (London: Mowbray, 1916).

The Fourth Year of the War: Hope Through Suffering, August 5th 1917 (Oxford: Mowbray, 1917).

Treasures of Hope for the Evening of Life (London: Longmans, Green & Co., 1918).

Cowley Retreats No. 1: The Incarnation and the Religious Life (Oxford: Society of Saint John the Evangelist, 1930).

"Loss and Gain: on the Passing of Fr Benson", in Anon., *Cowley Sermons: The Jubilee Volume of the Conventual Church of S. John the Evangelist, Oxford* (London: Mowbray, 1947), pp. 56–72.

The Being of God; Addresses at a Quiet Day (Oxford, Society of S John the Evangelist, no date).

George Congreve—published in collaboration

Congreve, George SSJE, and Longridge, William Hawks SSJE (eds), *Letters of Richard Meux Benson* (London: Mowbray, 1916).

George Congreve—papers published in *The Cowley Evangelist*

Congreve regularly published material in The Cowley Evangelist. This attempts to be a list of articles which appeared from 1902:

"Psalm cxix: An Address to the All Saints Sisters, Cape Town", February 1902, pp. 25–31.

"Meditation", July 1902, pp. 145–51.

"Christ Our Peace: On the end of the South African War", August 1902, pp. 169–77. "Desire", November 1902, pp. 241–8.

"The Need of God", February 1904, pp. 55–60 (reprinted from *The Church Chronicle of South Africa*).

"Epiphany", January 1911, pp. 1–6.

"The King", July 1911, pp. 145–54.

"An Address to the Sisters and Associates at the House of Charity, Knowle, Bristol", August 1911, pp. 170–9.

"Latent Force", September 1911, pp. 198–204.

"The Way of Repentance", October 1911, pp. 217–24.

"Light", November 1911, pp. 241–8.

"Union", December 1911, pp. 266–72.

"The First Word from the Cross", April 1912, pp. 73–7.

"A Door Open in Heaven", June 1912, pp. 122–6.

"*Deus Caritas Est*: an address at Knowle", August 1912, pp. 169–76.

"All Saints, All Souls", November 1912, pp. 241–7.

"Love Never Faileth", February 1913, pp. 25–30.

"The Power of Christ's Resurrection", April 1913, p. 73.

"For the Tree Hath Hope", August 1913, pp. 169–74.

"Prayer", September 1913, pp. 193–9.

"Progress", October 1913, pp. 217–26.

"I Believe in the Communion of Saints", November 1913, pp. 241–6.

"The Father of the Age to Come", January 1914, pp. 1–5.

"The Lord and Giver of Life", March 1914, pp. 50–4.

"Father Hollings", May 1914, p. 97.

"Seek Peace and Ensue It", August 1914, pp. 169–75.

"Mozley's Sermon on War", September 1914, p. 195.

"Planted Together with Christ", September 1914, p. 195.

"The Peace of Jerusalem", October 1914, pp. 217–24.

"*Salve*", January 1915, pp. 1–10.

"I Come from God", September 1915, pp. 193–9.

"I Go to God", November 1915, pp. 241–7.

"*Si Consurrexistis Cum Christo*", January 1916, p. 6.

"Salvation", February 1916, pp. 23–33.

"Lent", March 1916, pp. 53–60.

"Dying to Live", April 1916, p. 73.

"Some Fruits of the Resurrection", May 1916, p. 97.

"The God of All Comfort", July 1916, pp. 145–52.

"The Beauty of God", August 1916, pp. 170–9.

"Repentance and Hope: The Third Year of the War and the National Mission", September 1916, pp. 193–9.

"Sacrifice", October 1916, pp. 217–23.

"Behold the Lamb of God", November 1916, pp. 241–9.

"I Believe in the Communion of Saints", December 1916, pp. 265–72.

"Christ the Door of God's Fold", March 1917, pp. 53–9.

"The Interior Life", June 1917, p. 125.

"Newness of Life", August 1917, p. 173.

"The Call of God", September 1917, p. 197.

"The Hope that Saves", October 1917, p. 221.

"All Souls", November 1917, p. 245.

"Thy Commandment is Exceeding Broad", August 1918, p. 161.

"A Sermon Preached to the African Labourers lodging at S Columba's Cape Town in 1900", December 1919, pp. 221–2.

"Losing Christ and Finding Him Again (Preached on Robben Island 1902)", February 1922, pp. 28–34.

"Atonement, A Retreat Address", April 1922, pp. 74–9.

"S Paul's Gospel for Ordinary Christians (Sermon preached at S Philip's Cape Town on the XVI Sunday after Trinity 1900)", June 1922, pp. 201–7.

"The Open Door", April 1923, pp. 74–8.

"The Beauty of God", October 1923, pp. 217–21.

"The Will of God", November 1923, pp. 241–4.

George Congreve—introductions or prefaces contributed to published works

Anon., *By the Author of the Praeparatio, a Day-Book of Short Readings for use by Busy People, Advent to Trinity* (London: Masters and Co., 1906).

Anon., *By the Author of the Praeparatio, a Day-Book of Short Readings for use by Busy People, Trinity to Advent* (London: Masters and Co., 1906).

Anon., *In the House of my Pilgrimage and other Poems* (London: Longmans, Green & Co., 1922).

Anon., *My Communion: twenty-six short addresses in preparation for Holy Communion* (London: Longmans, Green & Co., 1905).

Anon., *Orient Leaves: A collection in memory of A. H. Mackonochie and R. F. Littledale* (London: Mowbray, 1900).

Anon., *Praeparatio, or Notes of Preparation for Holy Communion founded on the collect epistle and gospel for every Sunday of the Year* (London: Longmans, Green & Co., 1903).

Anon., *The Author of "The Sanctus Bell", "Seek me Early", etc., etc. The Soul's Escape, or Perfect Freedom, Psalm CXXIV 6* (London: Skeffington and Son, 1906).

Benson, Richard Meux SSJE, *The Divine Rule of Prayer* (Second Edition, London: Mowbray, 1916).

Comper, Frances M. M., *The Book of the Craft of Dying and other Early English Tracts Concerning Death* (London: Longmans, Green & Co., 1917).

Hepher, Cyril, *The Fruits of Silence: Being further studies in the common use of prayer without words, together with kindred essays in worship* (London: Macmillan & Co., 1915).

MacLeod, Flora Abigail, *The Riches of the House of God* (New York: Longmans, Green & Co., 1915).

Russell, Adeline Marie [Duchess of Bedford], *An Autumn Easter* (London: Mowbray, 1911).

Rousby, Lillian, *Under Table Mountain* (London: Mowbray, 1906).

White, Richard, [Richard Johnson], *Celestial Fire: Being a Book of Meditations on the hymn "Veni Sancte Spiritus", written in the Seventeenth Century,* ed. Green, E. M. (London: Longmans, Green & Co., 1913).

Wolff, Margaret, *A Schoolgirl Seeking God* (privately published, 1892).

George Congreve—unpublished material

*References refer to the archive index of Lambeth Palace Library,
which holds the archive of The Society of Saint John the Evangelist
at the Church of England Record Centre. <https://archives.
lambethpalacelibrary.org.uk/CalmView/Record.aspx?id=SSJE>,
accessed 14 June 2021. The material most cited is as follows:*

Personal papers, SSJE/6/5/1.

Correspondence with Father Benson, SSJE/6/5/2/1.

Letters to Brother John, SSJE/6/5/2/2/2–16.

General correspondence, SSJE/6/5/2/3.

Letters to Miss Kebbel, SSJE/6/5/2/4/1–24.

Letters to "N" (Selina Congreve), SSJE/6/5/2/5.

Letters to friends and associates, SSJE/6/5/2/6.

Copies of letters to friends and associates, SSJE/6/5/2/7.

Copy of correspondence between Father Congreve and Father Hodge
on war, SSJE/6/5/2/9.

Sermon notes, SSJE/6/5/3/1–18.

Notes of an Address to the Sisters of Bethany, SSJE/6/5/3/8.

Three Addresses on the Spiritual Life, St Faith's Chapel, Lent 1905,
SSJE/6/5/3/11.

Sermons at S Columba's and S Cyprian's Cape Town, SSJE/6/5/3/15.

South African sermons, SSJE/6/5/3/16.

Father Congreve's general Sermons, SSJE/6/5/3/17.

Address to the East and West Missionary Society at St Mary
Magdalene's Oxford, 1913, SSJE/6/5/3/18.

General notebooks, SSJE/6/5/3/19.

SSJE Summer Retreat, SSJE/6/5/4/5.

Paper "On Correspondence Between Fathers", SSJE/6/5/5/1.

Paper "Reminiscences", SSJE/6/5/5/2.

Letters to Richard Assheton, SSJE/6/5/5/9.

Miscellaneous items, SSJE/6/5/5/10.

Unpublished sources

To aid in locating references, this material is listed in the order in which it is catalogued in the SSJE Archive in Lambeth Palace Library.

Benson, Richard Meux SSJE, "Instructions upon the Rule of Life",
SSJE/1/1/1–2.

Statutes and Rule of Life of the Society of Mission Priests of St John the
Evangelist, 1884, SSJE/1/1/3.

General Chapter Minute Book, 1884–1905, SSJE/2/1.

Index to the General Chapter Minute Book, 1884–1905, SSJE/2/2.

General Chapter Minute Book SSJE, 1913–27, SSJE/2/5.

Benson, Richard Meux SSJE, Correspondence with Brother Beale,
1877–92, SSJE/6/1/2/4.

Benson, Richard Meux SSJE, Unpublished correspondence, 1860–87,
SSJE/6/1/2/7.

Benson, Richard Meux SSJE, Correspondence from Cowley, 1899–
1908, SSJE/6/1/2/9.

Benson, Richard Meux SSJE, Correspondence with Father Congreve,
1886–1903, SSJE/6/1/2/21.

Newspaper reviews for *Treasures of Hope for the Evening of Life*, 1919,
SSJE/6/5/5/4.

Letters of condolence on the death of Father Congreve, 1918,
SSJE/6/5/5/5.

Correspondence about the publication of Fr Congreve's letters,
1919–30, SSJE/6/5/5/6.

Correspondence about Congreve family history, 1927–9, SSJE/6/5/5/7.

Further correspondence about the publication of Fr Congreve's letters,
1919–30, SSJE/6/5/5/8.

Puller, Frederick William SSJE, letters on proposals to change the
Society, 1896, SSJE/6/9/1/2.

Puller, Frederick William SSJE, Correspondence with friends and
associates, 1890–1925, SSJE/6/9/1/23.

Waggett, Philip Napier SSJE, Correspondence with Father Page,
1898–9, SSJE/6/16/1/1.

Hodge, George Herbert SSJE, Correspondence with Father Page, 1899, SSJE/6/17/1.

Powell, Frederick Cecil SSJE, letter to Father Page, 1899, SSJE/6/18/1.

Benson, Richard Meux SSJE, "Advent Retreat 1875" in Retreats, Vol. 15, SSJE/8/1/15.

Cape Town Mission Accounts, 1884–5, SSJE/9/2/2.

Jones, William West, Correspondence with SSJE, 1881–96, SSJE/9/2/3/1.

Correspondence of Sisters of the All Saints Sisters of the Poor, 1881–98, SSJE/9/2/3/5.

John SSJE, Letters to Father Page, 1898–9, SSJE/9/2/3/6.

Correspondence regarding the election to the Bishopric of Zululand, 1891, SSJE/9/2/3/7.

Schofield, John M., "St Cuthbert's Mission: an Historical Sketch" (1971), SSJE/9/2/4/4.

Scrapbook of mission notices, 1869–1901, SSJE/10/1.

Walton, Lesley, "St Crispin's Home for Girls" (2007), SSJE/10/5.

Papers on the SSJE in World War I, SSJE/10/7.

Photographs, SSJE/11.

Secondary works

Anon., *An Alphabetical List of the Signatures to a Remonstrance Addressed to the Archbishops and Bishops of the Church of England on Occasion of the Report of the Judicial Committee of the Privy Council in re Herbert v. Purchas* (London: James Parker & Co., 1871).

Alington, Cyril, *Edward Lyttleton: An Appreciation* (London: John Murray, 1943).

Allchin, A. M., "R. M. Benson: The Man in his Time", in Smith, Martin L. SSJE (ed.), *Benson of Cowley* (Oxford: Oxford University Press, 1980), pp. 1–26.

Allchin, A. M., *The Dynamic of Tradition* (London: Darton, Longman & Todd, 1981).

Anson, Peter F., *Building up the Waste Places: The revival of monastic life on medieval lines in the post-Reformation Church of England* (London: Faith Press, 1973).

Anson, Peter F., *The Call of the Cloister* (London: SPCK, 1955).

Ajayi, J. F. A., *Christian Missions in Nigeria 1841–1891: The Making of a New Elite* (London: Longman, 1965).

Baker, F. Augustin OSB, *Sancta Sophia* (Doway: Patte and Fievet, 1657), ed. Sweeney, Norbert OSB (London: Burnes & Oates, 1876).

Bertouch, Beatrice Caroline, *The Monk of Llanthony: The Life of Father Ignatius OSB* (London: Methuen, 1904).

Benson, Richard Meux SSJE, *A Short Account of the Life and Work of George Edmund Sheppard* (London: J. T. Hayes, 1889).

Borsch, Frederick H., "Ye Shall be Holy", in Rowell, Geoffrey (ed.), *Tradition Renewed: The Oxford Movement Conference Papers* (Allison Park, PA: Pickwick Publications, 1986), pp. 64–77.

Brown, D. K., *Before the Ironclad: Warship design and development 1815–1860* (Barnsley: Seaforth Publishing, 2015).

Bull, Henry Power, "George Congreve", *The Cowley Evangelist*, May 1918, pp. 97–101.

Bull, Henry Power, "In Memory of Father Congreve: A sermon preached in substance by the Father Superior General in the Society's church at Oxford on the 3rd Sunday after Easter April 21 1918", *The Cowley Evangelist*, May 1918, pp. 101–8.

Butler, Perry, "The History of Anglicanism from the Early Eighteenth Century to the Present Day", in Sykes, Stephen and Booty, John (eds), *The Study of Anglicanism* (London: SPCK, 1988), pp. 28–47.

Chadwick, Owen, *The Pelican History of the Church, Vol. 3: The Reformation* (London: Penguin Books, 1964).

Comper, J. Ninian, *Of the Atmosphere of a Church* (London: Sheldon Press, 1947).

Congreve, William (Billy), *Armageddon Road: a VC's Diary*, ed. Norman, T. (Barnsley: Pen & Sword, 2014).

Dunstan, Peta, *The Labour of Obedience: The Benedictines of Pershore, Nashdom and Elmore, A History* (Norwich: Canterbury Press, 2009).

Garner, Rod, "Gilding the Cages of Others: the life and work of a philanthropic duchess compelled by her faith", *Church Times*, 20 August 2020.

Gibbard, Mark SSJE, "Richard Benson: Man of the Bible", in Smith, Martin L. SSJE (ed.), *Benson of Cowley* (Oxford: Oxford University Press, 1980), pp. 61–74.

Green, Brian, "Launching the Lifeboats: A History of the Public School Mission Movement", unpublished BA dissertation, (Birkbeck College, London, 2000).

Hamilton, R., *Victoria Cross Heroes of World War One* (Croxley Green: Authentic Publishing, 2015).

Haws, Steven CR, The Cowley Fathers in Philadelphia (Bloomington, IN: Author House, 2019).

Hinchliff, Peter, "The Selection and Training of Missionaries in the early Nineteenth Century", in Cuming, G. J. (ed.), *Studies in Church History, Vol. 6: The Mission of the Church and the Propagation of the Faith* (Cambridge: Cambridge University Press, 1970), pp. 131–5.

Hinchliff, Peter, "Church-State Relations", in Sykes, Stephen and Booty, John (eds), *The Study of Anglicanism* (London: SPCK, 1988), pp. 351–63.

Holland, Tom, *Dominion: The Making of the Western Mind* (London: Little, Brown, 2019).

Hylson-Smith, Kenneth, *The Churches in England from Elizabeth I to Elizabeth II, Vol. 2: 1689–1833* (London: SCM Press, 1997).

James, Serenhedd, *The Cowley Fathers: The History of the English Congregation of the Society of Saint John the Evangelist* (Norwich: Canterbury Press, 2019).

Johnson, William (Cory), "A Study of Boyhood", in *Ionica* (London: Smith Elder & Co., 1858).

Kemsley, R. SLG, "The Religious Life: Aspects of Father Benson's Teaching", in Smith, Martin L. SSJE (ed.), *Benson of Cowley* (Oxford: Oxford University Press, 1980), pp. 98–118.

Lloyd, Roger, *The Church of England in the Twentieth Century, Vols. 1 & 2* (London: Longmans, Green & Co., 1946, 1950).

Longridge, William Hawks SSJE (ed.), *Further Letters of Richard Meux Benson* (London: Mowbray, 1920).

Longridge, William Hawks SSJE (ed.), *Spiritual Letters of Richard Meux Benson* (London: Mowbray, 1924).

Longridge, William Hawks SSJE (ed.), *Spiritual Letters of Father Congreve* (London: Mowbray, 1928).

MacKay, H. F. B., "Fr Congreve", *The Oxford Journal*, May 1918.

Maturin, Basil [SSJE], *The Price of Unity* (London: Longmans, Green & Co., 1912).

Miller, Luke, *The Sorrow of Nature: The Way of the Cross with George Congreve and Thérèse of Lisieux* (Oxford: The Catholic League, 2014).

Miller, Luke, "The Winds of Change 1914–45", in Davage, William (ed.), *In This Sign Conquer: A History of the Society of the Holy Cross 1855–2005* (London: Continuum, 2006), pp. 120–44.

Mission Priests of S. John the Evangelist (eds), "Retreats", *The Evangelist Library* (London: J. T. Hayes, undated).

Newman, John Henry, *Discourses Addressed to Mixed Congregations* (Birmingham: Birmingham Oratory, 1849).

Nias, John, *Flame from an Oxford Cloister: The Life and Writings of Philip Napier Waggett SSJE* (London: Faith Press, 1961).

Nockles, Peter, "The Oxford Movement, Historical Background, 1780–1833", in Rowell, Geoffrey (ed.), *Tradition Renewed: The Oxford Movement Conference Papers* (Allison Park, PA: Pickwick Publications, 1986), pp. 24–50.

O'Brien, William Braithwaite SSJE, "Some Anglican Forms of Religious Life for Men", *Holy Cross Magazine*, July 1937.

Oliver, Roland and Atmore, Anthony, *The African Middle Ages* (Cambridge: Cambridge University Press, 1981).

Pakenham, Thomas, *The Boer War* (London: Weidenfeld & Nicolson, 1979).

Pendleton, Eldridge H. SSJE, *Press On, the Kingdom: The Life of Charles Chapman Grafton* (Cambridge, MA: Society of Saint John the Evangelist, 2014).

Puller, Frederick William SSJE, *The Anointing of the Sick in Scripture and Tradition, with some Considerations on the Numbering of the Sacraments* (London: SPCK, 1904).

Ramsey, A. M., "Bruising the Serpent's Head: Father Benson and the Atonement", in Smith, Martin L. (ed.), *Benson of Cowley* (Oxford: Oxford University Press, 1980), pp. 54–60.

Reed, John Shelton, *Glorious Battle: The Cultural Politics of Victorian Anglo-Catholicism* (Nashville, TN: Vanderbilt University Press, 1996).

Rowell, Geoffrey, *The Vision Glorious: Themes and Personalities of the Catholic Revival in Anglicanism* (Oxford: Oxford University Press, 1983).

Scotland, Nigel, *Squires in the Slums: Settlements and Missions in late Victorian London* (London: I.B. Tauris, 2007).

Smith, Martin L. (ed.), *Benson of Cowley* (Oxford: Oxford University Press, 1980).

Smith, H. Maynard, *Frank, Bishop of Zanzibar* (London: SPCK, 1926).

Spear, Percival, *A History of India: Vol. 2* (Harmondsworth: Penguin, 1965).

Symondson, Anthony SJ, "'An Ass or a Devil'? Sir Ninian Comper and Charles Eamer Kempe", *Journal of Stained Glass* Vol. 34 (2010), pp. 53–78.

Symondson, Anthony SJ and Bucknall, Stephen, *Sir Ninian Comper: An Introduction to his Life and Work, with Complete Gazetteer* (Reading: Spire Books, 2006).

Taylor, Brian, "The Cowley Fathers and the First World War", in Sheils, W. J. (ed.), *Ecclesiastical History Society, Studies in Church History, Vol. 20: The Church and War* (Oxford: Oxford University Press, 1983), pp. 383–90 (SSJE/10/6).

Teale, Ruth, "Dr Pusey and the Church Overseas" in Butler, Perry (ed.), *Pusey Rediscovered* (London: SPCK, 1983), pp. 185–209.

Thomas, Hugh, *The Slave Trade: The History of the Atlantic Slave Trade 1440–1870* (London: Papermac, 1988).

Thornton, Leslie H. and Fraser, Pamela, *The Congreves, Father and Son* (London: John Murray, 1930).

Trenholm, Edward Craig SSJE, *The Story of Iona* (Edinburgh: David Douglas, 1909).

Waggett, Philip Napier SSJE, "Father Congreve", *The Cowley Evangelist*, May 1918, pp. 127–32.

Warren, Max, "The Church Militant Abroad: Victorian Missionaries",
in Symondson, Anthony (ed.), *The Victorian Crisis of Faith*
(London: SPCK, 1970), pp. 57–70.

Wavell, Archibald, *Allenby: A Study in Greatness* (London: Harrap,
1940).

Weeder, Michael Ian, *The Palaces Of Memory: A reconstruction of
District One, Cape Town, before and after the Group Areas Act* (MA
mini-thesis, University of the Western Cape, 2006); <https://core.
ac.uk/download/pdf/58912907.pdf>, accessed 14 June 2021.

Woodgate, Mildred Violet, *Father Benson of Cowley* (London: Geoffrey
Bles, 1953).

Woodgate, Mildred Violet, *Father Congreve of Cowley* (London:
Geoffrey Bles, 1956).

Illustrations

Permission to reproduce pictures held there has been given by the Lambeth Palace Library and the Trustees of the Fellowship of St John. I am grateful to the Vicar of S Matthew Bilton and the Assheton family for permission to reproduce the picture of Richard Assheton.

Figure 1: George Congreve. SSJE/11/1/1/2/34/14.
Figure 2: Richard Assheton.
Figure 3: The Mission House from Marston Street. SSJE/11/1/1/2/15.
Figure 4: Simeon Wilberforce O'Neill. SSJE/11/1/2/2 f. 1.
Figure 5: George Congreve. SSJE/11/1/2/5 f. 2.
Figure 6: The Mission House Chapel. Author's photograph.
Figure 7: SSJE in 1887. SSJE/11/1/1/2/34/14.
Figure 8: Fr Maturin SSJE/11/1/2/6 f. 1.
Figure 9: Fr Page. SSJE/11/1/2/3 f. 1.
Figure 10: St Philip's Mission Cape Town. SSJE/11/1/3/7/6.
Figure 11: Fr Waggett. SSJE/11/1/2/16/1.
Figure 12: Lydia Williams. SSJE/9/2/4/5.
Figure 13: Walter Congreve. Thornton, Leslie H. and Fraser, Pamela, *The Congreves, father and son* (London: John Murray, 1930). Frontispiece.
Figure 14: Fr Congreve. SSJE/11/1/2/5 f. 8.
Figure 15: Billy Congreve. Thornton, Leslie H. and Fraser, Pamela, *The Congreves, father and son* (London: John Murray, 1930) p. 312.
Figure 16: Nofamile Noholoza. SSJE/6/5/2/4/13 f. 6.
Figure 17: Congreve in extreme old age. SSJE/11/1/2/5 f. 5.
Figure 18: The Cloister at Cowley St John. SSJE/11/1/1/1/2.
Figure 19: S Philip's Mission House Garden. SSJE/11/1/3/4.
Figure 20: The Cowley Fathers' Burial Plot. Author's photograph.

Index

Lightning Source UK Ltd.
Milton Keynes UK
UKHW020201010222
398006UK00010B/514/J